ADMINISTRATIVE PROCEDURES FOR THE LEGAL PROFESSIONAL

WEST LEGAL STUDIES

Options.
Over 300 products in every area of the law: textbooks, CD-ROMs, reference books, test banks, online companions, and more – helping you succeed in the classroom and on the job.

Support.
We offer unparalleled, practical support: robust instructor and student supplements to ensure the best learning experience, custom publishing to meet your unique needs, and other benefits such as West's Student Achievement Award. And our sales representatives are always ready to provide you with dependable service.

Feedback.
As always, we want to hear from you! Your feedback is our best resource for improving the quality of our products. Contact your sales representative or write us at the address below if you have any comments about our materials or if you have a product proposal.

Accounting and Financials for the Law Office • Administrative Law • Alternative Dispute Resolution Bankruptcy • Business Organizations/Corporations • Careers and Employment • Civil Litigation and Procedure • CLA Exam Preparation • Computer Applications in the Law Office • Contract Law Court Reporting • Criminal Law and Procedure • Document Preparation • Elder Law • Employment Law • Environmental Law • Ethics • Evidence Law • Family Law • Intellectual Property • Interviewing and Investigation • Introduction to Law • Introduction to Paralegalism • Law Office Management Law Office Procedures • Legal Nurse Consulting • Legal Research, Writing, and Analysis • Legal Terminology • Paralegal Internship • Product Liability • Real Estate Law • Reference Materials Social Security • Sports Law • Torts and Personal Injury Law • Wills, Trusts, and Estate Administration

---

West Legal Studies
5 Maxwell Drive
Clifton Park, New York 12065-2919

For additional information, find us online at:
www.westlegalstudies.com

THOMSON
DELMAR LEARNING

ADMINISTRATIVE PROCEDURES FOR THE LEGAL PROFESSIONAL

By Judy A. Long, J.D.

THOMSON

DELMAR LEARNING™   Australia   Brazil   Canada   Mexico   Singapore   Spain   United Kingdom   United States

THOMSON

™

DELMAR LEARNING

WEST LEGAL STUDIES

Administrative Procedures for the Legal Professional
Judy A. Long

Vice President, Career Education Strategic Business Unit:
Dawn Gerrain

Director of Learning Solutions:
John Fedor

Managing Editor:
Robert Serenka, Jr.

Acquisitions Editor:
Shelley Esposito

Editorial Assistant:
Melissa Zaza

Director of Content and Media Production:
Wendy Troeger

Senior Content Project Manager:
Glenn Castle

Art Director:
Joy Kocsis

Technology Project Manager:
Sandy Charette

Director of Marketing:
Wendy E. Mapstone

Channel Manager:
Gerard McAvey

Marketing Coordinator:
Jonathan Sheehan

Cover Design:
Elizabeth Wood

Library of Congress Cataloging-in-Publication Data

Long, Judy A., 1937–
  Administrative procedures for the legal professional / Judy A. Long.
      p. cm. — (West legal studies)
  Includes index.
  ISBN-13: 978-1-4180-1833-7
  ISBN-10: 1-4180-1833-3
  1. Legal assistants—United States. 2. Law offices—United States. I. Title.
  KF320.L4L656 2008
  340.068—dc22

                                    2007006108

NOTICE TO THE READER

Publisher does not warrant or guarantee any of the products described herein or perform any independent analysis in connection with any of the product information contained herein. Publisher does not assume, and expressly disclaims, any obligation to obtain and include information other than that provided to it by the manufacturer.

The reader is notified that this text is an educational tool, not a practice book. Since the law is in constant change, no rule or statement of law in this book should be relied upon for any service to any client. The reader should always refer to standard legal sources for the current rule or law. If legal advice or other expert assistance is required, the services of the appropriate professional should be sought.

The publisher makes no representations or warranties of any kind, including but not limited to, the warranties of fitness for particular purpose or merchantability, nor are any such representations implied with respect to the material set forth herein, and the publisher takes no responsibility with respect to such material. The publisher shall not be liable for any special, consequential, or exemplary damages resulting, in whole or part, from the reader's use of, or reliance upon, this material.

DEDICATION

To my granddaughter

Ariana

Brief Contents

Contents

PREFACE

Administrative procedures are the responsibility of all members of the law office team. The legal professional is generally given the task of coordinating these responsibilities into the workings of the law firm. The goal of this text is to provide an overview of the operation of the law office and the duties of different members of the law office team.

In addition to a description of the importance of understanding the human relations dynamics of the law firm, the student is provided with some critical guidelines for becoming an efficient member of the law office team. Basic strategies are provided for establishing priorities and meeting deadlines. The importance of proper scheduling is stressed.

Trends in the law office setting are described. While large law firms may employ paralegals, legal assistants, and legal professionals in many different specialty areas, smaller firms may employ one individual who performs the function of the paralegal, the legal assistant, and the administrative assistant. For purposes of this textbook, the latter-described individual will be referred to throughout as the legal professional. However, the legal professional may be called a legal assistant, legal secretary, legal administrative assistant, or administrative assistant in different law offices.

ORGANIZATION OF THE TEXT

The text begins with a basic description of the operation of the law office, including the structure and types of offices, responsibilities of different members of the law office team, and liaison with support personnel. The most efficient methods of succeeding as a valuable member of the law office team are discussed, such as establishing priorities and meeting deadlines. Various scheduling systems are described, including computerized systems that efficiently track deadlines and provide dates for hearings and trials.

Client relations are discussed as well as the ethical guidelines to follow in dealing with clients. Client confidentiality is stressed in the performance of the responsibilities of the legal assistant.

A more in-depth study is provided of the actual duties of the legal assistant. The importance of using computers is explained, including document processing, the Internet, and e-mail.

The students are provided with an overview of the research responsibilities of the legal assistant, including the proper method for writing citations, the use of form books, and the use of the Internet for legal research. File management techniques are discussed, as well as ethical problems connected therewith.

The chapter on communications includes both written and oral communications. The last chapter includes the mail system and docket control systems. Some of the more popular docket control systems are discussed.

PROJECT NOTEBOOKS

Students should be required to prepare a reference notebook that will be useful both during this course and later on the job. A notebook logo will appear next to those projects that should be torn out and kept in the notebook, which should be a three-ring binder with sections that coincide with the chapters in the text. Making a skeleton notebook with each tab marked with a chapter heading should be the student's first assignment in the course. The student should be required to hand in all notebook assignments for a grade. After each project is graded, it should be placed under the appropriate heading in the notebook. At the end of the semester, the instructor should check the notebook for a major grade.

Students should be encouraged to add to the notebook as they take additional courses in the program. Some of the material encountered in subsequent courses will fit under the headings established for this course. In some cases, new headings will be added as the student progresses through the course of study.

The notebook will prove valuable after graduation from the program. Most employers require writing samples to be submitted with the employment application. The assignments in the notebook can be used for this purpose. Since legal documents may be repetitive in nature, the student should be encouraged to file a copy in the notebook of each new document prepared on the job or in a subsequent class.

SPECIAL FEATURES

- **State Specific Information** boxes are included in each chapter. The student should complete the information on rules and procedures specific to the student's state.

- **Key Terms** are defined in the margins of the text and also appear at the end of each chapter and in a glossary.

- **Self Tests** at the end of each chapter help students to review the main concepts discussed.

- **Notebook Projects** provide students with practical experience in performing the tasks of the legal assistant. Notebook logos precede those projects that students should place in their notebooks.

- **Notebooks** must be prepared by all students and are explained in the preface. Pages in the text should be placed in the notebooks if the notebook logo appears therein.

SUPPLEMENTARY MATERIALS

This text is accompanied by support material that will aid instructors in teaching and students in learning. The following supplements accompany the text:

- **Instructor's Manual**—This supplement is designed for instructors to assist in presenting text material in an organized and comprehensive manner. The manual includes a detailed summary of each chapter, lesson plans (including suggestions for speakers and field trips), answers to the Self Tests, and suggestions for additional projects. A comprehensive test bank contains more than two hundred objective test questions and answers. The *Instructor's Manual* is also available online at

  http://www.westlegalstudies.com

  in the Instructor's Lounge under Resource.
- **Online Companion™**—The Online Companion Web site can be found at

  http://www.westlegalstudies.com

  in the Resource section of the Web site. The Online Companion contains study notes and outside activities for the students. Links are also provided to relevant Web sites.
- **Web page**—Come visit our Web site at

  http://www.westlegalstudies.com

  where you will find valuable information such as hot links and sample materials to download, as well as other West Legal Studies products.
- **Westlaw®**—West's online computerized legal research system offers students "hands-on" experience with a system commonly used in law offices. Qualified adopters can receive ten free hours of Westlaw®. Westlaw® can be accessed with Macintosh and Windows-based PCs. A modem is required.

ABOUT THE AUTHOR

Judy Long is a retired attorney and college professor. She developed an ABA-approved paralegal program at a California community college. She coordinated and taught courses in the program for many years. Prior to teaching, she spent twelve years working as a legal assistant/paralegal in private law offices and corporate law departments. Her first legal position was as a part-time legal secretary in a sole practitioner's office while she was in high school. She has written several legal textbooks, including:

1. *Basic Business Law* (co-author 2d edition), Prentice-Hall, 1994.
2. *Law Office Procedures,* West, 1997.
3. *California Supplement to Civil Litigation,* West, 1995.
4. *Legal Research Using the Internet,* Thomson/Delmar, 2000.
5. *California Legal Directory,* Thomson/Delmar, 2000.
6. *Computer Aided Legal Research,* Thomson/Delmar, 2003.
7. *Legal Research Using Westlaw,* Thomson/Delmar, 2001.
8. *Office Procedures for the Legal Professional,* Thomson/Delmar, 2005.
9. *Substantive Procedures for the Legal Professional,* Thomson/Delmar, 2008.

ACKNOWLEDGMENTS

Many individuals provided valuable assistance in the preparation of this textbook. I would first like to thank my editor, Shelley Esposito, for her numerous suggestions and considerable assistance in developing the ideas and background information for this book, as well as for her considerable support. Thanks so much to Robin Reed, my developmental editor, for her help and suggestions. Thanks to Brian Banks, editorial assistant, for his help in obtaining materials and other information.

The following reviewers furnished valuable recommendations in their reviews of the text:

Julie Abernathy
NALS

Dee Beardsley
Latham & Watkins LLP

Michele Bradford
Gadsden State Community College

Joni Montez
Lewis-Clark State College

Sharolyn Sayers
Milwaukee Area Technical College

Caryn Wolchuck
Thomas Whitelaw & Tyler LLP

Thanks very much to Sheila Cantrell for her sample topics for an Office Manual and sample time sheets. Thanks to the salespeople at Abacuslaw for their material on computerized docket control systems. Thanks to Kim at Compulaw for arranging our online and telephone meetings so that I might learn more about their computerized online calendaring and docket control systems. And a special thank-you to all others whose names have been inadvertently omitted.

FEEDBACK

The user may contact the author through e-mail at Jaler@aol.com with questions, suggestions, or comments about the text or its supplements.

Judy A. Long, J.D.

Please note that the Internet resources are of a time-sensitive nature and URL addresses may often change or be deleted.

Contact us at westlegalstudies@delmar.com

LAW PRACTICE OVERVIEW

CHAPTER OUTCOMES

As a result of studying this chapter, the student will learn:

1. the structure of different types of law offices.
2. the responsibilities of members of the legal team.
3. the responsibilities of different employees in the law firm.
4. the function of the administrative procedures manual.
5. how to maintain liaison with support personnel.

LAWYERS/ATTORNEYS

The terms **lawyer** and **attorney** are used interchangeably and have the same meaning. In order to call himself a lawyer or attorney, an individual must have graduated from law school and passed the state bar examination in the state in which he intends to practice. Once he passes the bar examination, the individual attends a swearing-in ceremony and becomes a member of the bar.

To practice in another state, the lawyer must pass the bar examination in that particular state and be admitted to practice in that state.

Typically, an individual who wishes to become an attorney must obtain an undergraduate degree to become eligible for law school. Once he graduates with a bachelor's degree, he may attend law school. In most states, law school consists of three years of intensive study in the various areas of law. After completing all of the requirements of law school, passing all of the examinations, and obtaining a law degree, one becomes eligible to take the state's bar examination. (A few states may have different requirements.)

In most states, the bar examination is given twice a year. A fee is charged to take the examination, and the results are either pass or fail. If one fails the examination, then it must be taken over again at the next scheduled time. Once the individual passes the examination, he receives notice from the state bar and is invited to attend a "swearing-in ceremony." After taking the state's oath of office at the ceremony, the individual becomes eligible to practice law in that particular state. Many states have special bar examinations for attorneys who are already licensed to practice in another state. These tests usually consist of questions about the new state's laws. Most states provide specialty

lawyer/attorney
individual who has graduated from law school and passed his state's bar examination

certification programs whereby attorneys may obtain a certificate in their specialty upon the completion of certain coursework or practice.

The rules of practice for each state may be found on the state bar's Web site. In order to find the requirements to practice law in your own state, search on the Internet using the name of your state and the words "state bar association." For example, if you are in Maryland, search for "Maryland state bar association." Other Web sites also contain links to state bar associations, such as

http://www.findlaw.com

discussed later in this text.

Research the requirements in your own state for an individual who wishes to become an attorney.

> STATE-SPECIFIC INFORMATION FOR THE STATE OF _____:
>
> In order to practice law in this state, one must follow the following steps:
>
> 1. _____
>   _____
>   _____
>
> 2. _____
>   _____
>   _____
>   _____
>
> 3. _____
>   _____
>   _____
>
> 4. _____
>   _____
>   _____

sole proprietorship
a law office operated by a single attorney who owns the practice

partnership a law firm that is composed of two or more attorneys who share the expenses and profits of the partnership

partner attorney owners of the law firm; they receive a percentage of the profits of the firm

LAW OFFICE ORGANIZATION

Law offices are organized based on whether they are private or public, their specialty (if any), and their form of business entity. Most private law firms are sole proprietorships, partnerships, or professional corporations. A **sole proprietorship** is operated by a single attorney who owns the practice.

A **partnership** organization is comprised of two or more attorneys who share the expenses and profits of the partnership. **Partners** may own equal or unequal shares of the partnership. However, all partners bear equal responsibility for the debts and liabilities of the partnership.

For example, if Partner A owns 60% of the partnership, he will receive 60% of the firm's profits. However, if the partnership cannot pay the firm's liabilities, each of the partners is individually liable for all of the debts, regardless of the percentage of ownership of each. The percentage of ownership of the partnership may be determined by a number of different means, such as the percentage of capital invested, the number of clients brought to the firm, the amount of seniority, or any other method determined by the partners.

Professional corporations are governed by state law and may be made up of attorneys, doctors, architects, accountants, or other professionals who form a special type of corporation to manage their business. The major advantage of a professional corporation over a sole proprietorship or a partnership is that the individuals who make up the professional corporation are not liable personally for the debts of the corporation, whereas the partnership members and the sole practitioner can be held personally liable if the assets of the business cannot pay the debts. An individual attorney may establish a professional corporation in most states. A number of variations on this basic structure exist, depending on state law.

Limited liability corporations are managed by the individual members; alternatively, management may be delegated to officers or managers, who are similar to corporate directors. The members of the corporation operate similar to partners but are not usually individually liable for company debts. Any income and losses are generally divided among the various members of the corporation. Taxes are paid by the individual members according to their shares of the business. A typical large law firm is illustrated in the law office organization chart found at Exhibit 1–1.

Research the law in your own state to determine what types of business entities are allowed for attorneys. You may find this information on the Web site for your state's bar association.

STATE-SPECIFIC INFORMATION FOR THE STATE OF _____ :

In the state of _____ , attorneys may operate the following types of business entities:

  1. sole or individual proprietorship _____

  2. partnership _____

  3. professional corporation _____

  4. other _____ .

---

professional corporation corporation governed by state law that may be made up of attorneys, doctors, architects, accountants, or other professionals to form a special type of corporation to manage their business

limited liability corporations corporations managed by the individual members, or their management may be delegated to officers or managers who are similar to corporate directors

THE SOLE PRACTITIONER

One-attorney law firms operate most frequently in smaller cities or towns. The typical organizational structure consists of an attorney and a combination paralegal and legal professional. In some offices, there may be other administrative support personnel, such as a law librarian and/or a bookkeeper.

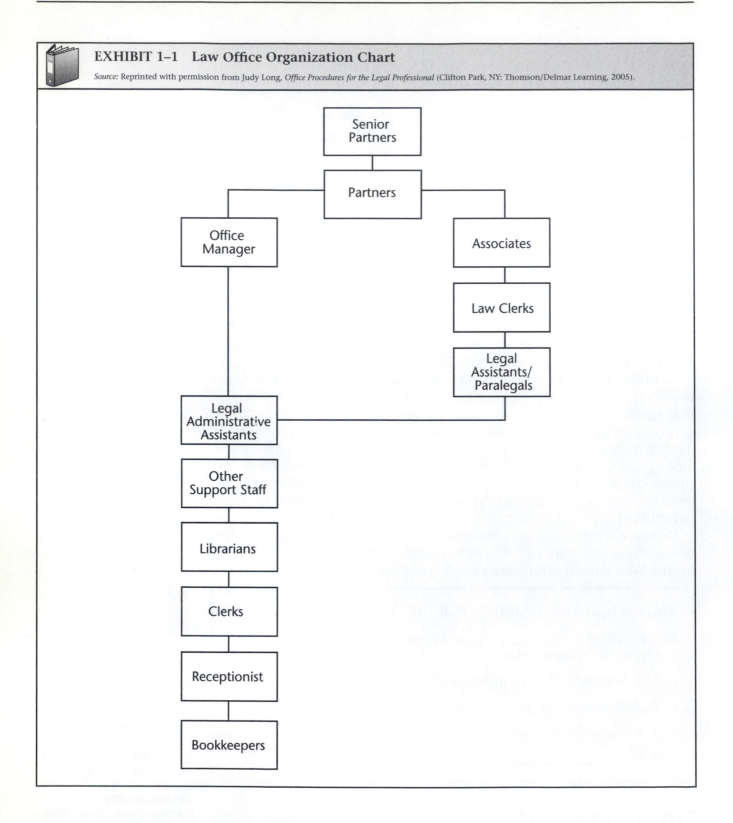

EXHIBIT 1–1 Law Office Organization Chart

Source: Reprinted with permission from Judy Long, *Office Procedures for the Legal Professional* (Clifton Park, NY: Thomson/Delmar Learning, 2005).

If an attorney practicing as a sole practitioner incorporates his practice, only the corporate assets will be liable in the case of a lawsuit against the firm. However, if the individual does not incorporate, his personal assets may also be liable. Because of this problem, many sole practitioners have chosen to incorporate and form a professional corporation.

Sole practitioners may specialize in one or several areas of law. Very few lawyers choose to become general practitioners, who practice in all legal areas. With today's complicated laws, many general practitioners have chosen to specialize in one or two areas.

THE LARGE PRIVATE LAW FIRM

Law firms come in various sizes and organizational types. Referring to Exhibit 1–1, note the different levels of responsibilities at a large firm. Typically, the **senior partners** are the founders of the law firm. They own the major percentage of shares in the firm and receive the majority of the profits. They are often the named partners in the law firm's name. Some of the founding partners may be retired or deceased, but may still maintain a partial ownership interest in the firm individually or through their heirs. Ownership interest varies considerably from one firm to the next, however; specific information may be found in the partnership agreement of the individual firm.

The larger the firm, the more levels of attorneys they employ. The very large law firms may have founding partners, senior partners, partners, junior partners, senior associates, associates, and junior associates. The higher-level partners typically receive a higher percentage of the firm's profits. **Associates** are employees of the firm and receive a salary. The more senior associates will receive a higher salary than the junior associates. In some firms, one must obtain a certain associate level before being considered for partnership status.

MANAGING ATTORNEYS

The day-to-day operations of the law firm are the responsibility of the **managing attorney.** This individual may review cases from other attorneys and hold staff meetings. He may be responsible for dividing the case load among the attorneys. If the firm does not employ an administrative law office manager, he may also be responsible for the administrative functions of the law firm.

ADMINISTRATIVE MANAGER/LAW OFFICE MANAGER/HUMAN RELATIONS

The **administrative manager** of the firm is responsible for managing all administrative functions of the office. This may include hiring and firing, managing the clerical staff, and any other day-to-day administrative decisions, including those involving the file room, library, accounting, and other administrative functions. The larger the firm, the more managerial responsibilities are accorded to this person. For instance, in a very large firm, the administrative manager may have responsibility for the managers of the various administrative departments. In a smaller firm, there would be no manager in the departments and the administrative manager would have the direct responsibility for those tasks. The administrative manager may be an individual with a

senior partners lawyers who are the founders of the law firm and have an ownership interest therein

associates lawyers who are employed by the firm; they receive a salary and not a percentage of the profits

managing attorney manages the law firm on a day-to-day basis

administrative manager individual responsible for managing all administrative functions of the office

business degree who has worked in a law office for a long period of time, a senior paralegal, or an individual with both legal and administrative experience.

Some law firms employ a **law office manager** instead of an administrative manager. This person would have the responsibilities of not only the administrative manager but the managing attorney as well. The law office manager may be a senior paralegal with a management background or degree, an attorney, or an individual with a business degree who has had extensive law firm experience.

Many firms also employ a human relations manager to oversee the employee relations functions of the law office. This individual is typically responsible for benefits and policies related to employees, such as medical insurance, vacations, labor relations, and personnel problems.

INFORMATION TECHNOLOGY/ COMPUTER EXPERT

Experts in information technology and computers are required in all firms. Small firms may outsource this function. These individuals are responsible for keeping the computers running, videoconference equipment issues, and telephone systems.

PARALEGAL/LEGAL ASSISTANT

Many firms use the job titles *paralegal* and *legal assistant* interchangeably. Some offices, however, distinguish between the paralegal and the legal assistant by giving more responsibility to the paralegal.

Paralegals are trained professionals who usually have either a four-year bachelor's degree and a paralegal certificate or a two-year associate's degree in paralegal studies. Some firms require a certification conferred by one of the national paralegal professional organizations, and some colleges and universities offer a bachelor's degree in paralegal studies.

Paralegals assist lawyers in many areas, including drafting documents, discovery, interviewing clients and witnesses, legal research, and investigation. Depending on the lawyer's specialty, the paralegal may also be involved in other activities. Generally, the paralegal's duties are diverse and vary considerably with the type of law practiced by the attorney.

LEGAL PROFESSIONAL

In those offices that distinguish between the paralegal and the **legal assistant**, the latter will generally assume less responsibility. In some cases, the legal assistant provides administrative support for the paralegal. Some modern-day law offices no longer use the term "legal secretary" and have substituted "legal administrative assistant" or "legal assistant" for this individual. For purposes of this textbook, the **"legal professional"** is a designation for a law office employee who performs administrative, secretarial, and some paralegal tasks.

law office manager individual with the responsibilities of not only the administrative manager but the managing attorney as well

paralegal trained professionals who usually have either a four-year bachelor's degree and a paralegal certificate or a two-year associate's degree in paralegal studies

legal assistant individual who provides administrative support for the paralegal and/or performs paralegal duties

legal professional law office employee who performs administrative, secretarial, and some paralegal tasks

In smaller law firms, the legal professional may perform many of the responsibilities of the paralegal, along with administrative responsibilities. In this case, the legal professional may perform legal research, draft documents, take notes at depositions, draft discovery materials, make travel arrangements, draft correspondence and reports, prepare the calendar, answer the telephone and take messages, schedule appointments and meetings, file, and type correspondence and reports. The duties may vary with different specialty areas of law and different size firms. In essence, the legal professional working in a small firm may have a combination paralegal and legal administrative assistant position.

In larger firms, the legal administrative assistant or legal professional will perform administrative functions. This individual may work for one or several attorneys, depending on the workload. Duties will include calendaring, making travel arrangements, drafting and typing correspondence and documents, scheduling appointments and meetings, and filing. This individual may also hold the designation of "legal secretary." Other responsibilities may be assigned depending on the individual firm.

The Internet is a valuable tool for one employed in either of these positions. The use of the Internet will be described extensively in Chapter 5.

NOTARY PUBLIC

Law offices employ a **notary public** to administer oaths and certify the authenticity of signatures. In order to become a notary, one must pass a test on the topic, post a bond, and pay a fee to the state. Some states require wills to be witnessed by a notary public.

Some offices require that their legal professionals and/or paralegals become notaries. Notary public is generally not a full-time position.

LAW LIBRARIAN

The **law librarian** is in charge of the library. This person usually has a degree in library science and/or paralegal training. In smaller firms, this position may be an added responsibility of the paralegal or legal assistant. Law librarians should be knowledgeable in the various computerized legal research systems, such as Westlaw and Lexis. Other responsibilities include ordering books, periodicals, and electronic publications, keeping track of volumes, law library structure, updating volumes, and generally maintaining the law library. A good system should be in place for checking books out of the law library. It can become particularly stressful when one is trying to meet a deadline and needs a particular volume, only to find that the volume is missing from the library and its whereabouts are unknown.

LAW CLERK

Law clerks are law school students who are working part time either in a law office or for a judge. Judges at all levels employ law clerks. Most

notary public one who has the power to administer oaths and certify authenticity of signatures

law librarian the individual who is in charge of the library and usually has a degree in library science and/or paralegal training

law clerks law school students who are working part time either in a law office or for a judge

firms require their law clerks to have completed their second or third year of law school. Their responsibilities may include performing legal research, investigating cases, and drafting documents. Some firms require that they file documents with the court and run errands for the attorneys. Sometimes their work includes responsibilities similar to those of the paralegal or law librarian.

Law clerks gain valuable experience in the real world environment of the law office that assists them in the practice of law once they become attorneys. Their assignment is usually temporary but may turn into a permanent position as an attorney after the individual graduates and passes the state bar examination.

RECEPTIONIST

Since the first contact that a client has with the law office is often with the receptionist, this position is one of the most critical in the firm. If the client encounters a rude receptionist on his first visit to the office, he may have a negative impression of the firm. This impression might make the meeting with the attorney very difficult. On the other hand, if the receptionist is cordial and personable, the client will be in a more positive frame of mind for the meeting with the attorney. The receptionist should receive training in how to handle difficult clients and situations. Good keyboarding skills and the ability to multitask are also important proficiencies to have. In a busy office, the telephones may be ringing, a client may come in for a meeting, and someone else may be calling on the intercom. The receptionist must be able to handle all of these situations in a friendly, efficient, and professional manner.

ACCOUNTING/PAYROLL/BOOKKEEPER

While the very large firm may have its own accounting department, a small firm may have one individual who handles the combined position of **bookkeeper** and payroll clerk. Some smaller firms employ an outside service to manage their accounting and payroll functions. The functions of this person or department include keeping the books of the firm, preparing the firm's payroll, billing clients after compiling data from time sheets of attorneys and paralegals, and keeping track of expenses of the firm.

GOVERNMENT LAW OFFICES

All branches of the government have lawyers employed in their various departments. At the county level, district attorneys prosecute criminal cases, public defenders defend individuals accused of crimes if they cannot afford an attorney, and attorneys employed as county counsels, defend lawsuits against the county. Cities also employ attorneys as city attorneys who take care of all legal business for that city. Other local government departments may also require the services of an attorney.

bookkeeper individual who keeps the firm's books and payroll

Many state departments employ attorneys in various capacities. They may work in the state courts or the administrative offices of the courts. In those states that have a state bar court, attorneys may handle disciplinary actions and appear in court for actions within the state bar.

The state attorney general is the chief attorney for that particular state. Other offices in the state that employ attorneys include the offices of the legislative counsel, governor, lieutenant governor, secretary of state, state treasurer, state controller, legislature, department of corporations, department of industrial relations, workers' compensation board, and any other state offices that may require legal services.

In addition to positions in the federal courts as prosecutors or public defenders, attorneys are employed in most departments of the federal government. Many federal government departments have local offices throughout the country. A few examples include the Federal Bureau of Investigation (FBI), Federal Trade Commission (FTC), Treasury Department, Internal Revenue Service (IRS), Immigration and Naturalization Services (INS), Patent and Trademark Office, and any other federal department that requires legal services. The Justice Department is one of the country's largest employers of legal assistants.

Research the offices of government in your own county and state and list departments that employ lawyers.

STATE-SPECIFIC INFORMATION FOR _____:

The state government employs attorneys in the following departments and positions:

_____

_____

_____

_____

_____

_____.

The county of _____ employs attorneys in the following capacities:

_____

_____

_____

_____

_____

_____

CORPORATE LAW DEPARTMENTS

Large corporations will have their own **corporate law departments** that handle the legal business of the corporation. Their work is as varied as the corporations themselves. The law department of a corporation is one of many different departments that exist in the organization. Corporations that are sued frequently and those that involve a considerable amount of legal service will most likely have their own legal department. Pharmaceutical companies, airlines, and large banks

corporate law departments law departments in corporations; handle the legal business of the corporation

are examples of those organizations that will probably have a law department.

The attorney who heads the law department is usually called the vice president of law, general counsel, or general attorney. Although this individual is an attorney, he will generally have a considerable amount of administrative responsibility for the running of the department. The law department personnel usually will not perform peripheral tasks such as timekeeping and accounting because there is a separate department in the corporation for those functions. Although the human resources department will perform initial screening of applicants for the law department, the prospective supervisor in the department will make the final hiring decision.

Employees who work in the law department will perform legal tasks for one client: the corporation. They may be involved in litigation for or against the corporation, labor law, patent law, or corporate law. These offices generally handle matters relating to corporate stock, corporate minutes, articles of incorporation, bylaws, and stock option plans. The specialty of the individual parts of the law department will depend on the specialty area of the corporation itself. For example, an insurance company's law department will deal heavily in litigation cases.

POLICIES AND PROCEDURES MANUAL ■

A large firm or corporation will usually have a policies and procedures manual that it provides to all employees. It will include employee benefits and employment policies of the office. The manual may include any or all of the following items:

1. **Hours**
   This includes the hours of work and whether overtime hours are compensated. Typically, one is paid overtime if he is an hourly employee who is considered non-exempt. If the employee is paid a straight monthly salary and is considered exempt, overtime may not be paid. In some firms "comp time" is issued for extra hours worked. That is, the employee is compensated by receiving the same amount of time off as he worked in extra hours. For instance, if the employee accumulates eight hours of "comp time" at the end of the week, then he will be entitled to an extra day off. The method of computing "comp time" varies with each firm but should be included in the manual.

2. **Time off, including holidays, vacation, and sick days**
   Each firm will have set holidays as well as policies on vacation time. The number of sick days that are paid each year will also vary by the firm.

3. **Employee benefits**
   Some firms provide medical insurance for employees. Some offices will also provide retirement plans as well as other types of insurance, such as life insurance, vision insurance, and dental insurance. In some cases, spouses or domestic partners are also included in these insurance programs.

4. **Templates**

Many procedures manuals have a section for templates of the proper format for correspondence and documents. These templates may include letters, different types of court documents, signature lines, headings, or pleadings. Since so many of the documents prepared in the law office have repetitive formats, templates will help you prepare written material quickly and efficiently.

5. **Confidentiality and Ethics**

Law office employees may be required to sign a confidentiality agreement that states that all information obtained at the firm cannot be repeated outside of the office. One must protect the confidences of the clients. Ethics will be discussed more extensively in Chapters 2 and 4.

6. **Forms**

Some states have many forms that are used for filing with the courts. Large offices have forms to be used for expense accounts, time sheets, travel requests, book requests, and other items. These forms will generally be provided as part of the manual.

Many other items may also be included in this manual. If you are newly hired in a firm that does not have a manual, then once you learn office procedures and policies, you might want to write one, with the permission of your supervisor. The table of contents from a manual in a large Los Angeles law firm is included herein as Exhibit 1–2.

SUPPORT PERSONNEL

As a member of the legal team, the legal professional will be required to provide liaison with other employees of the firm. In a very large firm, many support functions will be handled by other departments, such as clerical, word processing, library, transportation, and messengers. The legal professional must be knowledgeable in the purpose of the various departments as he will likely be responsible for coordinating the tasks assigned to each area. For instance, if a very long document must be keyboarded and the task is assigned to the word processing area, it may be the responsibility of the legal assistant to coordinate this assignment, being sure that the instructions are clear and that the job is completed in a timely manner. The legal professional must follow through diligently to assure that the effectiveness of the team is not put at risk by an assignment not being completed when it is due.

Whenever the legal professional enters another department to make a request, he must be courteous and adhere to that department's rules and regulations. For instance, if the librarian has a check-out procedure established for taking books from the library, the legal assistant should not take a book from the shelves of the library without utilizing this procedure. If the office has a central file room, the legal assistant should always request a file from the file clerk in charge of dispensing files and should not just remove it from the files. A cheerful and courteous

EXHIBIT 1–2   Office Manual Table of Contents

Source: Reprinted with permission from Sheppard, Mullin, Richter, & Hampton LLP.

OFFICE MANUAL
TABLE OF CONTENTS

continued

Exhibit 1–2 *continued*

attitude is important in dealing with individuals of whom a request is being made. It is important to remember that a last-minute request is often not met favorably by the requested individual. Therefore, try to establish reasonable timelines for all requests.

OUTSOURCING

Some firms **outsource**, using outside firms to complete some of their support functions. For instance, a long litigation keyboarding project may be turned over to a printing company to reproduce. It is often the responsibility of the legal assistant to be sure the project is completed correctly and in a timely fashion. The returned material should be read carefully and errors noted.

Travel agencies are sometimes used to make travel arrangements for the law firm. In this situation, the legal assistant is often the one who is making the preparations and discussing the trip with the travel agent. Be sure that the agency being utilized is reputable and has a good reputation in the community. Some agencies provide full travel services, such as hotel reservations, airline reservations, and car rentals. Others might provide only some of these services. If the legal assistant is making travel arrangements on his own, the Internet provides invaluable tools for this purpose. Chapter 5 will discuss the use of the Internet more extensively.

Outside messenger services may be used to transport items to a location in another part of the city or to another city. In order to meet a deadline, the service may be called upon to deliver a document to the adverse party's attorney for service, to file a document or pleading with the court, or to serve a party to the action. Clear instructions must be given by the legal assistant as to the time to deliver the item as well as the correct address and telephone number. Last-minute requests should be avoided to allow for the meeting of crucial deadlines, which are especially critical when filing documents with the court or making service on adverse parties.

Other examples of outside vendors that support the law office include records retrieval companies, process servers, trial specialists, scanning and coding companies, and overflow copy vendors.

LEGAL RESEARCH SERVICES

Attorney specialists in legal research offer **legal research services** to assist law firms with large research projects. These firms may provide large-scale research for major cases, or more specific services for smaller but highly specialized cases. In some situations, the firm may hire one of these services to assist in one specific aspect of a large case with many different issues.

FREELANCE PARALEGALS

Freelance paralegals work independently in their own businesses and are not permanent employees of a particular law firm, although they

outsource using outside firms to complete some support functions

legal research services specialists in legal research with services available to assist law firms with large research projects

freelance paralegals individuals who work independently in their own businesses and are not permanent employees of a particular law firm, although they may work for a firm on a temporary basis

may work for a firm on a temporary basis. These paralegals work in many areas of law, including probate, domestic relations, workers' compensation, immigration, and landlord/tenant law. Law offices often employ freelance paralegals as independent contractors to work for them on a large case or for highly specialized work.

Freelance paralegals work either for attorneys on an as-needed basis or directly with their own clients, who appear in court without attorney representation (*pro per*). Paralegals who work independently of attorneys and have their own clients have received much criticism in recent years because many state bar associations have become concerned that unlicensed individuals are engaging in the unauthorized practice of law. Some states are requiring paralegals to be certified or licensed in certain specialty areas to alleviate this problem.

Freelance paralegals working independently may not give a client legal advice. They must inform the client that they are paralegals and not attorneys. They may help the client complete the forms and/or documents required by the court for a particular case; however, they may not advise the client about whether to litigate an action, what settlement is realistic, or any other issues that require them to give legal advice or do anything that might be considered the practice of law or the exercise of independent legal judgment. The client, and not the paralegal, signs the forms and documents. Freelance paralegals should consult with an attorney when their client requires legal advice.

Some states restrict the ability of paralegals to practice on a freelance basis and to operate their own offices. It is important to find out the rules of your own state to determine the requirements. Record the requirements in the box below.

STATE-SPECIFIC INFORMATION FOR THE STATE OF _____

The requirements for freelance paralegals in this state are

_____

_____

_____

_____.

HUMAN RELATIONS ISSUES ■

The legal assistant is often the person called upon to coordinate activities of outside personnel, whether it is individuals in another department or those employed by other firms. It is important to remember that although your project may be the most critical to you at that moment, the outside person with whom you are making arrangements will have many other projects to complete and may not give yours the same priority as you feel it should have. Your deadlines are not necessarily amenable with their deadlines. Therefore, try to avoid last-minute requests that are critical to the outcome of a case. For instance,

---

EXHIBIT 1–3 Sample Activity Log

CASE NAME: _____
Company/
Department

Activity	Date Sent	Date Due	Follow-up	Completed
Acctg.Financial	4/8/06	4/20/06	4/15/06	4/18/06
LSMCaseRes	4/1/06	4/15/06	4/10/06	4/15/06

---

if your paperwork must be filed with the court on the tenth of the month, try not to give it to the printing company on the ninth and expect it to be ready the next day. Reasonable requests are met with considerably more cooperation than unreasonable ones.

When the firm is employing several outside sources to complete a particular project, a log of activities should be kept, so that at any given point in time, the deadline for the completion of each part of the project is available. A sample activity log is shown in Exhibit 1–3.

FORMS USED IN THE LAW OFFICE

Microsoft Word has a section entitled "Legal Pleadings" that may be found by using the following instructions:

> Click on the **"File"** menu at the top of the page; then click on **"New."**
>
> The **New Document** file will appear on the right. Click on **"New from template"** and then click on **General Templates**.
>
> Click the **Legal Pleadings** file tab and double-click on **Pleading Wizard**.
>
> Follow the steps in the wizard.

The instructions in the wizard are easy to follow. To demonstrate, if you have access to a computer running Microsoft Word, try creating a pleading using the Pleading Wizard.

1. First, click on "next" and then select "Create a pleading in another court." Name the court *County Court of Your State*.
2. Complete the caption as it pertains to the court in which you are filing the case.
3. Check the proper parties for this document and click "next."
4. Insert the names of the parties and click "next."
5. Insert the case number, the number of firms filing, the title of the pleading, and the title of the summary and click "next."
6. Insert the name of the attorney and the firm's name and address, and click "next."
7. Click "Finish."

EXHIBIT 1–4   Completed Pleading

```
 1   JOHN B. GOOD
     2433 Main Street
 2   White Plains, NY 1111
     Telephone:  (444) 123-4567
 3

 4   County Court of Your State

 5

 6   SAMUEL PLAINTIFF,                    ) Case No.: No. 12-3-456789-1
                                          )
 7             Plaintiff,                 ) COMPLAINT
                                          )
 8        vs.                             )
                                          )
 9   SALLY DEFENDANT,                     )
                                          )
10             Defendant                  )
                                          )
11   _____

12

13

14

15                          Dated this 4ᵗʰ day of October, 2006

16
                                          _____
17                                        2433 Main Street
                                          White Plains, NY 1111
18                                        Telephone:  (444) 123-
                                          4567
19                                        John B. GOOD

20

21

22

23

24

25
```

EXHIBIT 1–5 United States District Court Proof of Service—Summons and Complaint
Source: http://www.uscourts.gov

**UNITED STATES DISTRICT COURT
CENTRAL DISTRICT OF CALIFORNIA**

CASE NUMBER:

Plaintiff(s)

v.

**PROOF OF SERVICE
SUMMONS AND COMPLAINT**
(Use separate proof of service for each person/party served)

Defendant(s)

1. At the time of service I was at least 18 years of age and not a party to this action and **I served** copies of the *(specify documents)*:

    a. ☐ summons   ☐ complaint   ☐ alias summons   ☐ first amended complaint
    ☐ second amended complaint
    ☐ third amended complaint

    ☐ other *(specify)*:

2. **Person served:**

    a. ☐ Defendant *(name)*:

    b. ☐ Other *(specify name and title or relationship to the party/business named)*:

    c. ☐ Address where papers were served:

3. **Manner of Service** in compliance with *(the appropriate box **must** be checked)*:

    a. ☐ Federal Rules of Civil Procedure

    b. ☐ California Code of Civil Procedure

4. **I served** the person named in Item 2:

    a. ☐ By **Personal service**. By personally delivering copies. If the person is a minor, by leaving copies with a parent, guardian, conservator or similar fiduciary and to the minor if at least twelve (12) years of age.

       1. ☐ **Papers were served on** *(date)*: _____ at *(time)*: _____

    b. ☐ By **Substituted service**. By leaving copies:

       1. ☐ **(home)** at the dwelling house, usual place of abode, or usual place of business of the person served in the presence of a competent member of the household, at least 18 years of age, who was informed of the general nature of the papers.

       2. ☐ **(business)** or a person apparently in charge of the office of place of business, at least 18 years of age, who was informed of the general nature of the papers.

       3. ☐ **Papers were served on** *(date)*: _____ at *(time)*: _____

       4. ☐ **by mailing** *(by first-class mail, postage prepaid)* copies to the person served in Item 2(b) at the place where the copies were left in Item 2(c).

       5. ☐ **papers were mailed** on (date): _____

       6. ☐ **due diligence**. I made at least three (3) attempts to personally serve the defendant.

PROOF OF SERVICE - SUMMONS AND COMPLAINT

CV-1 (04/01)

PAGE 1

continued

Exhibit 1–5   *continued*

c. ☐ **Mail and acknowledgment of service**. By mailing *(by first-class mail or airmail, postage prepaid)* copies to the person served, with two (2) copies of the form of Waiver of Service of Summons and Complaint and a return envelope, postage prepaid addressed to the sender. **(Attach completed Waiver of Service of Summons and Complaint)**.

d. ☐ **Service on domestic corporation, unincorporated association (including partnership), or public entity. (F.R.Civ.P. 4(h)) (C.C.P. 416.10)** By delivering, during usual business hours, a copy of the summons and complaint to an officer, a managing or general agent, or to any other agent authorized by appointment or by law to receive service of process and, if the agent is one authorized by statute and the statute so requires, by also mailing, by first-class mail, postage prepaid, a copy to the defendant.

e. ☐ **Substituted service on domestic corporation, unincorporated association (including partnership), or public entity. (C.C.P. 415.20 only)** By leaving during usual office hours, a copy of the summons and complaint in the office of the person served with the person who apparently was in charge and thereafter by mailing *(by first-class mail, postage prepaid)* copies to the persons at the place where the copies were left in full compliance with C.C.P. 415.20. Substitute service upon the California Secretary of State requires a court order. **(Attach a copy of the order to this Proof of Service)**.

f. ☐ **Service on a foreign corporation**. In any manner prescribed for individuals by FRCP 4(f).

g. ☐ **Certified or registered mail service**. By mailing to an address outside California *(by first-class mail, postage prepaid, requiring a return receipt)* copies to the person served. **(Attach signed return receipt or other evidence of actual receipt by the person served)**.

h. ☐ **Other** (specify code section and type of service):

5. Service upon the **United States, and Its Agencies, Corporations or Officers**.

a. ☐ by delivering a copy of the summons and complaint to the clerical employee designated by the U.S. Attorney authorized to accept service, pursuant to the procedures for the Office of the U.S. Attorney for acceptance of service, or by sending a copy of the summons and complaint by registered or certified mail addressed to the civil process clerk at the U.S. Attorneys Office.

Name of person served:

Title of person served:

Date and time of service: *(date)*: _____   at *(time)*: _____

b. ☐ By sending a copy of the summons and complaint by registered or certified mail to the Attorney General of the United States at Washington, D.C. **(Attach signed return receipt or other evidence of actual receipt by the person served)**.

c. ☐ By sending a copy of the summons and complaint by registered or certified mail to the officer, agency or corporation **(Attach signed return receipt or other evidence of actual receipt by the person served)**.

6. At the time of service I was at least 18 years of age and not a party to this action.

7. Person serving *(name, address and telephone number)*:

    a. Fee for service: $

    b. ☐ Not a registered California process server

    c. ☐ Exempt from registration under B&P 22350(b)

    d. ☐ Registered California process server

8. ☐ I am a California sheriff, marshal, or constable and I certify that the foregoing is true and correct.

I declare under penalty of perjury that the foregoing is true and correct.

Date: _____

_____
(Signature)

A copy of a completed pleading prepared using these steps is included as Exhibit 1–4.

A sample form for the Federal District Court for the Central District of California for a Proof of Service, Summons and Complaint is shown as Exhibit 1–5.

◼ KEY TERMS

Administrative manager	Legal research services
Associates	Limited liability corporation
Bookkeeper	Managing attorney
Corporate law departments	Notary public
Freelance paralegals	Outsource
Law clerks	Paralegals
Law librarian	Partners
Law office manager	Partnership
Lawyer/attorney	Professional corporation
Legal assistant/legal administrative assistant	Senior partners
Legal professional	Sole proprietorship

◼ SELF TEST

Describe the items that you would include in an administrative procedures manual that you would prepare for a firm in which you were employed as a legal assistant.

What are the different types of law offices? Explain the advantages and disadvantages of each one. Include different types of private firms, corporate law departments, and government law offices.

What would be your ideal position in the law office, and why?

Explain the purpose of the administrative procedures manual.

◼ NOTEBOOK PROJECT

Obtain a three-ring binder with subject tabs. As you progress through this course, put headings on the binders with chapter titles from the text and insert items that will be of use to you in a future position. Be sure to include those items marked with a notebook logo in the text. Also include the exhibits from this chapter. Periodically, your instructor will review the notebook for a grade.

For additional resources, visit our Web site at **www.westlegalstudies.com**

MANAGEMENT OF THE LAW OFFICE

CHAPTER OUTCOMES

As a result of studying this chapter, the student will learn:

1. the billing function of the law office.
2. how to keep billable hours.
3. the methods of timekeeping utilized in law offices.
4. the importance of trust accounts and their function.
5. the importance of privileged communications and confidentiality.
6. the professional associations for legal assistants.

ETHICAL ISSUES

Attorney/Client Privilege

The most important aspect of ethical consideration in the law office is the practice of attorney-client privilege. The law protects disclosure of privileged statements made to the attorney by the client. The law also applies to the attorney's employees who are working on a particular client's case. The basic rule to follow is: when in doubt about whether a communication is privileged, do not disclose any part of it to anyone except the attorney.

The law protects the revealing of privileged information relating to a client under any circumstances. For instance, if you are subpoenaed in a court proceeding and he asked to reveal privileged communications received from the client, you are protected by the law so that you do not have to reveal this information.

The attorney-client privilege is so inclusive that it protects all information received from the client from being revealed at any time or place. Exceptions to this rule include the situation in which a client reveals that she is about to cause bodily harm to herself or another person, that she is about to commit a crime, or that she is about to commit a fraudulent act. In those cases, the attorney may be obligated to report the information. The exception also applies if the client is seeking the assistance of the attorney in these fraudulent or illegal activities. Since there is a considerable amount of

Continued

controversy surrounding several aspects of this ethical rule, it is advisable to not reveal information unless directed to do so by the attorney or after receiving the attorney's approval. Realistically, it is highly unlikely that the client would tell the legal assistant this information. In most cases, she would tell the attorney.

The client's confidential information should not be compromised accidentally in the law office. For instance, never answer questions on the telephone or give information about a client's case unless you are sure the person calling is the client. Someone may call you pretending to be the client and ask for confidential information. If you are not sure the person is the client, tell her you will call her back, or ask her to send you a letter or stop into the office so that you can be sure of her identity.

Be careful about speaking on the telephone about one client's case when another client can listen. In fact, if one client asks you if another individual is a client of your firm, you may not reveal that fact or anything about the case. For instance, suppose there are two different clients waiting in your office to see the attorney. If one of them asks you the nature of the other's visit, you may not divulge this information. You may say, "I'm sorry, but I cannot reveal any information about a case or a client."

However, suppose one client proceeds to discuss her case with the other client in the office. In that case, the client herself is revealing the information. Only the client may reveal the information to a third party because the privilege belongs to the client. You should never reveal information received from the client unless directed to do so by the attorney.

TIMEKEEPING SYSTEMS ■

Each employee who bills time is responsible for keeping track of her own hours in order to bill the client properly. Hours spent on matters pertaining to a client's case are billed to the client. These hours are called **billable hours.** In most firms, administrative and clerical work is not billed to clients, but legal work is billed. For example, the time spent drafting and revising a document for the client might be considered billable hours, while the time spent typing the document would not. **Time sheets** will be utilized by some employees of the firm to keep track of their billable hours. In most firms, these sheets are computerized so that a total bill may be prepared for the client that includes all billable hours for that client. Exhibit 2–1 shows a typical time sheet for a large law firm. In this form, hours are recorded manually. Some small firms utilize manual recording; however, in many firms computer programs are used to track billable hours. Computerized systems are described in Chapter 10. Using such systems, attorneys and other employees input their own time directly into the computer on the appropriate form.

Nonbillable hours are the hours spent working in the law office that cannot be billed directly to a client. For instance, the legal assistant

billable hours the hours that are spent working on a client's case that may be billed to the client.

time sheet used by each employee of the firm to keep track of the billable hours; may be computerized or done by hand

nonbillable hours the hours spent working in the law office that cannot be billed directly to a client

EXHIBIT 2–1 A Sample Time Sheet

Source: Reprinted with permission from Sheppard, Mullin, Richter, & Hampton LLP.

TIMESHEET

NONCHARGEABLE CATAGORIES

Client/File No.	Description
001-00001*	Public and Alumni Activities
002-00002*	Recruiting
003-00003*	Client Development
004-00004*	Professional Activities
005-00005	Travel Branch
006-00006	Sick Day
007-00007	Vacation Day
009-nnnnn*	Pro Bono

Client/File No.	Description
00A-00008	Billings and Collections
00B-00009*	Department/Practice Group/ Firm Meetings
00C-00010*	Firm Committee Work
00D-00011*	Internal Education
00E-00012*	Firm's Own Account
00F-00013	Other Office Time
00G-90061*	MCLE
00H-00014*	Zero Hour Weekend Time

GLOSSARY LIST — CHARGEABLE AND NONCHARGEABLE

aa	– Acquisition Agreement	ea	– Employment Agreement	pf	– Prepared for
af	– Arranged for	ep	– Estate Plan	pld	– pleadings
ag	– Agreement	exh	– exhibits	r	– Reviewed
arb	– Arbitration	fi	– file	ri	– Response to Interrogatories
att	– Attended	fin	– finalized	rr	– Reviewed and revised
az	– Analyzed	hea	– hearing	rs	– Researched
c	– Court	int	– Interrogatories	rv	– Revised
cd	– Closing Documents	ld	– Loan Documents	sa	– Security Agreement
ch	– Charter Documents	loi	– Letter of Intent	sag	– Settlement Agreement
clo	– Closing	m	– meeting	sl	– Sick time
cor	– Corresponded with	md	– motion documents	t	– Trial
cr	– Conferred re	mem	– memorandum	tcr	– Telephone conference re
cw	– Conferred with	n	– negotiated	tcw	– Telephone conference with
dep	– deposition	neg	– negotiations	tra	– Transcripts
doc	– documents	p	– Prepared	va	– Vacation time
drf	– Drafted	pd	– Prepared documents	wk	– Weekend
				wo	– Worked on

WORK LOCATION CODES:

LA – Los Angeles	SD – San Diego	OT – Other
OC – Orange County	SF – San Francisco	

SORT CODES:

DIS – Discovery	PRET – Pre-Trial	TRIAL – Trial
CLOSE – Closing	DOC – Documents	SETT – Settlements
	MEET – Meetings	OTH – Other

PAGE _____ OF _____ PAGES

* First File Number in a Series — Additional File Numbers also exist.

NAME: _____ DATE: _____

NO.				TIME		CITY	SORT	WORK	FUNCTION	CON-
CLIENT #	FILE #	CLIENT/MATTER NAME		H	T	CODE	CODES	CODE	CODE	TIN

may be asked to update publications in the law library. This time is typically billed under a special administrative code.

It is important to keep track of all time spent working on each client's case. Sometimes employees are reluctant to complete a time sheet for a ten-minute telephone call. But if you spend a lot of time on the telephone, you may come up very short on billable hours if all calls are not noted and billed. Consider that six ten-minute calls in a day equal one hour that should be billed to clients.

New legal assistants and legal professionals are often reluctant to note the actual time spent preparing a document for the first time because they are concerned that the attorney will think they spent too long on that project. Obviously, preparing a given type of document for the first time will take longer than preparing it for the tenth time. The attorney is aware of this, and the firm may reduce the amount of time charged to the client. However, at the outset, all time spent on each client's case should always be noted on the time sheet.

In some firms, billable hours are recorded on the time sheet in tenths of hours; that is, every six minutes equals .1 hour. Thus, if the legal assistant spends an hour interviewing a client, it is recorded as 1.0 hour. If the assistant spends six minutes talking on the telephone with the client, that time is billed as .1 hour. Uneven amounts are generally rounded up to the next tenth. Therefore, if fifteen minutes are spent on a telephone call, the time is billed as .3 hour (which amounts to eighteen minutes.) Some firms may require a minimum amount of time to bill to each client for each item. For instance, a six-minute telephone call to the client might be charged as .3 hour if this minimum is 18 minutes. If the legal professional or legal assistant is performing a function that is not billable to the client, a special code will be used for that purpose. Other firms record their billable hours in fifteen-minute increments, or quarter-hours. Each firm may have a slightly different version of one of these methods of recording hours.

Some firms will only require employees to complete time sheets if they are charging the client an hourly fee. However, many firms prefer to keep track of the amount of time employees spend on each project and will require all individuals to prepare time sheets regardless of the method of billing clients.

Rather than trying to remember how each day was spent at the end of the day, the legal professional/assistant should record time as each task is completed. This can be accomplished by either keeping the computer program for time sheets open at all times on the computer or by keeping blank time sheets next to the telephone and recording time as each task is accomplished. It is easy to forget those short telephone calls when you are trying to recollect how you spent your time at the end of the day. If all of this time is not recorded, there will be no opportunity to bill the client accurately.

Many of the larger law firms require legal professionals/assistants to bill a minimum number of hours each year. These hours are used to determine whether to promote the assistant or whether to give her a raise. In some cases, if the number of hours billed is far below the minimum required, the legal professional/assistant may lose her job. It is not unusual for a firm to require the billing of 1,500 to 1,600 hours a year. Taking into account a two-week vacation, the billing requirement would be between 30 and 36 hours a week. Considering those hours that are not billable, the daily and weekly billable hours requirement in these firms is very large.

In order to calculate the number of hours that must be billed each week when the firm has a yearly billable hours requirement, calculate the number of weeks of vacation you will receive as well as any other days you might not be working, such as holidays. Deduct the number of weeks you are not working from 52. Divide the number of billable hours required each year by that number, and you will determine the number of weekly hours required to be billed to the client. In many large and busy law offices, staff may be required to work overtime to meet their yearly billable hours requirement.

For example, suppose you are entitled to one week's vacation and one week of holidays each year. When these two weeks are deducted from 52, the results are 50 weeks of work each year. If the firm's yearly billable hours requirement is 1,500, then you will be required to bill 30 hours a week to clients. (1500 divided by 50 = 30.) However, an absence of ten days during the year makes the billing requirement increase to 31.25 hours per week. Deductions must also be made for any hours spent working on nonbillable functions, such as attending conferences, taking care of personal business in person or by telephone, or attending to the business of a professional organization. Some firms are more liberal in the activities that they allow to be credited to the billable hours requirement. A number of firms, for instance, allow credit for hours spent at conferences or as an officer or committee member of a professional organization.

Most firms will give credit toward billable hours when the individual is performing work that benefits the law firm, such as attending training sessions or staff meetings, writing reports, updating the library, serving on committees that relate to the law office, or any other function that directly benefits the law firm. It is important to know what functions each law firm considers to be credited to the annual billable hours requirement.

CLIENT ACCOUNTING INFORMATION

Each client will have a ledger for her account. The client ledger should also have all time sheet information posted. If you are using a computer system for timekeeping, this task will automatically be accomplished each time you enter time billed to a particular client on your time sheet. At the end of the month, the bookkeeper can use this ledger sheet for billing purposes for each client. In some programs, the bills may be automatically reproduced by the utilization of a few key strokes on the computer keyboard.

ATTORNEY FEES

The most common types of attorney fee structures are hourly, contingency, and project-based. Some firms use a combination of these methods. One of the most common sources of dispute between clients and attorneys is fees. To avoid fee disputes with the client, all fee arrangements should be in writing and signed by both the attorney and the client at the initial client interview. Some states require that all fee arrangements with the client be written and signed by the attorney and the client.

Hourly Fees

The **hourly fee** is the most utilized type of fee. If the firm bills the client for each hour spent working on her case, the attorney will keep track of each of these hours. Generally, a lower hourly fee is charged for paralegal and legal assistant time than for attorney time. Some firms charge a lower hourly fee based on the level of expertise and/or experience of the individual working. Typically in a large law firm, different hourly amounts will be charged for senior partners, junior partners, associates, paralegals, and legal assistants. In most firms, non-attorney time is not billed directly to the client unless the individual is performing paralegal or legal assistant tasks. In firms that charge hourly fees, the paralegal and legal assistant must keep track of all billable hours so that the client may be charged appropriately.

Hourly rates vary considerably from one section of the country to the other and from large metropolitan areas to small towns. Attorney specialists in large metropolitan areas may charge $500 an hour or more, while a general practice attorney in a small town may charge less than $200 an hour. Other factors to consider are the amount of time to be billed to the client on the case, what other attorneys in the locality are charging, the level of expertise of the attorney, and the nature of the firm.

Contingency Fees

Contingency fees are used when the client is the plaintiff in a litigation action suing for money damages plus attorney fees and costs. These cases typically involve personal injury and/or property damage, such as automobile accidents, medical malpractice, or other incidents that may cause injury to person or property. The attorney's fee is a percentage of the award that the client receives from the defendant. For instance, if the attorney charges the client a 30 percent contingency fee and the client receives an award of damages of $300,000, the attorney would receive $90,000 and the client would receive $210,000. Typically, an attorney may charge one-third of the award (33-1/3%) if the case is settled before trial and two-fifths (40%) to one-half (50%) of the award if the case goes to trial.

Most attorneys who charge contingency fees require that clients pay the costs of litigation. This may include filing fees, court costs, copying charges, and fees for medical examinations. Contingency fees are not allowed in divorce, dissolution, probate, or criminal actions. Note that attorney fees in probate matters are set by state statute and are generally a percentage of the value of the estate.

Because doctors were being assessed high medical malpractice premiums, the state of California adopted legislation changing the fee structure for this type of case. The argument on the part of the doctors was that their medical malpractice premiums were forcing them to give up the practice of medicine. Attorneys argued that if medical malpractice awards were reduced, they could no longer take this type of case. The California legislature adopted a sliding-scale fee structure for medical malpractice whereby the attorney was paid a higher percentage for the

hourly fee   the fee the attorney bills the client for each hour spent working on her case

contingency fees   the attorney's fee is a percentage of the award that the client receives from the defendant

lower amounts of recovery. For example, the attorney could charge up to 40 percent for the first $50,000 recovered. The percentage would be reduced to 10 percent of any amount of recovery over $200,000. Fees between those recovery amounts were reduced accordingly. Other states are studying the fee structure in medical malpractice and other areas of litigation to determine whether similar restrictions should be adopted. Note that by the time this book is published other states may have adopted similar fee structures for medical malpractice cases.

Find the fee structure allowed in your state for different types of litigation cases and complete the State-Specific Information box below. Label any specific types of cases with their own fee structures.

STATE-SPECIFIC INFORMATION FOR THE STATE OF _____:

The mandated fee structures for this state are as follows:

_____

_____

_____

_____

_____

These limits apply to the following types of cases:

_____

_____

Retainer Fees

Some attorneys charge **retainer fees**, special fees that are payable at the outset of the case or at the time the client retains the attorney to work on her case. These fees may be in addition to the other amounts charged and are used to reserve the attorney's time to perform work on the case. They are deposited into the client trust account and drawn on, as needed, as the attorney works on the case. For instance, if the attorney charged the client a $10,000 retainer fee and performed $3,000 work of work, after the work was done she could draw the $3,000 from the client trust account, leaving $7,000 in the account for future work. As the retainer fee is used, the attorney will bill the client for additional fees to replenish the retainer. These fees are usually used in hourly fee arrangements, but some attorneys also use retainers in contingency fee cases.

A few attorneys may charge a retainer fee at the outset of the case and use that fee to reserve their time. In some cases, the fee is refundable, and in others it is not. State bar codes of ethics and/or rules of professional conduct differ in their treatment of nonrefundable attorney fees. Many states do not allow attorneys to charge nonrefundable fees for the reservation of their time. In most states, the retainer fee is used on the client's case and any amount not used is returned to the client.

retainer fees   special fees charged by some attorneys that are payable at the outset of the case or at the time the client retains the attorney to work on her case

The rules for accepting retainer fees are governed by the state bar of the state in which the attorney is working. Therefore, it is important to review the rules for retainer fees in the state bar codes for your state. Complete the State-Specific Information Box below.

ETHICAL RULES FOR RETAINER FEES FOR THE STATE OF _____:

The state bar of _____ has established the following rules for retainer fees charged in that state:

_____

_____

_____

_____

Project Fees (Flat Fees)

Project fees are a flat fee charged to the client based on the project to be completed. For instance, the attorney may charge a set fee for the preparation of a simple will, a living trust, or articles of incorporation. For instance, the attorney may charge a set fee for the preparation of a simple will, a living trust, or articles of incorporation.

Statutory Fees

Some attorney fees are set by state statute, such as those used in probate and workers' compensation cases. These state established fees are called **statutory fees.** In probate, they are based on the size of the estate and represent a percentage of the assets. In unusual situations that take extraordinary amounts of time, the attorney may petition the court to obtain fees greater than those set by statute in probate cases. Attorneys may ask the court for extraordinary fees for paralegal and other lay personnel time when these individuals performed work on the probate. Many states have reduced the attorney fees in workers' compensation cases to 25 percent or lower.

Find the statutory fees for probate and workers compensation in your own state and complete the box below:

project fees   a flat fee charged to the client based on the project to be completed

statutory fees   attorney fees set by state statute, such as those used in probate and workers' compensation cases

---

STATE-SPECIFIC INFORMATION FOR THE STATE OF _____:

Statutory fees for probate are the following:

_____

Statutory fees for workers' compensation are:

_____

ETHICAL ISSUES

Legal fees may not be shared with nonlawyers. In most states, nonlawyers are not allowed to own a law firm with an attorney. Ethical codes may be violated by a nonlawyer assuming control of a case and supervising the attorney on the case. Lawyers may not allow their independent judgment to be controlled by a nonlawyer.

Under the ethical rules of most states, a law firm employee who recommends a prospective client to the firm may not receive a fee for doing so ("capping"). One may find "cappers" in large metropolitan areas soliciting business for a particular attorney.

Any number of combination fee structures using the concepts described above may be found. For instance, a retainer may be required in other types of fee arrangements. Additional charges may be incurred for exceptional work or for cases completed quickly. Most states require that fee agreements be in writing and signed by both the attorney and the client. This system assists in the avoidance of controversy over the fees at a later date.

Several different types of fee contracts are shown in Exhibit 2–2, including a retainer fee contract, an hourly fee contract, and a fixed-fee (project) contract. Billing practices vary considerably from one firm to the next. Therefore, legal professionals and legal assistants should always confirm the firm's billing practices with the attorney before conveying this information to clients.

SHARING FEES

In some states, lawyers working in the same firm are allowed to share fees under certain circumstances. The method by which the fee is divided must be proportional to the amount of time each attorney spent working on the case. The client must be informed that both attorneys will be sharing the fee.

ADDITIONAL CHARGES TO CLIENTS

A number of large law firms may charge additional fees to client for special services rendered. However, these charges must be listed in the written fee agreement that the lawyer has with the client. Some firms charge an additional flat fee for various extra services.

A large litigation case may require the law firm to hire temporary litigation support personnel. This may include attorneys, paralegals, investigators, document control clerks, and special messengers for the filing and service of documents. Whether these services are billed to the client or absorbed in the firm's overhead will vary from firm to firm.

Some law firms charge the client for the reproduction costs of documents and other paperwork. Many lawyers charge clients for telephone calls to and from the client or to and from others if the call relates to the client's case. Postage fees are charged to the client in some firms.

**EXHIBIT 2–2   (a) Nonrefundable Retainer Fee Contract
(b) Hourly Fee Contract (c) Fixed-Fee Contract**

Source: Reprinted with permission from Pamela Everett-Nolkamper, *Fundamentals of Law Office Management, Systems, Procedures & Ethics*, 9th ed. (Clifton Park, NY: Thomson Delmar Learning, 2004).

Attorney-Client Fee Contract

This document (the "agreement") is the written fee contract that the law requires lawyers to have with their clients. We will provide legal services to you on the terms set forth below.

1. SCOPE OF SERVICES. You are hiring us as your attorneys, to represent you in the matter described on the attached Rate Schedule. We will provide those legal services reasonably required to represent you. We will take reasonable steps to keep you informed of progress and to respond to your inquiries. Unless you and we make a different agreement in writing, this agreement will govern all future services we may perform for you.

2. MINIMUM FEE/DEPOSIT. You agree to pay us an initial deposit of $_____ by _____. Of the initial deposit, $_____ will be our minimum fee, paid in exchange for our agreement to represent you. The minimum fee is nonrefundable, but our hourly charges will be credited against it. The remainder of the initial deposit, as well as any future deposit, will be held in a trust account. You authorize us to use that fund to pay the fees and other charges you incur. Whenever your deposit is exhausted, we reserve the right to demand further deposits, each up to a maximum of $_____. You agree to pay all further deposits within _____ days of our demand. Except for the minimum fee, any unused deposit at the conclusion of our services will be refunded.

3. LEGAL FEES AND BILLING PRACTICES. You agree to pay by the hour at our prevailing rates for time spent on your matter by our legal personnel. Our current hourly rates for legal personnel (and other billing rates) are set forth on the attached Rate Schedule. The Rate Schedule also provides for periodic increases.

4. COSTS AND OTHER CHARGES.

   (a) In General—We will incur various costs and expenses in performing legal services under this agreement. You agree to pay for those costs and expenses in addition to the hourly fees. The costs and expenses commonly include long-distance telephone calls, messenger and other delivery fees, postage, parking and other local travel expenses, photocopying and other reproduction costs, clerical staff overtime, word processing charges, charges for computer time, and other similar items. Except for the items listed on the Rate Schedule, all costs and expenses will be charged at our cost.

   (b) Out-of-Town Travel—You agree to pay transportation, meals, lodging, and all other costs of any necessary out-of-town travel by our personnel. You will also be charged the hourly rates for the time legal personnel spend traveling.

5. BILLING STATEMENTS. We will send you periodic statements for fees and costs incurred. Each statement will be due within _____ days of its date. You may request a statement at intervals of no less than 30 days. If you do, we will provide one within 10 days.

6. DISCHARGE AND WITHDRAWAL. You may discharge us at any time. If you should discharge us, the minimum fee will not be returned to you. When our services conclude, all unpaid charges will immediately become due and payable.

7. DISCLAIMER OF GUARANTEE. Nothing in this agreement and nothing in our statements to you will be construed as a promise or guarantee about the outcome of your matter.

CLIENT   ATTORNEY

By _____   By: _____

Figure # _____

continued

Exhibit 2–2   *continued*

Attorney-Client Hourly Fee Contract

This ATTORNEY-CLIENT FEE CONTRACT ("Contract") is entered into by and between _____ ("Client") and _____ ("Attorney").

1. SCOPE AND DUTIES. Client hires Attorney to provide legal services in connection with _____. Attorney shall provide those legal services reasonably required to represent Client, and shall take reasonable steps to keep Client informed of progress and to respond to Client's inquiries.

2. DEPOSIT. Client shall deposit $_____ by _____. The sum will be deposited in a trust account, to be used to pay costs, expenses and legal fees. Client hereby authorizes Attorney to withdraw sums from the trust account to pay the costs and/or fees Client incurs. Any unused deposit at the conclusion of Attorney's services will be refunded.

3. LEGAL FEES. Client agrees to pay for legal services at the following rates: partners, $250 per hour; associates, $200 per hour; paralegals, $100 per hour; law clerks, $75 per hour. Attorneys and paralegals charge in minimum units of .2 hours.

4. COSTS AND EXPENSES. In addition to paying legal fees, Client shall reimburse Attorney for all costs and expenses incurred by Attorney, including, but not limited to, process servers' fees, fees fixed by law or assessed by courts or other agencies, court reporters' fees, long-distance telephone calls, messenger and other delivery fees, postage, in-office photocopying at $.30 per page, parking, mileage at $3 per mile, investigation expenses, consultants' fees, expert witness fees, and other similar items. Client authorizes Attorney to incur all reasonable costs and to hire any investigators, consultants, or expert witnesses reasonably necessary in Attorney's judgment.

5. STATEMENTS. Client shall pay Attorney's statements within 30 days after each statement's date. Client may request a statement at intervals of no less than 30 days.

6. LIEN. Client hereby grants Attorney a lien on any and all claims or causes of action that are the subject of Attorney's representation under this Contract. Attorney's lien will be for any sums due and owing to Attorney at the conclusion of Attorney's services. The lien will attach to any recovery Client may obtain, whether by arbitration award, judgment, settlement, or otherwise.

7. DISCHARGE AND WITHDRAWAL. Client may discharge Attorney at any time.

8. CONCLUSION OF SERVICES. When Attorney's services conclude, all unpaid charges shall become immediately due and payable. After Attorney's services conclude, Attorney will, upon client's request, deliver Client's file to Client, along with any Client funds or property in Attorney's possession.

9. DISCLAIMER OF GUARANTEE. Nothing in this Contract and nothing in Attorney's statements to Client will be construed as a promise or guarantee about the outcome of Client's matter.

Client   Attorney
By _____   By: _____
Figure # _____

continued

Exhibit 2–2 *continued*

Attorney-Client Fixed Fee Contract

This ATTORNEY-CLIENT FEE CONTRACT ("Contract") is entered into by and between _____ ("Client") and _____ ("Attorney").

1. SCOPE AND DUTIES. Client hires Attorney to provide legal services in connection with her dissolution of marriage. Attorney shall provide all services to bring the matter to conclusion, including filing all papers, appearing in court, and preparing a marital settlement agreement.

2. FIXED FEE. Client agrees to pay a fixed fee of $1,500 for Attorney's services under this Contract. The fixed fee is due by June 1. Attorneys shall have no obligation whatsoever to provide services to Client until the fixed fee is paid in full.

3. COSTS AND EXPENSES. In addition to the fixed fee, Client shall reimburse Attorney for all costs and expenses incurred by Attorney, including, but not limited to, long-distance telephone calls, messenger and other delivery fees, postage, in-office photocopying at $.50 per page, parking, mileage at $2.50 per mile, investigation expenses, consultants' fees, and other similar items. Client authorizes Attorney to incur all reasonable costs and to hire any investigators or consultants reasonably necessary in Attorney's judgment.

4. DEPOSIT. In addition to the fixed fee Client shall deposit $500.00 by June 1. The sum will be deposited in a trust account, to be used to pay for costs and expenses. Client hereby authorizes Attorney to withdraw sums from the trust account to pay the costs Client incurs. Any unused deposit at the conclusion of Attorney's services will be refunded.

5. STATEMENTS. Client shall pay Attorney's statements within 10 days after each statement's date.

6. DISCHARGE AND WITHDRAWAL. Client may discharge Attorney at any time. If Attorney withdraws before completing Attorney's duties under this Contract, Client may be entitled to a refund of some or all of the fixed fee, depending on the facts and circumstances.

7. DISCLAIMER OF GUARANTEE. Nothing in this Contract and nothing in Attorney's statements to Client will be construed as a promise or guarantee about the outcome of Client's matter.

Client

By _____

Attorney

By: _____

Figure # _____

Some cases require the attorney to travel to distant locations. Clients may be charged for travel time, travel expenses, airline or automobile expenses, hotels, and meals.

Plaintiffs' attorneys who work in litigation generally charge the client a contingency fee. However, the client is usually required to pay the costs of litigation if the case is decided in favor of the defendant. Some states allow attorneys to advance the costs of litigation to the client, but clients must sign a promissory note to repay the firm from the proceeds of the judgment. If the judgment is in favor of the defendant, then the client must pay the attorney the sum of the promissory note. Other states do not allow attorneys to advance any fees to the client. Find the rules in your own state and complete the state-specific information box below.

After the interview with the client where fees are discussed, the legal assistant should send a letter to the client specifying all fees and charges. A typical letter is shown in Exhibit 2–3.

Clients should be sent detailed bills describing the services performed by the attorney. A typical example of a detailed bill for hourly billing services is shown in Exhibit 2–4.

STATE-SPECIFIC INFORMATION BOX FOR THE STATE OF _____:

The state of _____ 's rules governing an attorney's advancing costs to the client follow:

_____

_____

_____

_____

_____

Client files are generally reviewed for payment by the office manager on a monthly basis. If the client has not paid the bill 30 days after it was sent, a letter should be sent by the firm reminding the client of the charges due. A typical example of a 30-day reminder letter is shown in Exhibit 2–5.

If the account has not been paid within 60 days, a more forceful reminder letter may be sent to the client. An example is shown in Exhibit 2–6.

In extreme cases of nonpayment, the attorney may withdraw from the case (see Exhibits 2–7 and 2–8). However, most states have strict ethical guidelines regarding withdrawal that relate to jeopardizing the client's case. Some considerations include the client's financial condition, the length of time the fees have been outstanding, whether the client disputes the fees, and whether the client has received notice of the period of time the fees are outstanding. Some states do not allow an attorney to withdraw from the case if the client is unable to pay the fee. Many states do not allow an attorney to withhold the client's property if fees are outstanding.

Find your own state's ethical rules for withdrawal from a case by the attorney and insert them below. They may be found on your state bar's Web page.

STATE-SPECIFIC REQUIREMENTS FOR THE STATE OF _____.

Ethical rules for this state require that attorneys may withdraw from the case for nonpayment of fees under the following circumstances:

_____

_____

_____

_____

_____

_____

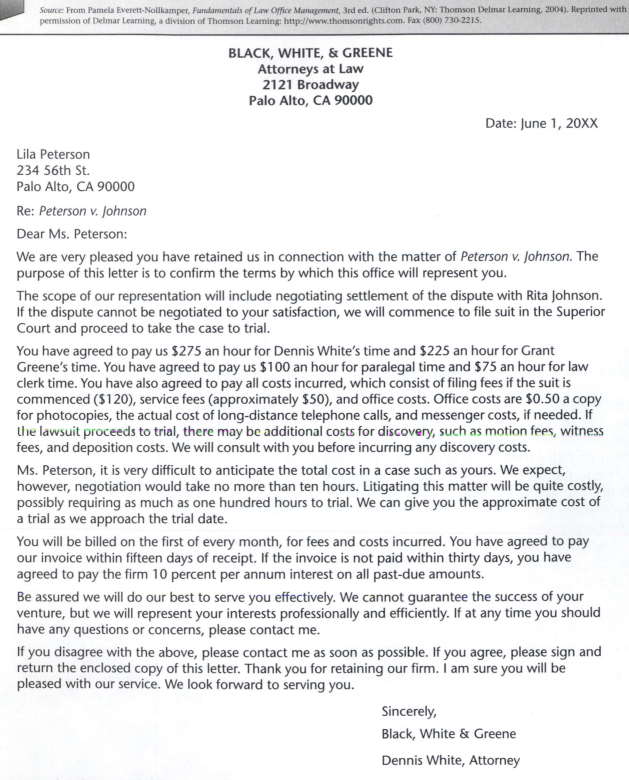

EXHIBIT 2–3 Engagement Letter

Source: From Pamela Everett-Nollkamper, *Fundamentals of Law Office Management*, 3rd ed. (Clifton Park, NY: Thomson Delmar Learning, 2004). Reprinted with permission of Delmar Learning, a division of Thomson Learning: http://www.thomsonrights.com. Fax (800) 730-2215.

BLACK, WHITE, & GREENE
Attorneys at Law
2121 Broadway
Palo Alto, CA 90000

Date: June 1, 20XX

Lila Peterson
234 56th St.
Palo Alto, CA 90000

Re: *Peterson v. Johnson*

Dear Ms. Peterson:

We are very pleased you have retained us in connection with the matter of *Peterson v. Johnson.* The purpose of this letter is to confirm the terms by which this office will represent you.

The scope of our representation will include negotiating settlement of the dispute with Rita Johnson. If the dispute cannot be negotiated to your satisfaction, we will commence to file suit in the Superior Court and proceed to take the case to trial.

You have agreed to pay us $275 an hour for Dennis White's time and $225 an hour for Grant Greene's time. You have agreed to pay us $100 an hour for paralegal time and $75 an hour for law clerk time. You have also agreed to pay all costs incurred, which consist of filing fees if the suit is commenced ($120), service fees (approximately $50), and office costs. Office costs are $0.50 a copy for photocopies, the actual cost of long-distance telephone calls, and messenger costs, if needed. If the lawsuit proceeds to trial, there may be additional costs for discovery, such as motion fees, witness fees, and deposition costs. We will consult with you before incurring any discovery costs.

Ms. Peterson, it is very difficult to anticipate the total cost in a case such as yours. We expect, however, negotiation would take no more than ten hours. Litigating this matter will be quite costly, possibly requiring as much as one hundred hours to trial. We can give you the approximate cost of a trial as we approach the trial date.

You will be billed on the first of every month, for fees and costs incurred. You have agreed to pay our invoice within fifteen days of receipt. If the invoice is not paid within thirty days, you have agreed to pay the firm 10 percent per annum interest on all past-due amounts.

Be assured we will do our best to serve you effectively. We cannot guarantee the success of your venture, but we will represent your interests professionally and efficiently. If at any time you should have any questions or concerns, please contact me.

If you disagree with the above, please contact me as soon as possible. If you agree, please sign and return the enclosed copy of this letter. Thank you for retaining our firm. I am sure you will be pleased with our service. We look forward to serving you.

Sincerely,

Black, White & Greene

Dennis White, Attorney

Agreed and accepted this _____ day of _____, 20XX.

_____

Lila Peterson

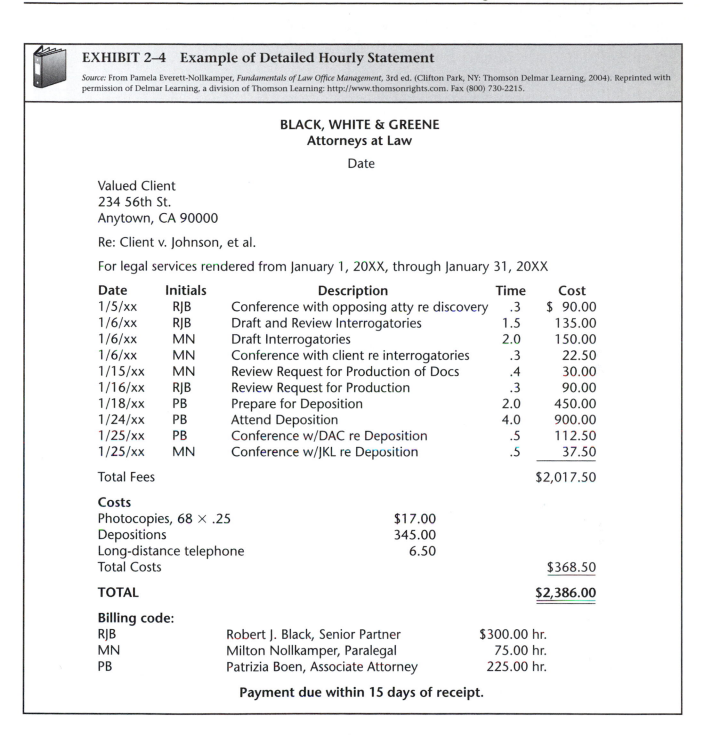

EXHIBIT 2–4   Example of Detailed Hourly Statement

Source: From Pamela Everett-Nollkamper, *Fundamentals of Law Office Management*, 3rd ed. (Clifton Park, NY: Thomson Delmar Learning, 2004). Reprinted with permission of Delmar Learning, a division of Thomson Learning: http://www.thomsonrights.com. Fax (800) 730-2215.

BLACK, WHITE & GREENE
Attorneys at Law

Date

Valued Client
234 56th St.
Anytown, CA 90000

Re: Client v. Johnson, et al.

For legal services rendered from January 1, 20XX, through January 31, 20XX

Date	Initials	Description	Time	Cost
1/5/xx	RJB	Conference with opposing atty re discovery	.3	$ 90.00
1/6/xx	RJB	Draft and Review Interrogatories	1.5	135.00
1/6/xx	MN	Draft Interrogatories	2.0	150.00
1/6/xx	MN	Conference with client re interrogatories	.3	22.50
1/15/xx	MN	Review Request for Production of Docs	.4	30.00
1/16/xx	RJB	Review Request for Production	.3	90.00
1/18/xx	PB	Prepare for Deposition	2.0	450.00
1/24/xx	PB	Attend Deposition	4.0	900.00
1/25/xx	PB	Conference w/DAC re Deposition	.5	112.50
1/25/xx	MN	Conference w/JKL re Deposition	.5	37.50

Total Fees				$2,017.50

Costs

Photocopies, 68 × .25	$17.00	
Depositions	345.00	
Long-distance telephone	6.50	
Total Costs		$368.50

TOTAL	**$2,386.00**

Billing code:

RJB	Robert J. Black, Senior Partner	$300.00 hr.
MN	Milton Nollkamper, Paralegal	75.00 hr.
PB	Patrizia Boen, Associate Attorney	225.00 hr.

Payment due within 15 days of receipt.

CLIENT TRUST ACCOUNTS ■

Attorneys are required to maintain a separate bank account for their operating expenses. Clients' funds are kept in the **client trust account**. When the client pays the attorney a retainer fee, this fee is deposited into the client trust account and may be drawn upon by the attorney when she performs work on that client's case. However, the client must be provided with a statement indicating the amount in the trust

client trust account   a separate bank account for client's funds that must be kept separate from the fund of the firm

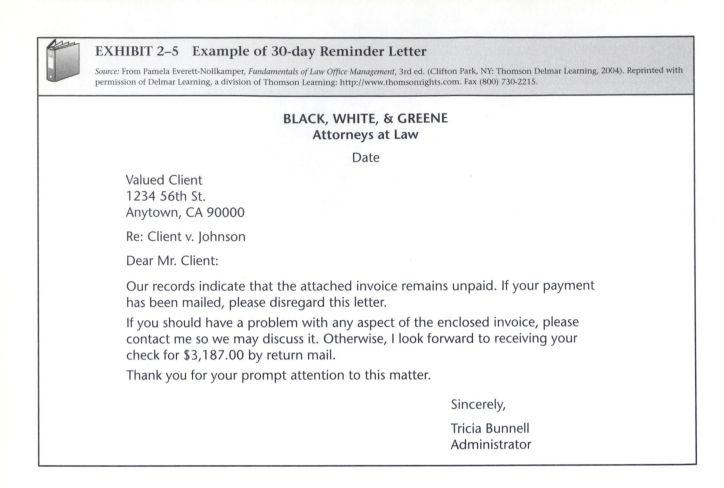

EXHIBIT 2–5   Example of 30-day Reminder Letter

Source: From Pamela Everett-Nollkamper, *Fundamentals of Law Office Management*, 3rd ed. (Clifton Park, NY: Thomson Delmar Learning, 2004). Reprinted with permission of Delmar Learning, a division of Thomson Learning: http://www.thomsonrights.com. Fax (800) 730-2215.

BLACK, WHITE, & GREENE
Attorneys at Law

Date

Valued Client
1234 56th St.
Anytown, CA 90000

Re: Client v. Johnson

Dear Mr. Client:

Our records indicate that the attached invoice remains unpaid. If your payment has been mailed, please disregard this letter.

If you should have a problem with any aspect of the enclosed invoice, please contact me so we may discuss it. Otherwise, I look forward to receiving your check for $3,187.00 by return mail.

Thank you for your prompt attention to this matter.

Sincerely,

Tricia Bunnell
Administrator

EXHIBIT 2–6   Example of 60-day Collection Letter

Source: From Pamela Everett-Nollkamper, *Fundamentals of Law Office Management*, 3rd ed. (Clifton Park, NY: Thomson Delmar Learning, 2004). Reprinted with permission of Delmar Learning, a division of Thomson Learning: http://www.thomsonrights.com. Fax (800) 730-2215.

BLACK, WHITE, & GREENE
Attorneys at Law

Date

Valued Client
1234 56th St.
Anytown, CA 90000

Re: Client v. Johnson

Dear Mr. Client:

Your account with our firm is seriously past due.

Please remit $3,187.00 by return mail, or we will be forced to take further action on this account.

Your immediate attention to this matter is imperative.

Sincerely,

Tricia Bunnell
Administrator

EXHIBIT 2–7   Attorneys Withdrawing from Representation

Source: Reprinted from Westlaw with permission of Thomson/West.

Court of Appeal, Second District, Division 3, California.
ESTATE OF John A. FALCO, Deceased.
G. Dana HOBART, et al., Petitioners and Appellants.
v.
Mahria DECKER, et al., Objectors and Respondents; **B012138**.

Jan. 20, 1987.

Attorneys who had **withdrawn** from representation of parties in will contest action filed petition seeking reimbursement of their costs and $48,000 in **attorney** fees. The Superior Court, Los Angeles County, George Xanthos, J., allowed **attorneys** to recover costs pursuant to provisions of contingent fee agreement, but denied recovery of **attorneys'** fees. **Attorneys** appealed. The Court of Appeal, Lui, J., held that: (1) **clients'** failure to accept settlement did not justify **attorneys' withdrawal** for purposes of recovery of **attorney** fees; (2) **attorneys** could be entitled to quantum meruit recovery if they **withdrew** in adherence to **ethical** mandates; (3) **attorneys** did not have **ethical** cause for **withdrawal**; (4) **clients'** refusal to settle could not in itself constitute cause for **withdrawal**; (5) finding that settlement **clients** entered into was not direct result of **attorneys'** labor was supported by substantial evidence; and (6) substantial evidence supported finding that **clients'** conduct did not justify **attorneys' withdrawal**.

Affirmed.

West Headnotes

[1] Attorney and Client ⚷ 76(1)
45k76(1) Most Cited Cases

[1] Attorney and Client ⚷ 134(1)
45k134(1) Most Cited Cases
Clients' failure to accept settlement did not justify **attorneys'** voluntary **withdrawal** from **case** and entitle them to recover **attorneys'** fees on basis of

quantum meruit; crucial element was existence of justifiable reason for **withdrawal**, rather than quantity of time expended.

[2] Attorney and Client ⚷ 134(1)
45k134(1) Most Cited Cases
For purposes of awarding **attorney** fees, granting of **attorney's** motion to **withdraw** does not establish cause for **withdrawal**, and thus personality clash between parties does not necessarily constitute justifiable reason for **withdrawal**.

[3] Attorney and Client ⚷ 134(1)
45k134(1) Most Cited Cases
For an **attorney** to be able to recover **attorney** fees in quantum meruit for **case** in which **attorney** has **withdrawn** from representation in adherence to **ethical** mandates, **attorney** must show that **withdrawal** was mandatory, not merely permissive, under state bar rules or statute, that overwhelming and primary motivation for counsel's **withdrawal** was obligation to adhere to **ethical** imperatives under state bar rules or statute, that counsel commenced action in good faith, that **client** obtained recovery subsequent to counsel's **withdrawal**, and that counsel's work contributed in some measurable degree toward **client's** ultimate recovery.

[4] Attorney and Client ⚷ 166(2)
45k166(2) Most Cited Cases
Determination that **attorneys** did not have **ethical** cause for **withdrawal** for purposes of quantum meruit recovery of **attorney** fees was supported by sufficient evidence; despite opponent's knowledge of allegedly damaging deposition testimony and **attorneys'** belief that **case** lacked merit, all parties to will contest action entered settlement agreement under which **attorneys' clients** received 36% of net balance of estate.

[5] Attorney and Client ⚷ 134(1)
45k134(1) Most Cited Cases
A **client's** refusal to settle cannot in itself constitute cause for **withdrawal** for purposes of recovery of **attorney** fees in quantum meruit to **withdrawing attorney**; disagreeing with *Pearlmutter v. Alexander,* 97 Cal.App.3d Supp. 16, 158 Cal. Rptr. 762.

[6] Attorney and Client ⚷ 101(1)
45k101(1) Most Cited Cases

continued

Exhibit 2–7   *continued*

[6] Constitutional Law ⚷305(2)
92k305(2) Most Cited Cases
Determination.
A client's right to reject settlement is absolute, as limitation of right to reject settlement would deprive client of due process right to proceed to trial on the merits. U.S.C.A. Const.Amends. 5, 14; ABA Rules of Prof.Conduct, Rule 1.2(a).

[7] Attorney and Client ⚷101(1)
45k101(1) Most Cited Cases
Exercise of the right to reject settlement is implicit in contract between client and attorney and cannot constitute breach of contract.

[8] Attorney and Client ⚷134(1)
45k134(1) Most Cited Cases
While a client's exercise of the right to reject settlement is not cause for withdrawal, client should be required to make restitution to attorney under theory of unjust enrichment, if client subsequently accepts settlement terms substantially to those negotiated by attorney prior to his or her withdrawal.

[9] Attorney and Client ⚷134(1)
45k134(1) Most Cited Cases
Clients were not required to make restitution to attorneys who had withdrawn from representation under theory of unjust enrichment where settlement entered into by clients six months after withdrawal was not direct result of attorneys' labor, but rather was result of six weeks of negotiations supervised by trial judge in which clients appeared in propria persona.

[10] Attorney and Client ⚷174
45k174 Most Cited Cases
Decision as to whether an attorney's lien should be imposed lies within trial court's discretion.

[11] Attorney and Client ⚷166(2)
45k166(2) Most Cited Cases
Substantial evidence supported trial court's finding that clients' conduct did not justify attorneys' withdrawal sufficient to award attorney fees in quantum meruit; although attorneys claimed that clients refused to cooperate, clients' right to refuse settlement could not constitute failure to cooperate, there was mutual animosity between attorneys and clients, and there was dispute which arose over attorney fees specified in contract.

*1007 **808 G. Dana Hobart, in pro. per., and Oshman, Brownfield & Smith, Richard H. Oshman, Los Angeles, and Gerald H.B. Kane, Jr., Redondo Beach, in pro. per., for petitioners and appellants.

Patten, Faith & Sandford, Jules Sandford and Lorraine Grindstaff, Monrovia, for contestants and respondents McAbee and Falcon.

No appearance for contestants and respondents Decker and Reimholz.

LUI, Associate Justice.

In this appeal, we address the question of an attorney's right to a quantum meruit recovery of fees after the attorney has voluntarily withdrawn from a case and the case is subsequently settled. In deciding this appeal, we do not intend our opinion to apply to a related but different question regarding the circumstances in which an attorney has a right to withdraw from a case.

*1008 FACTUAL AND PROCEDURAL BACKGROUND

Four sisters, Mahria Decker, Silvia McAbee, Lyn Reimholz and Lee Falcon (respondents) [FN1] entered into a contingency fee agreement with appellants G. Dana Hobart (Hobart) and the law firm of Oshman, Brownfield & Smith (Oshman) (collectively appellants) in September 1979 for the purpose of contesting the will of their deceased brother, John Falco (decedent). Appellants filed a petition for revocation of probate of purported will in December 1979, on behalf of the four sisters. The decedent's fifth sister, Virginia Vosburg, appeared in propria persona.

> FN1. For ease of reference, we collectively refer to all four clients as "respondents," although only two of the sisters have appeared on this appeal.

Inter alia, the decedent's will bequeathed $2,000 to each of his five sisters, leaving the bulk of decedent's estate to his friend and secretary Phyllis Werden. The value of the estate at the time of death in August 1979 was $918,924. The will was witnessed by the mother of Phyllis Werden, and executed by the decedent in October 1971, ****809** while he was hospitalized for liver complications stemming from alcoholism.

continued

Exhibit 2–7   *continued*

The contingency agreement provided that appellants would be obligated to "handle the Will contest up to and through the trial thereof and a Motion for a new trial, if any." Noting that neither the clients nor appellants knew the value of the estate, the contract specified that appellants "may withdraw as attorneys for the Contestants, if they discover that there are not sufficient assets subject to the contingency fee arrangement portion of the Estate to warrant them to prosecute said action."

In April 1983, all parties appeared in court prepared to begin trial, but stipulated to postpone trial until September due to an overcrowded court calendar. Thereafter, on May 11, Hobart then conducted an investigation and met with Dr. Telfer Reynolds, one of many physicians who examined the decedent in the hospital in October 1971, during the time decedent executed his will. Dr. Reynolds expressed his opinion that the decedent was competent at that time and able to execute a will, and was not in a mental or physical condition rendering him susceptible to influence.

Dr. Reynolds' evaluation prompted Hobart to advise respondents by letter dated May 13, 1983: ". . . In short, [Dr. Reynold's] testimony is directly contrary to our best interests in *every* respect.

". . . [T]here is at least one mutual friend that John Falco and Ginny Vosburg had, the name of whom escapes me at the moment without digging ***1009** into the file, who has unequivocally stated that during the last five or more years of your brother's life was [*sic*] angered with his sisters and intended to disinherit them.

"The foregoing are facts of life. Whether or not you like the facts of life is of no importance. My role and responsibility is to attempt to evaluate the win/lose potential of any litigation. Only a fool would not see the handwriting on the wall and reject settlement negotiations when confronted with this kind of evidence and testimony. For these reasons I am asking that each of you communicate to me your immediate willingness to accept any settlement that I can put together. If you do not do so, I will be forced to withdraw from a [*sic*] case on the basis that it is unethical for me and Mr. Oshman to proceed with litigation that we consider to be without merit . . . .

". . .

"Finally, please understand that my position is unequivocal and cannot be changed by discussing irrelevant issues with you and listening to each of you tell me how much John Falco cared for and loved each.

"Your failure to respond within 10 days, in writing, will leave me with no choice but to file a motion in court setting forth the reasons why Mr. Oshman and I are seeking permission to be relieved as counsel. Please understand that under these circumstances the court will have no alternative but to grant our motion and you will be faced with representing yourself or securing new trial counsel at this late date." (Emphasis in original.)

Hobart deposed Dr. Reynolds in two sessions, on May 18 and June 1, 1983, and concluded that Dr. Reynolds' testimony and reputation were unshakeable.

Appellants contend that prior to June 9, 1983, Hobart discussed settlement with his clients, who predicated their authority to settle upon appellants reducing their attorneys' fees, and upon the fifth sister, Vosburg, sharing in the payment of attorneys' fees. Respondents deny authorizing settlement and contend that they requested a reduction of attorneys' fees because the amount specified in the contract was unconscionable. The contract provided for appellants to receive 33-1/3 percent of the decedent's gross estate if the case was settled before trial. Respondents allege that they requested appellants to amend the contract to provide for the attorneys' fees to be based on a percentage of respondents' recovery rather than a percentage of the value of the gross estate. [FN2]

> FN2. Based on the valuation of the decedent's estate of $918,924 stated in the Inventory and Appraisement, upon any settlement before trial under the terms of the contingent fee agreement, appellants' fees would have been one-third of the gross estate, or approximately $306,305. Had respondents settled for 50 percent ($459,462), respondents would have received $153,157 after paying appellants $306,305. In comparison, if appellants' fees were calculated on the basis of the clients' recovery, in a settlement before trial of

continued

Exhibit 2–7   *continued*

50 percent, the clients would receive $306,310 and the appellants' fee of one-third would total $153,152.

**810 *1010 The facts in the record shed no light on the incidents which led Hobart to write to his clients on June 9, 1983, that "[b]ased on the authority previously given us, Mr. Oshman has made a settlement offer to the attorney for Phyllis Werden that we settle the claim on a 50/50 basis." [FN3] Hobart's letter further stated that he and Oshman agreed to "the modifications which [respondents] requested," [FN4] and that appellants would not need to file a motion to withdraw if the settlement negotiations were successful. Hobart informed respondents that he would be leaving the United States for a period of one year on July 28, 1983. He then warned respondents that "if something should occur which would nullify our settlement discussions or otherwise terminate them, you are placed on notice that I will not be available for trial under any circumstances."

FN3. The record on appeal contains no documentation of a settlement authorization given by any of the four sisters.

FN4. Appellants contend that respondents agreed to proceed with settlement on the condition that Virginia Vosburg agree to share in fees and costs. Since Ms. Vosburg refused, appellants decided to reduce their fees by 20 percent to give their clients the equivalent of their request. The record does not indicate whether respondents agreed to the 20 percent reduction as an equivalent of Vosburg's contribution.

By certified mail on June 14, 1983, Mahria Decker immediately denied that she ever gave appellants the authority to settle, and intended to take the case to trial.

By letter dated June 20, 1983, Hobart wrote to Mahria Decker informing her that her denial of settlement authority left him with no alternative but to withdraw as attorney of record, and reiterating that he would be leaving the United States in August for a year and would not be available for trial under any circumstances. [FN5]

FN5. "Dear Mrs. Decker:
"I am afraid you have finally placed me at the end of a rope. Needless to say, I am referring to your letter of June 14, 1983.
". . .
"To set the record straight I refer to your express authority to me to settle this matter on a '50/50' basis *if* your sister agreed to pay a one-fifth share of fees and expenses . . .
"I am fed up with your saying one thing and doing another . . . . *I am through with you.*
" . . .
"I will file our motion to be relieved on June 27, 1983, unless you have someone substituted in as your attorney before that date. " . . .
". . . You have made no secret of your dislike for me and I can't help but speculate that your change of position was intended to interfere with my planned sabbatical. Irrespective of your motives, I repeat that I will be leaving the country around August 1st and under no circumstances will I be available for trial in September." (Emphasis in original.)

*1011 On June 29, 1983, two months prior to the scheduled trial date, appellants filed their motion to withdraw as attorneys of record, on the basis that they believed that respondents' "case was, at best, on the *very* short end of being marginally meritorious." (Emphasis in original.) They argued that this belief became "cemented" by Dr. Reynolds' deposition testimony. Hobart contended that "[d]espite [respondents'] constant refusal to cooperate, Mr. Oshman and I have diligently prosecuted this cause. Not until we became convinced that we had no reasonable chance to prevail did we seek to be relieved as [respondents'] counsel."

Appellants contended that it was their legal duty to withdraw from prosecuting an action which they believed lacked merit, alleging "[n]ot only would it [have been] detrimental to [respondents] to be represented by counsel without faith in their cause, it would [have been] unethical for said attorneys to [have taken the] matter to trial."

Respondents, without benefit of legal counsel, did not file an opposition to appellants' ****811** motion to withdraw, but sent letters in opposition to the motion to the trial judge without serving copies on

continued

Exhibit 2–7 *continued*

appellants. Respondents' sister, Virginia Vosburg, who never retained appellants as counsel, filed a formal opposition and appeared at the hearing.

Appellants' motion to withdraw was granted on the basis that the attorney-client relationship had completely broken down. [FN6] Trial was continued until January 1984. All parties to the will contest action were served with copies of appellants' motion to withdraw, and as a result were aware of appellants' evaluation of the merits of the case.

> FN6. At the hearing of the motion, the trial court stated, "[I]t appears to the court . . . the attorney-client relationship is completely broken down. And I see no advantage to foisting either counsel on the clients and clients on the counsel and continuing what appears to be a totally irresolvable matter. [¶] Accordingly, the motion will be granted . . . ."

The mandatory settlement conference was held in December 1983, with respondents appearing in propria persona. Under the supervision of the trial court, the parties entered in a settlement agreement which specified, inter alia, that the decedent's five sisters would each receive one-fifth of a 36 percent share of the net balance of the estate.

In September 1984, appellants filed a petition seeking reimbursement of their costs and $48,000 in attorneys' fees. Appellants argued that their withdrawal was justified, entitling them to recover fees in quantum meruit because (1) their withdrawal was mandated by rules of professional conduct as a result of appellants' evaluation that the case was meritless; and (2) their clients did not cooperate and failed to authorize them to enter into settlement**1012** negotiations. In summarizing the important role appellants' work played in the eventual settlement of the case, appellants contended that there was a two percent chance their clients would prevail at trial as a result of their vigorous discovery work. [FN7] The trial court allowed appellants to recover their costs pursuant to the provisions of the contingent fee agreement, but denied recovery of attorneys' fees. This appeal followed.

> FN7. On the hearing of appellants' petition for attorneys' fees, Hobart commented on

the settlement of the case by the Bank of America, trustee for decedent's trust set up for the benefit of Werden: " . . . the Bank of America and the executor [were] in a position where at least they had to be concerned about what the outcome of the case would be, not what they saw or didn't feel confident they'd win the case, because I'm sure they knew what I knew, that they would probably win the case 98 times out of 100. [¶] But there was still a 2 percent chance. Now, whatever motivated them to settle this case—not the sisters—whatever motivated the Bank of America to settle this case is what you should be considering. And what motivated them was my deposition taken of the doctors, what I solicited from those doctors, the strangleholds that I had to fight with and come to grips with, the work that [Oshman] did, in connection with that."

CONTENTIONS ON APPEAL

Appellants contend that they are entitled to recover fees in quantum meruit because:

1. Appellants withdrew in adherence to ethical mandates stemming from their belief that respondents' case was meritless;

2. Respondents repudiated settlement authority and refused to settle;

3. Subsequent to appellants' withdrawal, respondents settled under terms similar to those negotiated by appellants; and

4. Respondents refused to cooperate.

DISCUSSION
I
California Decisions Concerning an Attorney's Right to Fees Following Discharge Or Withdrawal from a Contingent Fee Arrangement

In _Francasse v. Brent_ (1972) 6 Cal.3d 784, 100 Cal.Rptr. 385, 494 P.2d 9, our Supreme Court articulated the respective rights of an attorney and client engaged in a contingent fee agreement when the attorney is discharged. A client's right and power to discharge his or her attorney at any time, with or without cause, is absolute. (**812** _Id.,_ at p. 790, 100 Cal.Rptr. 385, 494 P.2d 9, citing Code Civ.Proc., § 284.) *1013 Such a discharge does not constitute a breach of contract for the

continued

Exhibit 2–7 *continued*

reason that it is a basic term of the contract, implied by law. However, an attorney discharged with or without cause is entitled to recover, in quantum meruit, the reasonable value of services rendered up to the time of the discharge. (*Id., at* p. 791, 100 Cal.Rptr. 385, 494 P.2d 9.)

Appellants, who voluntarily withdrew from representing respondents, now wish to extend the policy laid down in *Fracasse.*

Subsequent to the *Fracasse* decision, only two California cases, *Hensel v. Cohen* (1984) 155 Cal.App.3d 563, 202 Cal.Rptr. 85, and *Pearlmutter v. Alexander* (1979) 97 Cal.App.3d Supp. 16, 158 Cal.Rptr. 762, have analyzed whether an attorney who voluntarily withdraws from a contingency fee contract is entitled to recover attorney's fees from his client's subsequent recovery. [FN8] Appellants wish to distinguish *Hensel v. Cohen,* and rely heavily upon *Pearlmutter v. Alexander,* decided by the Appellate Department of the Superior Court of Los Angeles County. We are not bound by *Pearlmutter* (9 Witkin, Cal.Procedure (3d ed. 1985) Appeal, § 777, p. 747) and, to the extent that it is inconsistent with the views expressed herein, we decline to follow its holding.

> FN8. Prior to the *Fracasse* decision, in *Moore v. Fellner* (1958) 50 Cal.2d 330, 325 P.2d 857, in dicta, our Supreme Court recognized the principle that "an attorney who wrongfully abandons or withdraws from a case which he has contracted to handle, or has been discharged for cause by the client, may not recover compensation [citations]." The Court noted that "this approach appears to have grown in part from situations in which the contract of employment was considered to be entire and indivisible." (*Id.,* at p. 341, 325 P.2d 857.)

We note in passing that, to the extent that it is inconsistent, *Moore* is overruled by the *Fracasse* decision. In analyzing whether an attorney discharged by the client was entitled to recover fees, the *Moore* court focused on whether the discharge was for cause, and whether the contract was divisible. However, the analysis in the *Moore* decision is dubious in view of the court's subsequent analysis in the *Fracasse* case, which did not consider divisibility of the contract as a factor, and specifically rejected cause as a factor when an

attorney is discharged. "In summary, we hold that an attorney discharged with or without cause is entitled to recover the reasonable value of his services rendered to the time of discharge. Cases to the contrary, commencing with *Baldwin v. Bennett* [1854] 4 Cal. 392, are overruled." (*Fracasse v. Brent, supra,* 6 Cal.3d at p. 792, 100 Cal.Rptr. 385, 494 P.2d 9.)

[1] In *Pearlmutter,* the court held that a client's failure to accept a settlement was justification for the attorneys' withdrawal, entitling them to recover attorneys' fees on the basis of the written lien executed by their clients. In dicta, the court concluded that the standard applied when a client discharges an attorney similarly applies to a case in which an attorney voluntarily withdraws; [FN9] we reject this conclusion.

> FN9. In allowing the attorney to recover on his lien, the *Pearlmutter* court reasoned, "While the trial court found that plaintiff was under no legal compulsion to withdraw from the case, there is no finding that his withdrawal was improper . . . . [¶] We see no reason to differentiate between the situation where the attorney is discharged and where the attorney is allowed to withdraw insofar as continuation of the attorney's written lien for fees is involved." (*Pearlmutter v. Alexander, supra,* 97 Cal.App.3d Supp. at p. 20, 158 Cal.Rptr. 762.)

*1014 The court in *Hensel, supra,* 155 Cal.App.3d at page 568, 202 Cal.Rptr. 85, specifically rejected the rubric of *Pearlmutter,* and embraced the general rule followed in other jurisdictions: recovery for services in quantum meruit is allowed only when the attorney has *justifiable* cause for withdrawing. An attorney who voluntarily abandons a case without good cause will be denied compensation. (*Id.,* at p. 567, 202 Cal.Rptr. 85, citing 7 Am.Jur.2d, Attorneys at Law, § § 262-266, pp. 298-303, Annot. (1978) 88 A.L.R.3d 246, § 2.)

In *Hensel, supra,* 155 Cal.App.3d 563, 202 Cal.Rptr. 85, the Cohen law firm filed a personal injury suit on behalf of Hensel. When efforts to obtain witnesses failed and the defendant's insurance company showed no interest in offering settlement, Cohen advised Hensel that the firm wished to **withdraw** from the **case**. Hensel engaged alternative counsel and subsequently

continued

Exhibit 2–7   *continued*

settled the **case**. Finding that the firm was ****813** not justified in its **withdrawal**, the Court of Appeal denied recovery of **attorneys'** fees through enforcement of the written lien signed by Hensel.

Appellants argue that *Hensel* is distinguishable on the basis that the **attorneys** in *Hensel* expended merely 25 hours on the **case** before their **withdrawal**, compared to appellants' extensive investigation and discovery during a four-year period. Appellants' emphasis is misplaced. In our view, the crucial element is the existence of a justifiable reason for **withdrawing**, not the quantity of time expended.

[2] Appellants contend that once a trial court grants an **attorney's** motion to **withdraw**, cause for **withdrawal** has been established for the purpose of awarding **attorneys'** fees. We disagree. As the court noted in *Hensel,* "employing the proper procedure in **withdrawing** from a **case** is not synonymous with **withdrawal** for justifiable cause." (*Id.,* at p. 568, 202 Cal.Rptr. 85.) To protect the best interests of the **client**, a trial court should have broad discretion in allowing **attorneys** to **withdraw**. In the **case** at bar, the court granted appellants' motion to **withdraw** on the basis that the relationship between the parties had completely broken down. It was not relevant who caused the breakdown for the purposes of determining whether appellants should be allowed to **withdraw**, but rather, the trial court's concern focused on the effects the rift would have on respondents' legal representation.

While a personality clash between the parties may provide good reason for allowing the **attorney** to **withdraw**, it is not necessarily a justifiable reason for purposes of awarding fees.

*1015 II
Attorneys May Be Entitled to Quantum Meruit Recovery If They **Withdraw** in Adherence to **Ethical** Mandates

To date, no court has addressed the question of whether an **attorney's** voluntary **withdrawal**, motivated by an adherence to professional **ethical** codes, constitutes a justifiable cause so as to permit a recovery of compensation.

Two crucial factors must be present for appellant to prevail. First, we must conclude that **withdrawal** for **ethical** reasons justifies an award of **attorneys'** fees; an **attorney** who **withdraws** voluntarily without cause forfeits recovery for services performed. (*Hensel v. Cohen, supra,* 155 Cal.App.3d at p. 567, 202 Cal.Rptr. 85.) Second, the facts in the instant **case** must be sufficient to establish that appellants did in fact **withdraw** for a justifiable reason.

Business and Professions Code section 6068, subdivision (c), specifies that an **attorney** has a duty to maintain only such actions, proceedings or defenses as appear to him or her to be legal or just. [FN10] Our Supreme Court has commented that "[w]hen an **attorney** loses faith in his cause he should either retire from the **case** or dismiss the action." (*Kirsch v. Duryea* (1978) 21 Cal.3d 303, 309-310, 146 Cal.Rptr. 218, 578 P.2d 935, citing *Larimer v. Smith* (1933) 130 Cal.App. 98, 101, 19 P.2d 825.) [FN11]

> FN10. Additionally, Rules of Professional Conduct, rule 2-111(C) provides for *permissive* withdrawal when the client insists upon presenting a claim that is not warranted under existing law and cannot be supported by good faith argument for extension, modification, or reversal of the law. Rule 2-110(B) provides that a member of the State Bar shall not accept employment to present "a claim or defense in litigation that is not warranted under existing law, unless it can be supported by good faith argument of an extension, modification or reversal of existing law."

> FN11. We refrain from determining the corollary issue of whether an **attorney** who is **ethically** prohibited from proceeding to trial in a **case** the **attorney** believes lacks merit is similarly prohibited from settling the **case**.

Appellants argue that an **attorney** hired under a contingent fee agreement who determines that a **case** is meritless, and thus **withdraws** from the **case** for **ethical** reasons is entitled to recovery in quantum meruit. In considering the merits of appellants' position, our concerns focus on two ****814** undesirable consequences of such a position.

First, **attorneys** faced with failing claims may attempt to abandon a losing cause under the guise of an **ethical** duty, hoping later to collect their fees

continued

Exhibit 2–7 *continued*

if the **client** eventually recovers at trial or through settlement. As the court aptly stated in *Hensel, supra,* 155 Cal.App.3d at page 564, 202 Cal.Rptr. 85, an **attorney** employed ***1016** on a contingency fee basis may not "determine that it is not worth his time to pursue the matter, instruct his **client** to look elsewhere for legal assistance, but hedge his bet by claiming a part of the recovery if a settlement is made or a judgment obtained . . . ."

Secondly, appellants' position would require trial courts to weigh the veracity of the attorney's contention of an ethical motivation against the possibility that counsel's withdrawal was motivated by a desire to reduce counsel's own losses. Both motivations may well co-exist in the minds of counsel faced with a "meritless" case. The trial judge is faced with the dilemma of determining the proportions of these two desires: ethical versus financial motivation.

As Professors Hazard and Hodes have noted, "[i]t is impossible to look into a lawyer's head, and it is unacceptable simply to take his word for his state of mind when the probity of his own conduct is at issue." (Hazard & Hodes, The Law of Lawyering: A Handbook on the Model Rules of Professional Conduct (1986 supp.) p. 342.) However, we must balance these considerations with the inequities which would result if **attorneys** compelled to **withdraw** from **cases** by the provisions of **ethical** codes, through no fault of their own, were denied the ability to recover compensation.

[3] Noting the difficulty facing a trial court in making a factual determination of an **attorney's** motivation, we nonetheless find that an **attorney's** **withdrawal** in adherence to **ethical** mandates is justified, entitling counsel to recover **attorney's** fees in quantum meruit. But, the **attorney** has the burden of proof to show: (1) counsel's **withdrawal** was mandatory, not merely permissive, under statute or state bar rules; [FN12] (2) the overwhelming and primary motivation for counsel's **withdrawal** was the obligation to adhere to these **ethical** imperatives under statute or state bar rules; (3) counsel commenced the action in good faith; (4) subsequent to counsel's **withdrawal**, the **client** obtained recovery; and (5) counsel has demonstrated that his work contributed in some measurable degree towards the **client's** ultimate recovery. [FN13]

FN12. See, e.g., <u>Business and Professions Code section 6068,</u> subdivision (c). Compare <u>Rules of Professional Conduct, rule 2- 111(C)</u> (permissive **withdrawal**) and rule 2-110(B) (mandatory **withdrawal**).

We do not rule out the possibility of awarding fees to an **attorney** who **withdraws** under permissive **withdrawal** provisions of state bar rules or statute. In **cases** involving permissive **withdrawal** it is within the discretion of the trial court, with heightened scrutiny consistent with the standards articulated here, to determine whether counsel's **withdrawal** was justified for the purpose of awarding fees.

FN13. This is not intended to be an exhaustive list of considerations which a trial court must utilize.

*1017 A. *The Trial Court's Determination that Appellants Did Not Have **Ethical** Cause for **Withdrawal** Is Supported by Substantial Evidence*

In denying appellants' petition, the trial court determined that the **case** was not, in fact, meritless, and further rejected appellants' contentions that their **withdrawal** was motivated by appellants' **ethical** duties. [FN14]

FN14. Turning first to the provisions in the contract allowing for **withdrawal**, the trial court noted that the only right to **withdraw** established by contract was in the event there were insufficient assets in the estate:

"There is nothing said in here about anything else except that. So, consequently, we then have the only other thing, and that is the right to withdraw for cause.

"Notwithstanding what Mr. Oshman and Mr. Hobart say, I am very clear in my mind that what happened at some point in time was that [appellants came] to the realization that this case, from a proof standpoint, was not the case that we [*sic*] had hoped it to be.

" . . .

"[W]hen the . . . four ladies refused to relieve the two attorneys, it was necessary that a motion be filed in this court . . . . [C]onsiderable length was taken in setting

continued

Exhibit 2–7   *continued*

forth the position that the research, the discovery that was done in this case, led the attorneys to believe that they did not have the triable case that they were hoping for.

"I don't want to use the word 'weak case' or 'no case,' but at least it wasn't what we [*sic*] had expected it would be."

**815 The trial court's conclusion that the case was not meritless is supported by substantial evidence.

Despite the opposing parties' knowledge of Dr. Reynolds' deposition testimony and appellants' belief that the case lacked merit, all parties to the will contest action subsequently entered into a settlement agreement in which the five contesting sisters received 36 percent of the net balance of the estate. [FN15]

> FN15. Subsequent recovery cannot, in itself, rebut counsel's allegations of cause for withdrawal on the basis of a meritless case, for the simple reason that counsel may *only* recover if their client subsequently recovers. However, the amount of the recovery and the facts which gave rise to the clients obtaining the recovery are valid considerations to be weighed by the trial court in determining whether counsel's withdrawal was justified.

Appellants did not consistently argue that the will contest was completely meritless. Appellants stated in their petition for attorneys' fees, that after fully explaining to the four sisters the liability aspects of the case, they refused to settle "in spite of [appellants'] advice that, in view of the very questionable liability, the proposed settlement amount was, in [appellants'] opinion, *far greater than any possible recovery that could be obtained in the trial of the Contest action.*" (Emphasis added.)

Appellants simultaneously argued that Dr. Reynolds' testimony "pulled out the final vestiges of *any* hope" that respondents could prevail at trial. (Emphasis added.) However, the credibility of Dr. Reynolds, one of a number of doctors who examined the decedent, and the totality of the circumstances ***1018** under which the decedent executed his will, were ultimately questions of fact to be determined by the trier of fact.

[4] Appellants' inconsistent contentions regarding the validity of respondents' case was a factor to be considered by the trial court in making a factual determination as to appellants' motivation for withdrawal. The presumption on appellate review favors the correctness of the judgment, and where there is a conflict in the evidence and the inferences to be drawn therefrom, an appellate court is bound to accept as true the evidence and inferences in accordance with the findings of the lower court. (*Price v. Hibbs* (1964) 225 Cal.App.2d 209, 216, 37 Cal.Rptr. 270.) We find the trial court's factual determination to be supported by substantial evidence.

III
A Client's Refusal to Settle Cannot in Itself Constitute Cause for Withdrawal

Appellants cite *Pearlmutter v. Alexander, supra,* 97 Cal.App.3d Supp. 16, 158 Cal.Rptr. 762, in contending that respondents' refusal to settle justified their withdrawal. As noted, we disagree with *Pearlmutter.*

[5][6][7] A client's right to reject settlement is absolute. [FN16] To hold otherwise would deprive the client of his due process right to proceed to trial on the merits. [FN17] The exercise of the right to reject settlement ****816** is implicit in the contract between a client and an attorney, and cannot constitute a breach of contract. This right is irreconcilable with the rule espoused in *Pearlmutter.* A client's exercise of this right cannot constitute cause for the purpose of awarding attorneys' fees. [FN18]

> FN16. An attorney may not surrender any substantial right of a client contrary to his instructions or declared desires (*Kohr v. Kohr* (1963) 216 Cal.App.2d 516, 31 Cal.Rptr. 85), and may not compromise the client's case without the client's knowledge and express consent. (1 Witkin, Cal.Procedure (3d ed. 1985) Attorneys, § 194, pp. 221-222.) See, also, American Bar Association, Model Rules of Professional Conduct, rule 1.2(a): "A Lawyer shall abide by a client's decision whether to accept an offer of settlement of a matter."

> FN17. Our finding is limited to an analysis of the relationship between attorney and client.

continued

Exhibit 2–7 *continued*

We have not considered the consequences facing a client who refuses to accept a good faith settlement, including the possibility of a levy of sanctions.

FN18. We note other jurisdictions which have adopted the rule. (See *Borup v. National Airlines* (S.D.N.Y.1958) 159 F.Supp. 808, 810 ["[t]he mere fact that clients refuse to accept a settlement recommended by the attorney is not ground for his withdrawal"]; *Burston v. Pinkis* (1941) 25 N.Y.S.2d 12, 13 ["[t]he exercise of a client's unfettered right to refuse a settlement secured by his attorney . . . does not warrant the latter's withdrawal from the case"]; *Holmes v. Evans* (1891), 129 N.Y. 140, 29 N.E. 233 [withdrawal after client refused settlement constituted voluntary abandonment, attorney forfeited compensation]; *Suffolk Roadways, Inc. v. Minuse* (1968) 56 Misc.2d 6, 287 N.Y.S.2d 965 ["[r]efusal of client to accept a settlement offer, even though favored by his attorney, is not cause for withdrawal by the attorney"].)

*1019 IV
An Attorney May Be Entitled to Recover Under a Theory of Unjust
Enrichment If a Client Who Repudiates Settlement Later Accepts the Terms Negotiated

[8] While a client's exercise of the right to reject settlement is not cause for withdrawal, a client should be required to make restitution to the attorney, under a theory of unjust enrichment, if the client subsequently accepts settlement terms substantially similar to those negotiated by the attorney prior to his or her withdrawal.

[9] In the case at bar, respondents were not unjustly enriched by the settlement they entered into six months after appellants' withdrawal. The trial court's finding that the settlement entered into was not the direct result of appellants' labor is supported by substantial evidence.

Appellants never solidified any settlement with the opposing parties. They merely offered settlement on behalf of four of the five sisters at a rate of 50 percent, three days prior to receiving word from respondents denying that appellants had authority

to negotiate settlement. The trial court concluded that the subsequent settlement agreement entered into by all five sisters was not a direct result of the settlement efforts made by appellants, but rather was the result of six weeks of negotiations, supervised by the trial judge, in which respondents appeared in propria persona. The trial judge had firsthand knowledge of the proceedings in their entirety, and was in a superior position to evaluate the circumstances which led the parties to enter into the settlement agreement. On review, we find no error in this factual determination.

V
Substantial Evidence Supports the Trial Court's Finding that Respondents'
Conduct Did Not Justify Appellants' Withdrawal

Appellants argue that their withdrawal was justified by respondents' failure to cooperate. Other jurisdictions have recognized, under some instances, that an attorney who cannot obtain the cooperation of a client may be justified in withdrawing from the case and entitled to recover compensation. (See Annot. (1978) 88 A.L.R.3d 246, § 7, p. 260.) [FN19]

FN19. See, *Borup v. National Airlines, supra,* 159 F.Supp. 808, 810 (clients' delays and lack of diligence made attorneys' duties unreasonably onerous, but, "[t]he mere fact that clients refuse to accept a settlement recommended by the attorney is not ground for his withdrawal"); *Ambrose v. Detroit Edison Company* (1975) 65 Mich.App. 484, 237 N.W.2d 520 (client's total failure to cooperate constituted cause for withdrawal); *Dempsey v. Dorrance* (1910) 151 Mo.App. 429, 132 S.W. 33 (client refused to speak to counsel, amounting to wrongful discharge); *Irwin v. Baruch* (1946) 60 N.Y.S.2d 223 (plaintiff/attorney was unwilling to relinquish authority to his retained counsel).

*1020 In their motion to withdraw, appellants contended that respondents refused to cooperate, claiming that one of their ****817** clients stated that she would not testify unless her transportation was paid for by appellants; that respondents denied appellants permission to incur jury fee and medical expert witness expenses; and that Mrs. Decker told

continued

Exhibit 2–7   *continued*

appellants " 'your contract with us requires you to pay the costs of litigation.' "

Appellants further contend that respondents' failure to take their advice regarding settlement constitutes failure to cooperate. Given that it was respondents' absolute right to refuse settlement, it would be anomalous to hold that their refusal to settle constitutes lack of cooperation sufficient to award attorneys' fees in quantum meruit.

Appellants' motion to withdraw was granted on the basis that the attorney-client relationship had completely broken down. It is clear from the record that there was mutual animosity between appellants and respondents. The harsh tone of Hobart's letters to respondents understandably did not improve their compatibility.

Adding to the troubled relationship was the dispute which arose over the attorneys' fees specified in the contract. In all likelihood the fees specified in the contract would have been substantially greater than any recovery gained by respondents. It does not appear from the record that this dispute was ever resolved.

It is reasonable to conclude that these factors adversely affected respondents' ability, and desire, to cooperate with appellants.

[10][11] The decision as to whether an attorney's lien should be imposed lies within the trial court's discretion. On review, we must resolve all conflicts in favor of the respondents, and indulge all legitimate and reasonable inferences to uphold the verdict. (*Crawford v. Southern Pacific Co.* (1935) 3 Cal.2d 427, 429, 45 P.2d 183.) We find no abuse of discretion in the trial court's implicit finding rejecting the contention that respondents' lack of cooperation justified appellants' withdrawal.

DISPOSITION
The order is affirmed.

KLEIN, P.J., and ARABIAN, J., concur.

188 Cal.App.3d 1004, 233 Cal.Rptr. 807, 55 USLW 2454

END OF DOCUMENT

account, the amount deducted, the purpose therefore, and the balance. Most states require that the attorney take money from the account for reimbursement on a monthly basis at the time the monthly statement is being sent to the client.

For instance, suppose Client A pays the attorney a $2000 retainer fee and the attorney charges $300 an hour for her time. After she works on the client's case for three hours, she may withdraw $900 from the client trust account and deposit it into her own business account.

If the attorney receives a settlement for the client in a litigation case, the check should be deposited in the client trust account. The attorney may pay those fees advanced to the client or on behalf of the client from these proceeds. For example, in a personal injury case the attorney often either advances fees for doctor bills and medical expenses or has an arrangement with the doctor that she will be paid when the case is settled. In either case, the attorney would take the amount of the fee from the settlement and provide the remainder to the client after the attorney fees are distributed.

For instance, suppose Dr. X provided medical services to the client with an arrangement that her fee would be paid after the case was

EXHIBIT 2–8   Law Firm Withdrawing Representation

Source: Reprinted from Westlaw with permission of Thomson/West.

C

Kiernan v. KiernanN.Y.A.D. 4 Dept.,1996.
Supreme Court, Appellate Division, Fourth
Department, New York.
Patricia B. KIERNAN, Respondent,
v.
Stephen M. KIERNAN, Defendant.
Ange & Gordon, Appellant.
Nov. 8, 1996.

Law firm moved to withdraw representation of
wife in matrimonial action. The Supreme Court,
Erie County, Notaro, J., denied motion. Law firm
appealed. The Supreme Court, Appellate Division,
held that law firm was entitled to withdraw as
counsel for wife and was entitled to charging lien
for legal services rendered to her.

Reversed, motion granted and remitted.
West Headnotes
[1] Attorney and Client 45 ⬦⟜ **76(1)**

45 Attorney and Client
   45II Retainer and Authority
      45k76 Termination of Relation
         45k76(1) k. Act of Parties. Most Cited
Cases
Law firm was entitled to withdraw as counsel for
wife in matrimonial action and was entitled to
charging lien for legal services rendered to her
where wife did not pay counsel fees and
questioned her attorneys' competence, strategy
and ethics, rendering it unreasonably difficult for
firm to carry out its employment effectively.
N.Y.Ct.Rules, § 1200.15(c)(1)(iv) [DR 2-110, subd.
C, par. 1 d].

[2] Attorney and Client 45 ⬦⟜ **76(1)**

45 Attorney and Client
   45II Retainer and Authority
      45k76 Termination of Relation
         45k76(1) k. Act of Parties. Most Cited
Cases
Nonpayment of counsel fees alone will not entitle
attorney to withdraw from representation of
client. N.Y.Ct.Rules, § 1200.15(c)(1)(iv) [DR
2-110, subd. C, par. 1 d].

**612 Ange, Gordon and Adams by John Adams,
Buffalo, for Appellant.

Brown & Kelly by Philip Abramowitz, Buffalo, for
Respondent.

Before PINE, J.P., and LAWTON, CALLAHAN,
DOERR and BOEHM, JJ.
**613 *867 MEMORANDUM.
[1][2] Supreme Court improvidently exercised its
discretion in denying the motion of Ange &
Gordon to withdraw as counsel for plaintiff in this
matrimonial action.   While nonpayment of
counsel fees alone will not entitle an attorney to
withdraw ***868** from representation (*see, George v.
George,* 217 A.D.2d 913, 629 N.Y.S.2d 602), the
record demonstrates that the questioning by
plaintiff of her attorneys' competence, strategy
and ethics has rendered it unreasonably difficult
for the firm to carry out its employment effectively
(*see,* Code of Professional Responsibility DR
2-110[C][1][d] [22 NYCRR 1200.15(c)(1)(iv)];
Ashker v. International Bus. Machs. Corp., 201
A.D.2d 765, 766, 607 N.Y.S.2d 488; *Mars Prods. v.
U.S. Media Corp.,* 198 A.D.2d 175, 176, 603
N.Y.S.2d 487; *Bankers Trust Co. v. Hogan,* 187
A.D.2d 305, 589 N.Y.S.2d 338).

We therefore grant the motion of Ange & Gordon
to withdraw as plaintiff's counsel.   The firm is
thereby entitled to a charging lien (*see, Kahn v.
Kahn,* 186 A.D.2d 719, 720, 588 N.Y.S.2d 658;
Katsaros v. Katsaros, 152 A.D.2d 539, 543 N.Y.S.2d
478), and we remit the matter to Supreme Court
for a hearing to determine the reasonable value of
the legal services rendered to plaintiff.

Order unanimously reversed on the law without
costs, motion granted and matter remitted to
Supreme Court for further proceedings.

N.Y.A.D. 4 Dept.,1996.
Kiernan v. Kiernan
233 A.D.2d 867, 649 N.Y.S.2d 612

END OF DOCUMENT

settled. Her bill amounts to $5000. The client receives $100,000, and the attorney charges a 30 percent contingency fee. The $100,000 would be deposited in the client trust account. The attorney would pay Dr. X $5000. The attorney would take $30,000 for her fee. The client would receive $65,000.

ETHICAL ISSUES

Ethical codes require that attorneys must keep their trust account completely separate from any other bank accounts maintained by the law office. Some states require that the account be in a separate bank from the attorney's other accounts. However, each client is not required to have a separate trust account. It is sufficient that the attorney have an account called "Client Trust Account," in which all money advanced by or on behalf of clients is deposited. However, if the attorney has many large probate cases, it may be more efficient to have a separate trust account for each of them. Typically, the executor of an estate will open an account called the "Estate of Decedent Trust Account," in which monetary assets of the decedent are deposited and expenses of the estate are paid.

States vary greatly on their requirements for client trust accounts Determine the requirements in your own state and complete the box below.

STATE-SPECIFIC INFORMATION BOX

The requirements for client trust accounts for the state of _____ follow:

1. _____

_____

2. _____

_____

3. _____

_____

4. _____

_____

5. _____

_____

LEGAL ASSISTANT/LEGAL PROFESSIONAL RESPONSIBILITIES WITH CLIENT TRUST ACCOUNTS

Legal professionals/assistants are sometimes required to maintain the client trust account. This may include depositing funds into the account and paying disbursements from the account. When a settlement check arrives in the office, the legal professional or legal assistant may be responsible for depositing the check into the account and notifying the attorney and the client that it has arrived. Many firms, however, do not allow their legal professionals or legal assistants to maintain signature authority for depositing client funds or maintaining client trust accounts.

In some firms, the legal professional/legal assistant may be required to manage the account in a well-organized manner so that proceeds and expenses are separated into each client's file. Client files should be reviewed on a monthly basis to determine whether all expenses have been paid and that funds have been disbursed.

All checks that are received should be copied and retained in the file. Receipts should be prepared for all disbursements and signed by the individual receiving the funds. It is imperative that a "paper trail" be maintained for all funds that are received in the office as well as those funds that are disbursed.

A typical client ledger sheet for a Client Trust Account is shown in Exhibit 2–9.

EXHIBIT 2–9   Client Ledger Sheet

Source: Pamela -From Fundamentals of Law Office Management, 3rd edition by EVERETT/NOLLKAMPER. 2004. Reprinted with permission of Delmar Learning, a division of Thomson Learning: http://www.thomsonrights.com. Fax 800 730-2215.

Name   Lila Peterson

Address   234 56th St., Palo Alto, CA 90000

Matter: *Peterson v. Johnson*

File No.   94-126R

Phone   555-1234

Date	Description	Chk. No.	FEES			COSTS			TRUST FUNDS		
			Charged	Rec'd.	Balance	Adv.	Rec'd.	Balance	Rec'd.	Paid	Balance
1/7/xx	Rec'd. from client	739							$1,500.00		$1,500.00
2/1/xx	Feb. billing		$465.00		$465.00	$ 56.92		$ 56.92			
2/1/xx	Payment of fees	840		$465.00	-0-		$ 56.92	-0-		$521.92	$ 978.08
3/1/xx	Mar. billing		$650.00		$650.00	$145.23		$145.23			
3/1/xx	Payment of fees	851		$650.00	-0-		$145.23	-0-		$795.23	$ 182.85
4/1/xx	Apr. billing		$295.00		$295.00	$ 31.90		$ 31.90			
4/1/xx	Payment of fees	863		$182.85	$112.15					$182.85	-0-

EXHIBIT 2–10   Statement of Trust Account

Source: From Pamela Everett-Nollkamper, *Fundamentals of Law Office Management*, 3rd ed. (Clifton Park, NY: Thomson Delmar Learning, 2004). Reprinted with permission of Delmar Learning, a division of Thomson Learning: http://www.thomsonrights.com. Fax (800) 730-2215.

BLACK, WHITE & GREENE
Attorneys at Law

February 1, 20XX

Lila Peterson
234 56th St.
Anytown, CA 90000

Re: Peterson vs. Johnson, et al.

Statement of Trust Account

January 1, 20XX to February 28, 20XX

Date	Description	Rec'd	Disbursed	Balance
1/7/xx	Received from client	$1,500.00		$1,500.00
2/1/xx	February attorneys' fees		$465.00	1,035.00
2/1/xx	February costs		56.92	978.08
Balance as of February 28, 20XX				**$978.08**

Each month the client should be sent a statement showing the amounts received and disbursed from their trust account. A sample statement is shown in Exhibit 2–10.

PROBATE ACCOUNTS

When an attorney is representing a personal representative of an estate, all money received for the estate must be placed in a **probate account** or separate bank account entitled "Estate Account for the Estate of <name of decedent>." All expenses paid for the benefit of the estate should be taken from this account. When creditors of the decedent pay a bill, those funds are deposited in the estate account. Funeral expenses are deducted from this account. The attorney will charge the estate the statutory fee established by that state for that size of estate. Determine the method of payment for your own state and write the information below.

probate account a separate bank account for the funds of an estate; used by the law office when the attorney is representing the personal representative of the decedent

STATE SPECIFIC INFORMATION FOR THE STATE OF _____:

Attorney fees in probate are paid as follows:

_____

_____

_____

CLIENT RECORDS

Client recordkeeping and billing is usually accomplished by utilizing various types of software. Even small offices will often have a computerized recordkeeping and billing system. However, some simple tasks may be required to be done by hand, especially in smaller law offices.

RECEIVING A CLIENT'S MONEY

When the client pays the attorney, it is generally by check. The check may be received in the mail or in person. Most attorneys require the client to pay certain fees at their initial interview. Therefore, the check must be obtained while the client is in the office. The person who receives the check should endorse it on the back. Usually this is accomplished by a stamp that indicates the name of the bank in which it will be deposited and the name of the firm.

If the legal assistant receives the check, she should follow the office's procedures for depositing it into the firm's account. It is imperative that this check go into the client trust account and not into the attorney's account. As the attorney works on the client's case, she may withdraw funds from this client trust account and deposit them into her account.

If the firm uses a computerized accounting system, the receipt information should be recorded therein. The system will automatically post the amount to the appropriate account. The transaction will be maintained in an electronic file. Most law office accounting applications will prepare and print various accounting reports from these files, such as statements to clients, balance sheets, income and expense reports, and records of clients' accounts.

In most cases, even in a small firm, a bookkeeper will be employed, sometimes on a part-time basis, to take care of all accounting and billing business of the firm. In that case, it will be the legal assistant's responsibility to accumulate material for the bookkeeper if she is not present on a daily basis. This might include time sheets, checks, bills, or any other items used in the accounting process.

PETTY CASH

From time to time, cash will be needed immediately to cover items required for the firm. These items might include taxi fare, supplies for the office, purchase of a form, postage, or any number of other items. A petty cash fund will hold a small amount of cash and will be in the possession of the receptionist or legal assistant. Each time cash is removed from the fund, a voucher must be completed showing who removed the cash, how much cash was removed, the date, the purpose of the expenditure, and who received it. If appropriate, the client account that should be charged for the item should also be noted. When the cash fund gets low, then the custodian of the account should have a check written to re-fund the petty cash account.

SOLICITATION

ETHICAL ISSUES

Solicitation of clients on behalf of the attorney is also forbidden. Although the attorney is allowed to advertise to the public at large, directly seeking a prospective client's business is prohibited. Therefore, the law office may not employ individuals who directly solicit business from prospective clients.

These individuals are called "cappers" and may operate near unemployment offices, hospitals, ambulances, and anywhere else where potential clients may be present. In some cases, they use radios with police bands that enable them to know when accidents happen or ambulances are dispatched. They are the modern-day "ambulance chasers."

If an attorney-employer tells you she will give you a monetary sum for getting clients for the attorney, this is considered to be **solicitation** and is forbidden by the ethical codes and also by statute in many states. You are not precluded from recommending the attorney if a friend asks you for a referral, but at no time may you take a monetary amount from the attorney for this recommendation.

The courts have consistently held that attorneys may not pay their employees for bringing business to the firm. However, the end-of-the-year bonus given by many large firms to their employees has been upheld by the courts as not qualifying under the solicitation provision even though this bonus is usually related to the firm's profits for the year.

The major difference lies in the direct solicitation of clients, either in person, by telephone, or by any other direct means. The exception to the rule in most states is in class action litigation, where contact may be made with those who are potential plaintiffs in the lawsuit. However, some jurisdictions forbid this practice. It is important to know your own state's rules in these situations.

Record the differences in your own state's ethical rules below.

solicitation directly seeking business from prospective clients for the attorney and being paid a fee for this service; this practice is not allowed by state law

STATE-SPECIFIC INFORMATION FOR THE STATE OF _____

The ethical rules that are different from the above-described rules for solicitation in this state are listed below:

_____

_____

_____

_____

LAW DEPARTMENTS OF CORPORATIONS

Most corporate law department employees spend their time providing legal services for many different departments of the corporation. Depending on the type of corporation, specialty law departments may be established to service these specialized requirements. For instance, some large manufacturing and electronics companies may have a patent law department to complete requirements for patents. If the company leases a large number of buildings or properties, a real estate department may be established for the preparation of these leases.

Some cases may justify court-awarded legal fees in a litigation case where the corporation prevails. Therefore, many companies now require that their attorneys and legal assistants keep accurate records of their work. Some law departments actually bill different departments for whom they provide legal assistance. In these cases, the legal assistant will be required to keep a time sheet with billable hours noted. Time sheet forms will generally be provided by those corporate law departments that have this requirement.

GOVERNMENT AGENCIES

The rules for timekeeping vary among different government departments and agencies. Some departments have detailed timekeeping systems that assist the department in the preparation of budgets and in performance appraisals. Others may require only attorneys to keep daily time sheets.

ETIQUETTE IN THE OFFICE AND THE COURTROOM

The legal professional, paralegal, and/or legal assistant should always represent herself as a professional both in and out of the office. She should dress professionally and refrain from chewing gum or practicing other annoying habits. When introduced to a client or other individual, extend your hand to shake hands and address the person by name. The client should be addressed by her last name unless she or the attorney tells you otherwise.

The attorney will either introduce you to the client or you will introduce yourself upon her first visit to the office. Greet the client politely and always shake hands. Smile when you are greeting the client or other individual.

On some occasions, the attorney may ask you to accompany her to court. Most courtrooms do not allow cell phones, gum chewing, wearing shorts or other unprofessional attire, and talking. As soon as you enter the court house, turn your cell phone off. You may not make or receive calls while the court is in session. If you have an urgent call, then quietly leave the courtroom and make or receive the call from the hallway outside. Breaks in the courtroom proceedings usually occur about every two hours, so you can usually wait to make any calls at the break.

During court proceedings you should refrain from whispering to the attorney. If the issue is critical at that point in time, keep a notepad handy and write her a legible note. Listen carefully during the court-room proceedings and take notes for the attorney. This may be done on a notepad or with a laptop computer. If you are using a laptop, be sure that you either have an electrical outlet for the computer or that your laptop's battery is fully charged. If you are using a portable mouse, be sure the batteries in it are fully charged and working properly. When you plan to use this equipment in the courtroom, be sure to test it before leaving for court to be sure it is operating suitably.

PROFESSIONAL ORGANIZATIONS

Professional organizations for legal assistants exist on both the national and local levels. Many national organizations have local branches. Membership is beneficial for keeping abreast of the latest developments within the profession and for career changes. Many of these organizations offer student memberships for those individuals enrolled in their chosen fields. Student members may attend meetings, meet individuals employed in the profession, and network for future employment.

Some well-known organizations that have been established specifically for the legal assistant profession are:

1. **NALS ... the association for legal professionals (formerly National Association of Legal Secretaries)**
   NALS ... the association for legal professionals has been the major association for legal assistant professionals for nearly 75 years. Most large metropolitan areas have chapters of NALS. Its Web site (http://www.nals.org) provides links to other interesting sites, including legal news, education, careers, online learning, ethical codes, certification, and membership. Information about professional certification is also available on this Web site.

2. **National Association of Legal Assistants (NALA)**
   The National Association of Legal Assistants (NALA) is a leading professional organization for legal assistants and paralegals. It provides continuing education and professional development programs. It comprises close to 20,000 legal professionals, including individual members of over 90 state and local affiliated associations. The Web site (http://www.nala.org) describes the organization and its education programs as well as a listing of local branches.

3. **National Federation of Paralegal Associations (NFPA)**
   The National Federation of Paralegal Associations (NFPA) is a leading organization of paralegals that is national in scope. Its website (http://www.paralegals.org) describes the organization and provides links to other legal resources, career opportunities, industry resources, membership, its certification program (PACE), continuing education, professional development, and its own publication, *National Paralegal Reporter*.

Exhibit 2–11 shows the Web site for NALS. Exhibit 2–12 lists the names, addresses, and e-mail addresses of the three professional organizations described here.

EXHIBIT 2–11   NALS Web Page (http://www.nals.org)

Source: Reprinted with permission of NALS . . . the association for legal professionals.

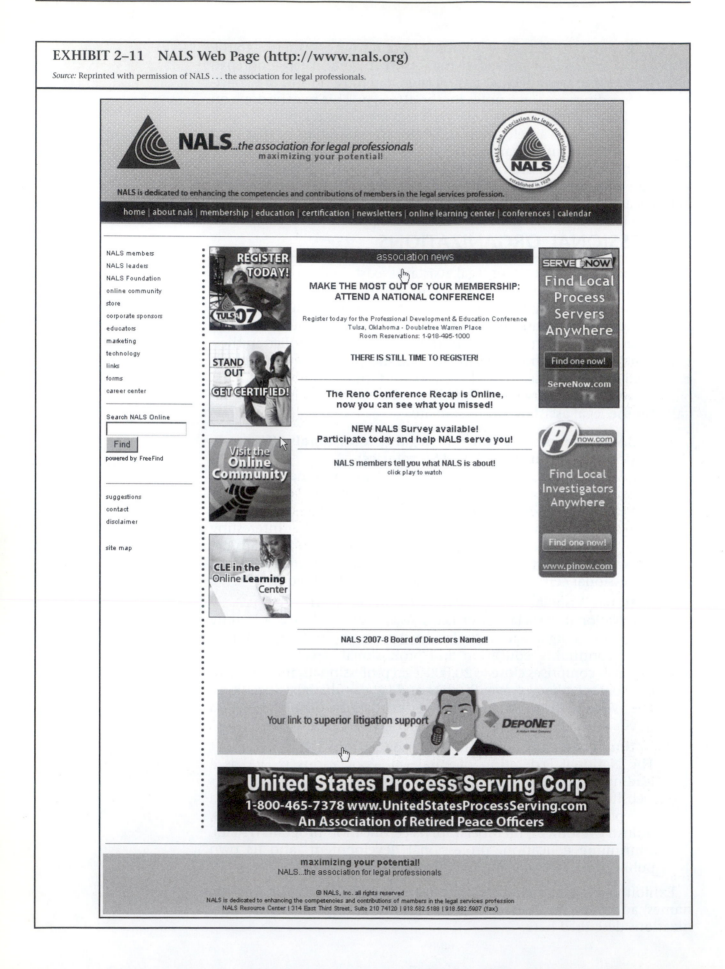

EXHIBIT 2–12   National Professional Organizations

NALS . . . the association for legal professionals
314 E. 3d Street, Suite 210
Tulsa, OK 74120
Phone: (918) 582-5188
E-mail: info@nals.org
NALA – National Association of Legal Assistants
1514 S. Boston, Suite 200
Tulsa, OK 74119
Phone: (918) 587-6828
E-mail: nalanet@nala.org
NFPA – National Federation of Paralegal Associations
PO Box 33108
Kansas City, MO 64114
Phone: (816) 941-4000
E-mail: info@paralegals.org

Note: Please check the organizations' Web sites to determine whether any of the information
has changed since the printing of this textbook.

■ KEY TERMS

Billable hours	Probate account
Client trust account	Retainer fees
Contingency fees	Solicitation
Hourly fees	Statutory fees
Nonbillable hours	Time sheet
Project fees	

■ SELF TEST

1. Complete all of the blanks for the state-specific information boxes in this chapter. Discuss them in class.

2. Write a memorandum to your instructor setting forth your understanding of the attorney-client privilege.

3. Send an e-mail to one of the three legal assistant organizations discussed in the chapter and ask them for information about local chapters of their organization.

■ NOTEBOOK PROJECTS

1. Contact local law firms, and obtain sample time sheets that they use. Blank time sheets should be obtained for three law firms, corporate law departments, or government law offices.

2. Using one of the samples obtained from the law firms in #1, complete a time sheet for one day this week for your own time. Be sure to record the time in tenths of hours.

3. Contact your local state bar organization and obtain information about student activities in which you might participate, such as seminars and classes. File your letter and their response in your notebook.

 For additional resources, visit our Web site at **www.westlegalstudies.com**

WORKING WITH ATTORNEYS AND OTHERS

CHAPTER 2

CHAPTER OUTCOMES

As a result of studying this chapter, the student will learn:

1. the duties and responsibilities of the legal professional.
2. the differences and similarities between a paralegal and a legal professional.
3. how to establish priorities.
4. the importance of meeting deadlines.
5. how to work with attorneys' expectations.
6. how to schedule appointments.
7. how to schedule assignments with deadlines.

DUTIES AND RESPONSIBILITIES

Legal professionals who work in large law firms will generally have more specialized responsibilities than those employed by small law offices. The small law office may employ legal professionals who do double duty as paralegals. Therefore, they will assume both administrative and paralegal responsibilities.

In general, legal professionals have considerable contact with the attorney's clients. It is imperative that the legal professional make his status known to the client each time they communicate. Most clients will not be familiar with the position, and some may assume that the legal professional is a junior attorney. Other individuals with whom the assistant is in contact may be in the same category. That is, they may not know the status and must be told. The legal assistant should explain his position as an assistant to the attorney but not an attorney. He would then enlighten the client or other individual on exactly what his responsibilities entail, as well as duties that he can and cannot perform. For instance, he should explain that he cannot give the client legal advice and that he may not speak with someone who is represented by counsel.

ETHICAL ISSUES

Bear in mind that the attorney or other law office employees working on a case may not speak with another individual who is represented by legal counsel unless permission is first received from that individual's attorney.

"Legal professional" is a relatively new term for one whose role is the modern successor to the traditional legal secretary. This individual assumes administrative and secretarial responsibilities in the large or small firm. In some cases, the term "legal assistant" is used interchangeably with "legal professional." Some offices refer to the legal professional as a "legal administrative assistant." Because of the different methods of identifying some members of the law office team, it is recommended that the duties and responsibilities be categorized prior to determining the individual's status. Some large firms may call their secretaries "legal administrative assistants" or "administrative assistants." If an individual has some paralegal duties, the term used for that person may be "legal assistant."

Other firms may distinguish between the paralegal and the legal professional by identifying their specific duties and responsibilities. In some firms, the legal assistant is a lower-level paralegal who may perform work for the paralegal. In other firms, these terms are used interchangeably.

Most large firms will have an organization chart that may be utilized to determine the individual work performed by each member of the law office team. Study this chart to determine whether your firm employs both paralegals and legal assistants, and whether the legal secretaries are called administrative assistants. In this manner, the organizational structure of the firm and identifying characteristics of the various members may be identified. In a smaller firm, duties will often overlap and it may be more difficult to distinguish among a legal secretary, legal professional, administrative assistant, legal assistant, and/or paralegal.

THE LEGAL PROFESSIONAL IN THE LARGE LAW FIRM

In the typical large law firm, the legal professional will usually have administrative responsibilities. Paralegals working in the office will handle the more substantive paralegal work. Some typical administrative duties of the legal professional in the large law firm include:

1. drafting correspondence.
2. scheduling appointments.
3. preparing and updating calendars.
4. answering telephones and taking messages.
5. making travel reservations.
6. arranging conferences.

7. taking minutes of meetings.

8. typing reports, pleadings, documents, and correspondence.

9. using the computer for word processing and document preparation and management.

In the typical small law firm, the legal professional may perform both administrative and paralegal duties. Paralegal duties generally include:

1. drafting documents.

2. performing legal research.

3. docket control.

4. completion of legal forms.

5. preparation of legal documents for service and filing with the courts.

6. arranging for service of process and court filings.

7. organizing the client files.

8. drafting legal documents and correspondence.

9. coordinating court dates with the attorney, witnesses, other attorneys, and parties to the suit.

10. preparation of exhibits for trial.

11. drafting summaries of depositions.

12. summarizing legal documents, such as written interrogatories.

13. drafting questions for depositions, written interrogatories, and other discovery documents.

14. attending court proceedings to assist the attorney.

15. research of legal issues.

The legal professional may also be called upon to perform other duties in various specialty areas. For instance, in the law office specializing in corporate work, he may maintain the corporation's minute books, draft articles of incorporation and bylaws, prepare and file tax documents, prepare documents for mergers and consolidations, or perform other duties specific to the corporate law office.

LEGAL ADVICE

Attorneys are the only members of the law office team who may give **legal advice** to clients. However, in certain situations, the paralegal or legal professional may communicate the attorney's advice to the client with specific instructions from the attorney. For instance, if the client calls the office and leaves a message for the attorney with a question that requires legal advice, and the attorney subsequently gets the message, he may tell the legal professional specifically what to tell the client. In a subsequent call to the client, it should be made clear that the advice is being communicated from the attorney.

legal advice   counsel given to clients telling them how to proceed in their case; advising the client regarding legal issues

ETHICAL ISSUES

If asked a question that is considered to be legal advice, the legal professional must inform the client, opposing counsel, or other party to whom he is speaking that he is not an attorney but will obtain the information requested from the attorney and relay the information back to the individual.

Only the attorney may appear in court to represent his client. Certain exceptions to this rule may exist in different states, such as at administrative hearings. Certain government agencies, such as the Social Security Administration, allow paralegals with specific training to represent a client before that body. Some states may also have different requirements.

STATE-SPECIFIC INFORMATION FOR THE STATE OF _____:

Legal assistants/paralegals may provide the following services in the courtroom in the state of _____:

_____

_____

_____

_____

Legal assistants/paralegals may represent clients in the courtroom at the following types of proceedings:_____

_____

_____

_____

Legal professionals, legal assistants, or paralegals may attend court proceedings with the attorney for the purpose of observing prospective jurors, taking notes, doing legal research, assessing clients and witnesses, keeping track of exhibits and documents, or any other administrative functions. Some attorneys require that their legal assistants/paralegals sit with them at the counsel table during the trial.

TRIAL BOOK

trial book a comprehensive notebook containing all pertinent information for a trial

The paralegal is usually in charge of the preparation of the **trial book** and may delegate certain administrative functions to the legal professional. In the small law office, the legal professional may be required to prepare the complete trial book. If the paralegal prepares the more technical parts of the book, the legal professional may be responsible for organizing the notebook with dividers representing the different aspects of the case. The attorney will determine the style of the book as well as the items that are included therein. Some typical items that are included are:

1. copies of all pleadings in the case.
2. copies of all discovery documents.
3. deposition transcripts and summaries.
4. notes on discrepancies in witness testimony.
5. outline of case issues.
6. index to and copies of exhibits.
7. chronological list of case events.
8. trial brief.
9. jury instructions.
10. witness schedule and possible questions.

If the legal professional attends the trial, he may be responsible for making sure the witnesses are in court at the scheduled time. The witness should always be provided with prior statements made in the case. For instance, if a witness's deposition was taken three months before the trial, a copy of the deposition transcript should be provided to the witness for review purposes before the witness testifies in court. Listed below are some of the potential responsibilities of the legal professional in preparation for a trial.

1. preparing the trial book.
2. providing witnesses with prior statements.
3. reading all witness and client statements to determine whether the accounts of facts presented are consistent, and informing the attorney of any discrepancies.
4. writing to clients and witnesses with the date and time they are scheduled to testify in court.
5. calling to remind clients and witnesses a day or two before the trial.
6. keeping a list of trial witnesses close at hand (in court or at the office) so that you may call witnesses with any scheduling problems. (For instance, if the court adjourns early one day, all witnesses may have to be called to appear on a later date.)
7. arranging for hotel lodging or travel for the attorney, witnesses, or clients.
8. keeping in touch with witnesses during the trial.
9. being prepared to make last-minute telephone calls or provide rush assistance to the attorney at trial or in the office during the trial.
10. coordinating labeling of trial exhibits with court clerk.

See Exhibit 3–1.

EXHIBIT 3–1　Sample Witness Schedule

CASE NAME: Smith V. Jones
TRIAL DATE: April 27, 2006

WITNESS SCHEDULE:

9:00 A.M.	Jane Nicholas	184 Melinda Lane Corning, New York 555-222-7777
10:00 A.M.	Joseph Diaz	9235 Sunset Drive Harmon, New York 555-345-6789
12:00 P.M.	Lunch Break	
2:00 P.M.	Continue Joseph Diaz testimony or Linda Jeffries	1122 Main Street Croton, New York 555-678-9999
3:00 P.M.	Linda Jeffries (continued)	
4:00 P.M.	Marie Rodman	5556 Grand Avenue Peekskill, New York 555-222-3333

AFTER THE TRIAL

The legal professional may draft various court documents related to the court decision after the trial. He may be required to schedule an appointment with the client and the attorney. Appeals documents might also have to be prepared.

ESTABLISHING PRIORITIES

Most work performed in the law office has a deadline. The deadlines are critical to each case. Not meeting a deadline may be the cause of a client's losing his case. One of the most frequent causes of malpractice cases against attorneys involve missed deadlines. For instance, if a document or pleading is filed a day late with the court, a client may not be allowed to maintain his case. If the legal professional hurries to the courthouse at the end of the day to meet a deadline and finds that the clerk's office is closed, the item may not be filed the next day and the client may be precluded from continuing the case. Legal professionals must therefore be aware of the opening and closing hours of the court clerk's office and plan accordingly to guarantee that filings are made on a timely basis.

EXHIBIT 3–2   Computerized Daily Log

October 22, 2005

Smith v. Jones	Deposition Summary Due on October 29, 2005
X v. Y Co.	Trial starts November 1, 2005
Abb v. Cee	Trial began October 20, 2005; keep track of witnesses (note: you will have a witness log)
Estate of J. Jones	Prepare Petition for Probate; contact executor regarding establishing estate account.

Law offices are usually very busy places, and the legal professional may be working on several cases with conflicting deadlines. Each project must be completed by its deadline date. If a "pending" log is kept on the computer, you should read your schedule on the computer each morning and determine what has to be done that day. As items are completed, they may be removed from the log. Some items may need to be removed later if others have deadlines subsequent to yours.

The legal professional should strive to complete items before their deadlines by reminding the attorney several days ahead of the date when a document is due at the court. A good rule to follow is to log items in the schedule in the following manner:

ten days before due date

three days before due date

morning of due date

In some cases, you might wish to log items two weeks before the due date if they are more complex. If you do not have a computer log, then either institute one or write notes on your calendar. A typical computer log is shown in Exhibit 3–2.

Many different methods exist for the preparation of the pending log. Whatever method works best for you should be utilized. As long as you remember to review the pending log each morning and to perform the tasks required therein, you should be able to keep track of deadlines and complete your work in a timely fashion.

SCHEDULING ASSIGNMENTS   ■

The assignments received first are not necessarily the ones that should be completed first. Often you will be working on one assignment and the attorney will give another with a more critical deadline. You may have to stop the first assignment and complete the second before going back to the first one. This scenario may occur several times a day.

ATTORNEY EXPECTATIONS

Attorneys sometimes do not give clear instructions, and the legal professional must ask questions if the assignment is not clear. All instructions should be written in a note pad and reviewed. A considerable amount of time is wasted on misunderstood assignments. New employees who have not worked with a particular attorney previously tend to have more problems of this sort. You should never be afraid or apprehensive about asking a question to further clarify an assignment. However, once the assignment is understood, do not ask the same question over and over again.

A former student of the author had extreme difficulty keeping a position as a legal assistant because he tended to ask the same question many times. Although this individual actually knew the answer, he did not have the confidence to proceed with assignments without extremely close direction by the attorney.

Whenever you get a new and different assignment, a copy should be made for your notebook, with the specific instructions given by the attorney at the time the assignment was prepared. In this manner, having to ask questions that were previously answered will be avoided. A copy of each new type of assignment should be added to your notebook for future reference.

Since most legal documents are repetitious, templates should be prepared of those that are prepared frequently. If you are using Microsoft Word, go to File>New>General Templates>Legal Pleadings, and either prepare a document using the template there or generate a new template and use it for that particular type of document.

If you are employed in a state that uses statutory forms for various documents, formatting information may be obtained from the West/Delmar Web site, which organizes the material for court documents by state. Go to http://www.westlegalstudies.com, click on Professional Center, then click on the Find State-Specific Resources & Forms button, find your own state, and look for the appropriate form on which to base your document.

Exhibit 3–3 shows a page from this Web site.

COURT DEADLINES

docket a list of cases scheduled for trial in court; an office document containing a summary of court dates, deadlines, and schedules

statute of limitations the maximum amount of time after an incident for it to be taken to court

barred banned, excluded

The most important schedules are those found in the court docket. The **docket** is the firm's schedule of important deadlines, meetings, and other scheduled events. Of critical importance are the deadlines set by state in the **statute of limitations** for filing various types of legal actions. Some states refer to this statute as "Limitation of Actions." The statute of limitations establishes the deadline by which a case must be filed with the court. Once the statute of limitations deadline is past, the case may not be filed. (There are some limited exceptions to this rule.)

Imagine the client who has been severely injured and wishes to sue the responsible party. If the attorney does not file the case by the statute's deadline, then the client is **barred** from filing the case later.

EXHIBIT 3–3   West Legal Studies Web Page for State Sources

Source: From http://www.westlegalstudies.com. Reprinted with permission of Thomson Delmar Learning.

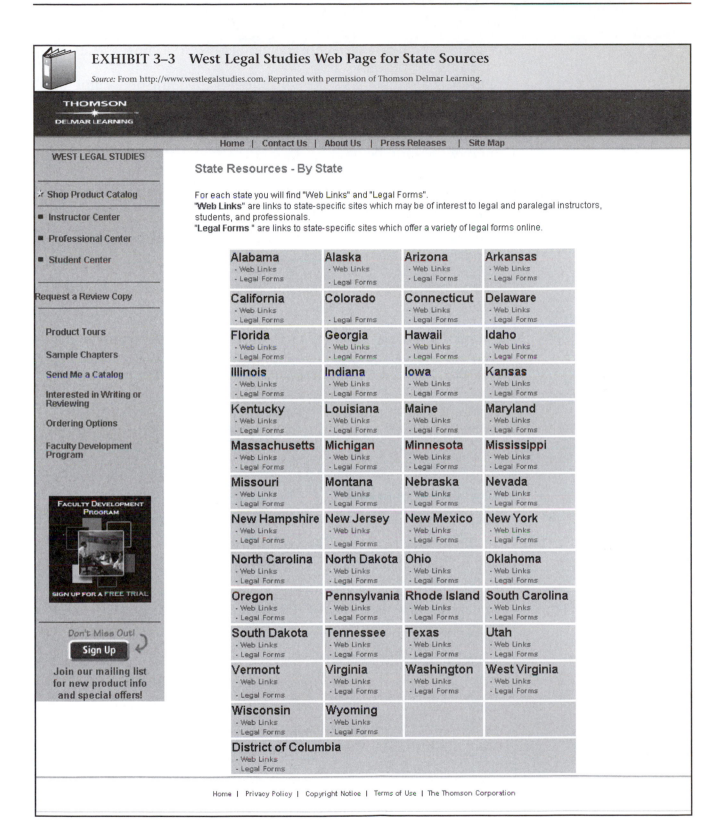

His next step might logically be a malpractice suit against the attorney for missing the deadline.

The court also imposes strict deadlines for the filing of documents in the lawsuit. If these deadlines are not met, the court may impose sanctions on the filing attorney or dismiss the lawsuit, depending on state law and local court rules. Determine your own state's sanctions and complete the form below.

STATE-SPECIFIC INFORMATION BOX

The state of _____ imposes the following sanctions for missed deadlines in its state courts:

_____

_____

_____

_____

A simple docket calendar system for a large law firm is shown in Exhibit 3–4. More sophisticated computerized systems and software

---

EXHIBIT 3–4   Docket Calendar System—Large Law Firm

NAME OF FIRM
DATE

Court Matter No.	Case Name	Attorney Team
Petition for Dissolution	*Adams v. Adams*	Jackson & Nicholas
Answer to Complaint	*Rodriguez v. Langley*	Jeffries & Martin

SCHEDULE FOR MS. JACKSON

9:00 A.M.	Client (Mrs. Adams) meeting	Jackson/office
10:00	Weekly attorney's meeting	All Attorneys
11:30	Weekly staff meeting	All Staff
12:30	Lunch with legal assistants	
	Re: Rodriguez case issues	
2:00 P.M.	Prepare questions for	
	Mr. Adams' deposition	
3:00 P.M.	Meeting with Adams witness –	Office
	Ms. Lang	
4:00 P.M.	Speech at Bar Association	State Bar Offices

packages are described in Chapter 10. Some of these more sophisticated systems are appropriate for use in both large and small law offices.

Most law offices use computer software packages for their calendars and deadlines. Larger offices often connect their computers on a network so that each staff member is able to find his own schedule. A **docket control clerk** may be required to maintain the program by

docket control clerk law firm employee whose responsibility is to maintain the docket control program by keying in court dates, deadlines, and attorney and staff schedules

---

EXHIBIT 3–5 Sample Master Calendar

Source: From Pamela Everett-Nollkamper, *Fundamentals of Law Office Management*, 3rd ed. (Clifton Park, NY: Thomson Delmar Learning, 2004). Reprinted with permission of Delmar Learning, a division of Thomson Learning: http://www.thomsonrights.com. Fax 800 730-2215.

Master Calendar				
Monday	**Tuesday**	**Wednesday**	**Thursday**	**Friday**
1 JFH—9:00 Trial, Black v. Claridge, Sup. Ct. D-56 - - - - - ERN—9:00 Trial— Gardner v. Larson, Cir. Ct D-87 * * * *	2 *} PDF—10:00 Dep., Brown v. Redd, 346 Capitol St. LA, #787	3 BSD—9:00 Hrg. Motion to compel, Sand v. Waters, Sup. Ct. D12	4 WAC—10:00 Dep., Jacks v. Yawl, here REN—2:00 Dep., Tru v. Falz, here	5 PDF 9:00 Motion to quash, Pert v. Yerl, Cir. Ct., D-5
8	9 LCN—9:00 Disso Marriage of Yale, Sup. Ct. D-33	10 xxxxxxxxxxxxxxxxxxxxxxxxxxxxxxxxxxxx} BSD—10:00 Dep., Young v. Osterholm 1600 Main St., LA	11 NAD—1:00 Hrg. ++++++++++++++++++ Luther v. Ti, Tax Ct., Rm. 9	12
15 ++++++++++++++} 2:00 REN Dep., Tooly v. Hale, here ^^^^^^^^^	16 ^^^^^^^^^^^^^^^^^^^^^^^^	17 ^^^^^^^^^^^^^^^^^^^] ^^^^^^^^^^^^^^^^^^	18 ^^^^^^^^^^^^^^^^^}	19
22 HOLIDAY	23	24	25	26

keying in the information for court dates, deadlines, and attorney and staff schedules. Generally, staff members are also able to key in their own information.

Computerized docket control systems have many features not available in a manual system. One advantage is that several individuals at different computer stations on a network may access the system and key in data at the same time. Fewer errors are likely to occur when the office uses a computerized system. See Chapter 10 for a more detailed explanation of specific computerized docket control systems.

An example of a master calendar is shown in Exhibit 3–5.

SIMPLE TICKLER FILES

In some small offices, a more simple type of reminder system may be utilized, called a **tickler file**. In some cases, the legal assistant may wish to use a card system, where the box contains a tab for each month as well as numbered tabs from 1 to 31. The legal professional would keep the current month in the front with the tabs for each day. The later months would be kept behind the last day of this month. Simple cards may be prepared with the information shown in Exhibit 3–6.

These reminder systems may be modified to meet the needs of the individual office. If the law office already has an adequate system in place, that system should be utilized and additions or modifications should be made as required.

A card box with inserts for a typical simple tickler system is shown in Exhibit 3–7.

EXHIBIT 3–6   Simple Tickler System Cards

REMINDER DATE   Month_____ Day _____ Year _____

DUE DATE: Month/Day/Year _____

CLIENT FILE: _____

OTHER _____

REMIND LAWYERS _____ Smith _____ Escovar _____ Langley

ITEM DUE _____

NOTES _____

Case Statute of Limitations _____

<Your name and initials>   Completion Date_____

---

tickler file   a reminder system that lists scheduled events and deadlines

EXHIBIT 3–7   Sample Manual Tickler System

Source: From Pamela Everett-Nollkamper, *Fundamentals of Law Office Management,* 3rd ed. (Clifton Park, NY: Thomson Delmar Learning, 2004). Reprinted with permission of Delmar Learning, a division of Thomson Learning: http://www.thomsonrights.com. Fax 800 730-2215.

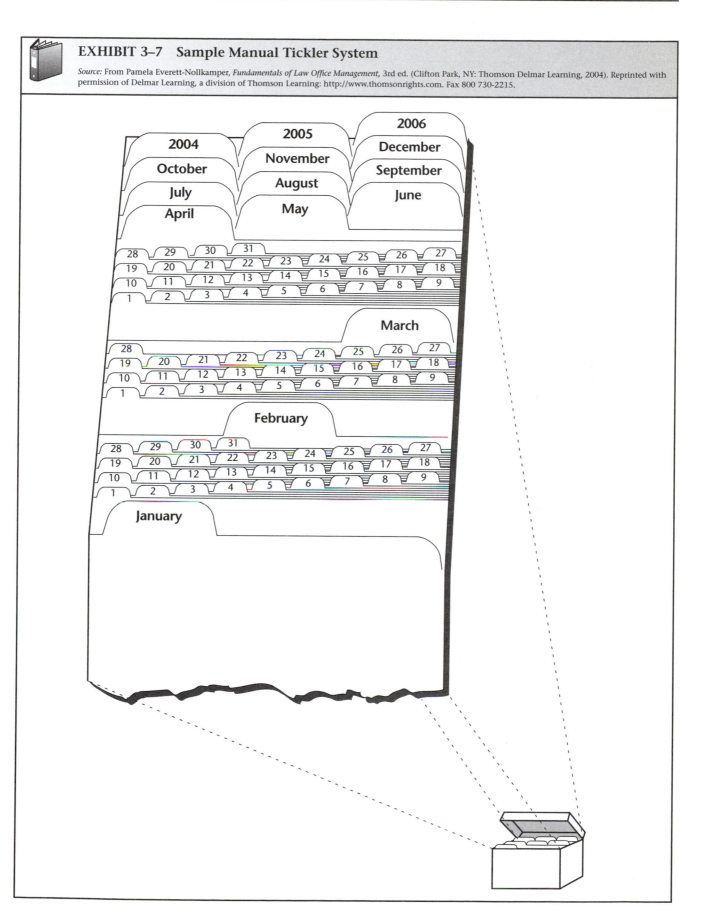

■ KEY TERMS

Barred

Docket

Docket control clerk

Legal advice

Statute of limitations

Tickler file

Trial book

■ SELF TEST

1. What is the difference between a paralegal and a legal assistant?

2. Describe the responsibilities of the paralegal and the legal assistant in a large law firm.

3. What is a trial book?

4. What items are included in the trial book?

5. What happens to the case when a court deadline is missed?

6. Prepare a schedule for yourself for one day this week using one of the samples given in the exhibits above.

■ NOTEBOOK PROJECTS

1. Complete the state-specific information boxes in the chapter and make a copy for your notebook.

2. Find the statutes of limitation for different types of cases in your state and prepare a table for your notebook.

For additional resources, visit our Web site at **www.westlegalstudies.com**

ETHICS IN CLIENT RELATIONS

CHAPTER OUTCOMES

As a result of studying this chapter, the student will learn:

1. the appropriate ethics practiced in a law office.
2. the concept of confidentiality as it relates to client relations.
3. the importance of reminders about upcoming deadlines and events.

ETHICS ISSUES

Legal ethics is defined as

1. professional standards of conduct for lawyers and judges...
2. standards of fair and honest conduct in general.[1]

These professional standards are also applicable to individuals who are in the employ of a lawyer, such as paralegals, legal assistants, librarians, bookkeepers, and others. Attorneys are regulated by their state bar association and by state statutes.

[1]Daniel Oran, *Oran's Dictionary of the Law,* 3rd ed. (Clifton Park, NY: West Legal Studies, an imprint of Thomson Delmar Learning, 2000), 281.

ETHICS

Legal assistants who work under the supervision of attorneys are also required to adhere to these standards of conduct. In most states, the highest state court in each state, generally called the state *supreme court,* is responsible for making the rules for admission to practice law and the attorneys' ethical code. Many state supreme courts rely on their state bar associations to govern the conduct of their attorney members. Violations of these ethical rules may result in several different sanctions, depending on their severity. Lawyers may be restricted from the practice of law for a certain period of time or may be **disbarred** from practicing law. In cases of minor violations, the attorney may be reprimanded with a warning. In some situations, the reprimand (known as a *reproval*) is public and in others it remains private. **Public reproval**

disbar take away a lawyer's right to practice law.

public reproval notice to the attorney's clients that the attorney has committed a violation of the ethical codes. Admonishment is also considered a punishment in some states.

includes a notice to the attorney's clients that the attorney has committed a violation of the ethical code.

Some states have paralegals employed in their state bar offices to act as investigators into claims against attorneys licensed in that state. These investigators may find that a complaint against an attorney has no merit; that it is a violation but not a serious one; or that it is a major violation that may lead to disbarment.

The American Bar Association (ABA) has developed model codes of ethics that are followed in most states. In general, the state codes may be more restrictive than the ABA Model Code, but they may not be less restrictive.

ETHICS ISSUES

The most important standard to remember is *attorney/client privilege,* which requires that all confidential information related to the client must not be repeated. The most important aspect of legal ethics is protecting the confidence of the client. Court cases have shown that individuals employed by the law firm may not be required to reveal information about confidential communications received from the client, even in a court case.

The exception to this rule relates to the rare situation where the client tells you or the attorney that she is planning to commit a violent act against another individual or herself. In that case, the recipient of the information is required to report the client's plan if she reasonably believes that the client will carry out the act.

This rule came about as a result of the case of *Tarasoff v. Regents of the University of California*, 131 Cal. Rptr. 14 (1976), where the parents of a murdered woman, who was killed by a psychiatric patient who had told his psychiatrist that he planned to kill the woman, instituted a civil action for her wrongful death. In this case, the court held that the therapist was required to warn the intended victim or others likely to apprise her of the danger, notify the police, or take whatever steps were reasonably necessary under the circumstances. The court held, on page 340 of its decision:

> . . . defendant therapists cannot escape liability merely because Tatiana herself was not their patient. When a therapist determines, or pursuant to the standards of his profession should determine, that his patient presents a serious danger of violence to another, he incurs an obligation to use reasonable care to protect the intended victim against such danger.

This rule has been extended to include attorneys dealing with clients. Therefore, if a client tells you he plans to leave the office and go home and kill his wife, you should immediately notify the attorney of his intentions if you believe they were made with the intent to carry them out.

MALPRACTICE

In addition to the ethical considerations required by the state and the state bar, attorneys may be faced with a civil lawsuit for **malpractice** by clients and/or former clients. One of the major reasons for malpractice suits against attorneys is missed deadlines. Other grounds for these suits include misconduct, negligent handling of a lawsuit, and incompetence. In most cases, the attorney may be disciplined by the court or state bar, and subsequently be sued by the client for malpractice.

COURT SANCTIONS

If a lawyer demonstrates unethical behavior in the courtroom or in relation to issues before the court, she may be charged with **contempt** of court. The judge may reprimand the attorney for failure to adhere to the court rules in the questioning of witnesses or for other unethical behavior.

LEGAL PROFESSIONALS AND ETHICS

Although legal professionals, legal assistants, and legal secretaries are not bound by their state's ethical codes for attorneys, they should strive to perform with the highest standards of conduct since the attorney who employs them would be responsible for any violations. Attorneys may be subject to discipline if their non-attorney staff members violate the ethical code.

Some professional organizations have developed their own ethical codes. The NALS ethical codes may be found in Appendix A. The National Association of Legal Assistants developed its own Code of Ethics for legal assistants several years ago. A copy of the association's Web page may be found at Exhibit 4–1. It is located at

http://www.nala.org

Their model standards for ethics may be found in Appendix B.

The National Federation of Paralegal Association's ethical codes are administered by its more than one hundred local organizations. Each group maintains its own method of sanctions for those members who violate the codes. The codes may be found at the association's Web site, located at

http://www.paralegals.org

A copy of their Web site's home page is shown here as Exhibit 4–2. Their Model Code is shown in Appendix C.

malpractice professional misconduct or unreasonable lack of skill

contempt an act that obstructs a court's work or lessens the dignity of the court; court sanction for inappropriate behavior in court.

EXHIBIT 4–1   NALA Web Page

Source: Reprinted with permission from NALA.

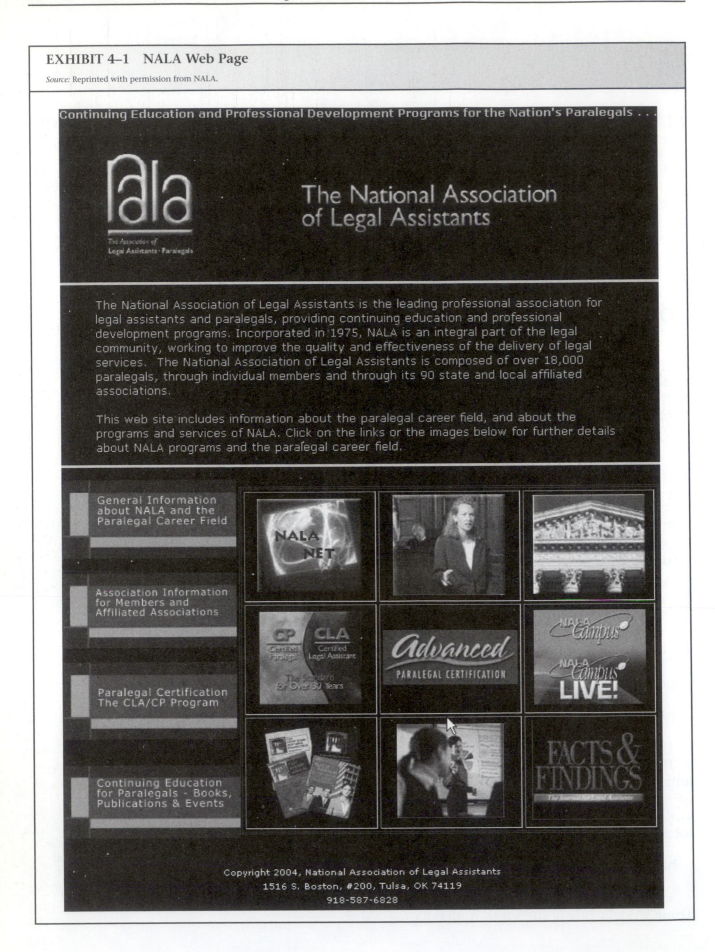

EXHIBIT 4–2 NFPA Web Page

Source: Reprinted with permission. Copyright National Federation of Paralegal Associations, Inc.

ETHICS ISSUES

Lawyers are required by state law and ethical codes not to assist in the unauthorized practice of law. Therefore, the lawyer will be responsible for training the legal assistant as well as supervising her work. The attorney may only delegate that work to the legal assistant that is allowed to be completed by nonlawyer personnel. It is the responsibility of the attorney to teach and supervise the legal assistant, especially with respect to confidentiality and the finished work product. The attorney is responsible for making sure that the legal assistant does not engage in activities that may only be performed by the attorney. Listed below are those activities in which the legal assistant may not engage. Please note that there may be limited exceptions to these rules in your own state's laws.

1. The legal assistant may not represent a client in court.
2. The legal assistant may not sign any document or pleading for the client if the document or pleading is filed with the court.
3. The legal assistant may not give legal advice.
4. The legal assistant may not represent a client at a deposition or other similar proceeding.
5. The legal assistant may not set the fee to be charged to the client.
6. The legal assistant may not give a legal opinion to the client.
7. The legal assistant may not establish a lawyer/client relationship with the client.
8. The legal assistant may not be paid for bringing new clients into the firm.

Look up the ethical codes for your own state and complete the blanks below.

STATE-SPECIFIC INFORMATION FOR THE STATE OF _____:

In addition to Nos. 1–8 above, the legal assistant may not engage in the following activities:

_____

_____

_____

_____.

Exceptions exist in the state of _____ to No. 1–8 above in the following areas:

_____

_____

_____

Some federal government agencies may allow nonlawyers to practice before them in the representation of clients. The specific agencies that allow this practice change over time. Some states also allow non-lawyers to represent clients before certain state agencies. Complete the form below in relation to your own state.

STATE-SPECIFIC INFORMATION FOR THE STATE OF _____:

The following state agencies allow the representation of clients by nonlawyers:

_____

_____

_____

_____.

If a legal professional, legal assistant, or secretary (hereinafter re-ferred to as legal professional) is involved in a situation that might be considered the unauthorized practice of law, it should be discussed with the attorney. The most important consideration, of course, is maintaining confidentiality. The legal professional is required to pre-serve the client's secrets. Divulging confidential information may be done inadvertently. For instance, a law firm employee may be in an elevator discussing a case with a co-worker. An employee of the op-posing counsel in that case may also be in the elevator and may hear information about the case that is confidential. The same scenario may take place in a restaurant, in the courthouse, or in any other public place. It is important to not discuss the firm's cases outside the office.

If a client is in the office and another client calls on the telephone, no confidential information may be discussed. The client on the tele-phone should not be called by name. If the client in the office (Mrs. Smith) knows the client on the telephone (Mrs. Jones), who is ad-dressed by her name, then Mrs. Smith may find out confidential infor-mation about her friend.

Papers or other items about one client's case should never be left on the legal professional's desk when another client is in the office. For in-stance, the legal professional may have been working on a client's file and have the folder open on the desk when another client arrives to sign papers in her own case. The folder must be closed and there can be no items visible with the client's name on them for the second client to see.

If someone calls the office and requests information on a client's case, she should be referred to the attorney. It is not the responsibility of the legal professional to determine what information should be given to outside sources. This problem is prevalent in well-publicized cases. A newspaper reporter may call to attempt to obtain information that should not be divulged.

Particular care is necessary when communicating by e-mail with clients. An adequate firewall (sometimes known as an "ethical wall") should already be installed on your law office's computers. Alternatively, software packages are available that will encode outgoing messages.

If faxes are sent to the client, the legal professional should verify the correctness of the fax number prior to sending. The author has received faxes on several occasions that were meant for someone else. Transposing a telephone number is easy to do when you are rushed. If you have your frequently called numbers on speed dial, be sure you don't key the wrong number when you send the fax. Perhaps the client's number is one digit different from that of the adverse party's attorney. The legal professional might hit the latter number by mistake and send that attorney confidential information about the client.

Extreme caution should be taken when using the telephone. Confidential information should not be given over the telephone. You may not be able to identify the person to whom you are speaking. Perhaps the caller is using the client's name but is not the client. If in doubt whether or not you are speaking to the client, ask the caller for her telephone number and if she is at that number presently, and say that you will find the information she wants and call her back. You should then check the telephone number against the one you have for the client in your file. In this way, you will be able to determine whether it is the client calling. Sometimes you will recognize the client's voice and know the person on the telephone is actually the client. In most situations, the caller will be who she says she is; however, if you are working on a high-profile case, there may be devious methods utilized to get inside information about the case.

■ KEY TERMS

Contempt	Malpractice
Disbar	Public reproval

■ SELF TEST

1. Explain the concept of attorney/client privileged communications.

2. Are there any exceptions?

■ NOTEBOOK PROJECTS

1. Find the ethical codes for the state bar in your state. Make a copy and file them in your Notebook.

2. Write a memorandum to Jane Sanchez, a new legal assistant in your firm, explaining the ethical codes obtained in question 1.

For additional resources, visit our Web site at **www.westlegalstudies.com**

USING COMPUTERS

CHAPTER OUTCOMES

As a result of studying this chapter, the student will learn:

1. how to prepare documents on the computer.
2. how to find court forms on the Internet.
3. how to prepare e-mail for use in the law office.
4. how to arrange travel and conferences using the Internet.
5. how to find legal information on the various sites available on the Internet.

WORD PROCESSING PROGRAMS

For many years, the most widely used software in law offices was Word Perfect. However, over the years Microsoft Word has become the program utilized in the majority of law offices. In a 2003 survey conducted by *Legal Assistant Today*, a leading magazine dedicated to the legal assistant profession, 31.3% of the law firms that responded use Corel Word Perfect and 66.4% use Microsoft Word. Since both programs are similar in their method of operation, instructions in this chapter will relate to the Microsoft Word program.

OTHER SOFTWARE

Depending on the type of law firm in which the legal assistant is employed, he may also be called upon to use programs for spreadsheets, databases, billing, timekeeping, legal research, and docket control. Civil litigation firms utilize various types of litigation support applications in the management of their more complex cases. For purposes of this text, only the more basic software programs will be discussed. The student should have previously taken a basic computer keyboarding class and learned how to make, save, revise, and view a document.

FORMAT OF LEGAL DOCUMENTS

Law offices use similar basic formats for their legal **pleadings.** Civil rules of individual states dictate the format for their pleadings. Check your office files or the civil rules to find the appropriate heading for

pleading formal legal document of allegations by the parties in a lawsuit where they state their claims and defenses and documents

your state. Most states use legal pleading paper, called **legal cap,** wherein certain items are put on the numbered lines as shown in Exhibit 5–1. Some law firms have pleading paper letterhead with the name and telephone number of the law firm imprinted in the upper left corner, starting on line 1. Some states have this letterhead at the bottom of the page. Always refer to your own state's guidelines to determine the proper format.

> STATE-SPECIFIC INFORMATION BOX
>
> The proper format for legal pleadings in the state of _____ follows:
>
> _____
>
> _____
>
> _____

DOCUMENT PREPARATION

In order to prepare a legal document using Microsoft Word, one must access the legal template by clicking "File" at the top left of your screen. In the pull-down menu, click "New." A list of available documents will appear on the right of your screen. Under "New from template," choose "General Templates" and then "Legal Pleadings." The Pleading Wizard will guide you through the process of preparing the document. Exhibit 5–1 shows a sample document created using the Pleading Wizard.

Once a specific template has been developed, the legal professional may use it each time a document or pleading is prepared. For instance, the name and address of the law firm may be keyed starting on line 1. The same attorney's name may be used in the signature line. In a large case with multiple pleadings, a template may be developed for that case with the heading and caption. Whenever the legal professional finds himself typing the same information over and over again, a template should be developed for that information.

In most states, the name and address of the law firm should appear on lines 1–4. The court name and address should be centered on line 8. The case caption begins on line 11 and includes the name of the parties, case number, and document name. See the example in Exhibit 5–1.

legal cap lined and numbered paper used for preparing pleadings and legal documents in most states

caption the heading of the document or pleading that identifies it

PLEADING CAPTIONS

Most cases involve one plaintiff against one defendant and use a **caption** similar to that found in Exhibit 5–1. However, other specialized cases use different captions, which are shown as follows.

1. **Minors**
   PATRICIA ZARKON, as Guardian ad litem for
   RAY ZARKON, a Minor,

   > Plaintiff,

   > v.

   JAMES JEFFRIES,

   > Defendant.

2. **Class Action Suits**
   JANET MUNOZ, on behalf of herself
   And all Plaintiffs similarly situated,

   > Plaintiffs,

   > v.

   DELANO CONSTRUCTION COMPANY,

   > Defendants.

3. **Executor of an Estate**
   CAROLYN MARTINSON, Executor of the Estate of
   MARK ROBINSON,

   > Plaintiff,

   > v.

   ANTHONY GALLO,

   > Defendant.

MULTIPARTY ACTIONS

In cases where there are several plaintiffs and/or several defendants, all of their names must be mentioned in the first pleading filed with the court. Thereafter, most courts allow the use of the term *et al.,* which means "and others." Check with the court in which you are filing the document to be certain of their procedures. You may also use the term when you are writing a letter, e-mail, or memorandum about the case. When you are including the name of the case within correspondence or documents, it should always be underlined or italicized. Here is an example of a case name with multiple parties written within a document:

Jacob B. Able, et al. v. Alexander W. Charles, et al., Case No. PI-25555

PREPARATION OF PLEADINGS

The complaint (or petition as it is called in a few states) and answer or answering documents in a civil case are called pleadings. Pleadings introduce the case and define the character and scope of the matters being litigated by narrowing disputed issues.

The complaint notifies the defendant of the claims asserted by the plaintiff and petitions the court for jurisdiction of the matter. To establish a cause of action, the attorney must first determine which court has jurisdiction, whether the plaintiff has in fact raised valid contentions, and what issues are being litigated. In most states, pleadings

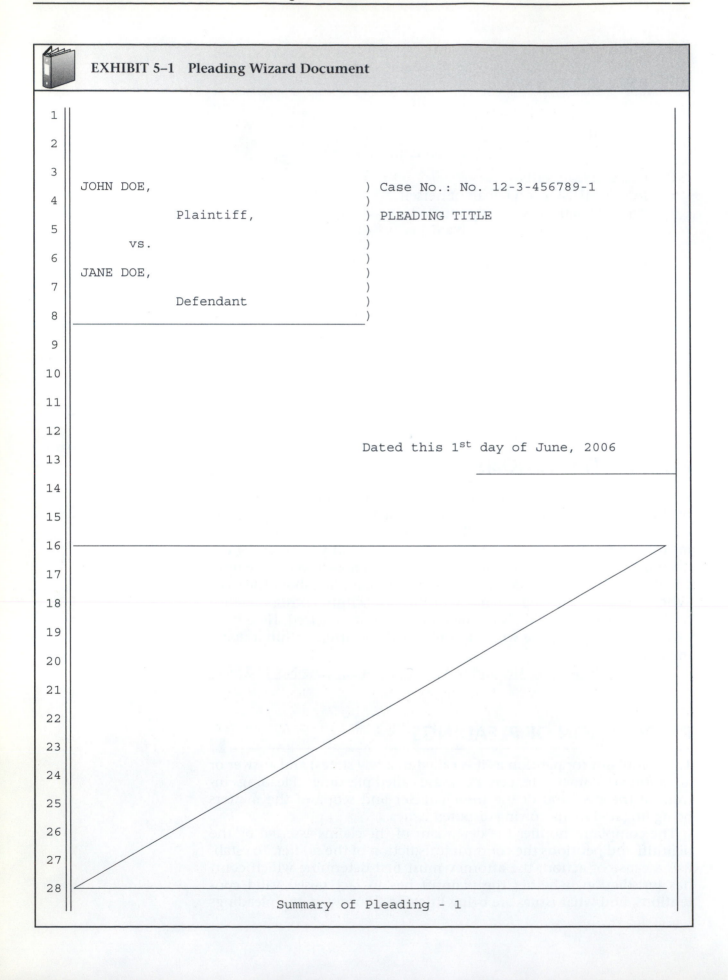

EXHIBIT 5–1 Pleading Wizard Document

```
 1
 2
 3
      JOHN DOE,                              ) Case No.: No. 12-3-456789-1
 4                                           )
                    Plaintiff,               ) PLEADING TITLE
 5                                           )
              vs.                            )
 6                                           )
      JANE DOE,                              )
 7                                           )
                    Defendant                )
 8    _____   )
 9
10
11
12
                                      Dated this 1st day of June, 2006
13
                                      _____
14
15
16
17
18
19
20
21
22
23
24
25
26
27
28    _____
                            Summary of Pleading - 1
```

must be prepared on lined and numbered pleading paper unless the state court has forms for this purpose.

Z-RULINGS OR SLASH MARKS

Signature lines for pleadings or other legally binding documents may not be typed on a separate page from the document itself. At least two lines of the document should be placed on the same page as the signature line.

Pleading paper contains 28 numbered lines. If you find your document ending on line 26, stop typing the document on line 24 and include the last two lines on the following page, along with the signature lines. Three slash marks should be typed on each numbered line below line 24 down to and including line 28.

If the document ends several lines earlier, however, and the signature line does not fit on that page, some law offices prefer the use of "Z rules" from the last line of the text to the end of that page. Two examples follow:

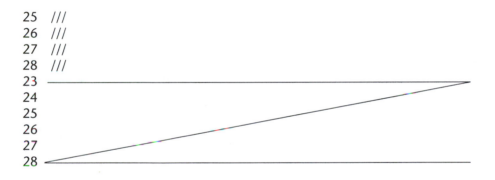

Some states do not use Z rulings or slash marks but place the words "Intentionally Left Blank" when there is a large break between pages.

SIGNATURE LINES

Two types of signature lines may be found on legal documents and pleadings. The first is used by a sole practitioner and the second by a member of a law firm, government agency, or corporation. The signature line begins in the middle of the page and continues to the right margin as follows.

1. **Sole practitioner**

DANIELLE ALICE MICHAELS
Attorney for Plaintiff

2. **Law firm**

JEFFRIES AND WILLIAMS
By: _____
JOHN W. PRICE
Attorney for Defendant

PROOFREADING

All documents that are filed with the court must be accurate or they may be rejected. Be sure to proofread all correspondence and documents for accuracy and spelling. Remember that even though you use spell check on the computer, if the word you wish to use is spelled incorrectly but is an actual word, it will not be corrected by spell check. After typing a letter or document, read it twice, once for spelling and the second for accuracy. Listed below are particular items that you should check carefully:

1. **Names and addresses**
   Be sure all names and addresses are spelled correctly. Check them against the name and address in the client's file.

2. **Capitalization**
   If a specific word is capitalized at the beginning of the document, be sure it is capitalized throughout.

3. **Parties**
   Parties' names are usually placed in all capital letters throughout the document.

4. **Captions**
   Check parties' names for spelling and designations. Legal names should be used. Be sure the case number is correct.

5. **Citations**
   Check each citation for accuracy. Judges may ignore the case information if they cannot find it in their books because the citation has been typed incorrectly. Transposing numbers on citations is easy to do and difficult to find. If necessary, go back to each individual case to be sure its citation is correct.

6. **Grammar and sentence structure**
   Read the document a second or third time for grammatical correctness.

SPECIALIZED LEGAL SOFTWARE

Specialized legal software packages exist for the preparation of various types of legal documents. For instance, if you are employed in an estate planning firm, you may use a package that assists in the writing of wills. The format of the will is given in the template, and you would complete the form with the individual's name and distinguishing information. The newer software packages will provide guides on your screen to make the process quite simple to use.

Forms packages are also available for the preparation of various court forms. The forms software packages sometimes have interactive forms that may be completed as they appear on your screen. If a package is not available in your office, you may find several forms, by state, at

http://www.westlegalstudies.com

You may copy the forms and complete them.

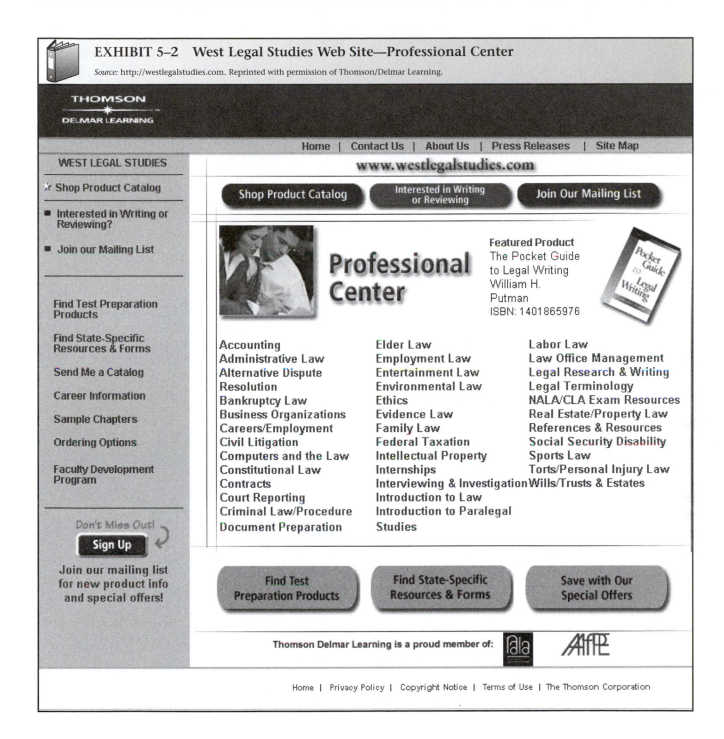

EXHIBIT 5–2   West Legal Studies Web Site—Professional Center
Source: http://westlegalstudies.com. Reprinted with permission of Thomson/Delmar Learning.

Once you get to the above-cited Web site, click the link for "Professional Center." At that point, you may obtain a considerable amount of information about different specialty areas of law. If you click on the box for "Find State Specific Resources & Forms," you will arrive at the page that lists all states. You may then click on either the Web links or on legal forms for a particular state. Exhibit 5–2 shows the Professional Center Web site, and Exhibit 5–3 shows the Web page you will reach by clicking on the "Find State-specific Resources & Forms" box.

If the legal professional wants to find Web links for the state of New York, he would click on the link for "New York Web Links." The Web

EXHIBIT 5–3   West Legal Studies Web Site—State Sources

Source: http://westlegalstudies.com. Reprinted with permission of Thomson/Delmar Learning

links page, shown in Exhibit 5–4, shows links to various pages dealing with the state of New York, as well as descriptions to the Web sites. If using the link to "Attorney General," it will go to the official Web site for the New York State Attorney General's office.

If the legal professional is looking for legal forms for the state of California, the link entitled "California Legal Forms" would be used.

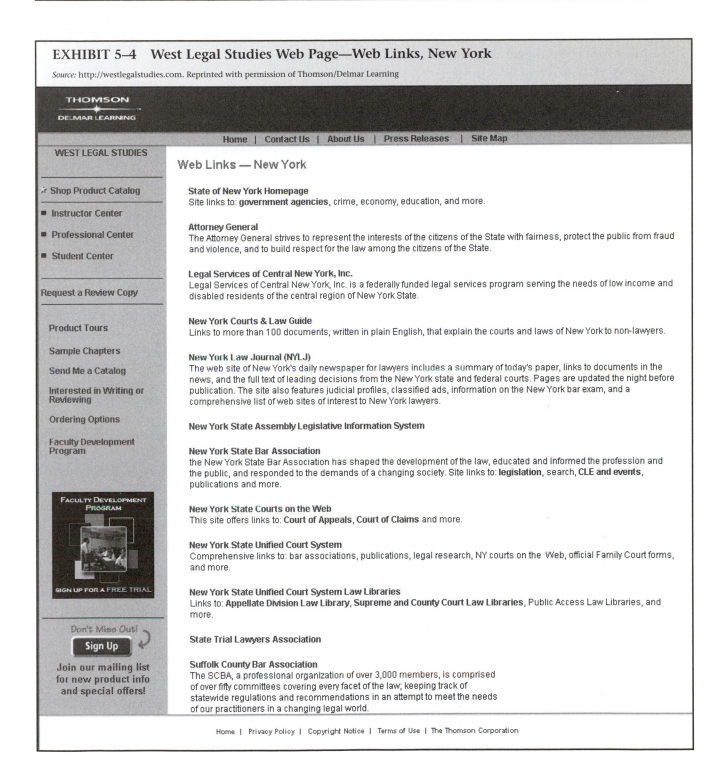

EXHIBIT 5–4   West Legal Studies Web Page—Web Links, New York

Source: http://westlegalstudies.com. Reprinted with permission of Thomson/Delmar Learning

This would connect to the Web page shown at Exhibit 5–5. The first link on that page ("Judicial Council of California") will take you to the pages shown in Exhibit 5–6. These pages list some of the available court forms for California in alphabetical order. Note that only the first page of 46 pages of forms links is provided herein.

Instructions are provided on the relevant page for the completion of the forms. Each form has its own specific instructions.

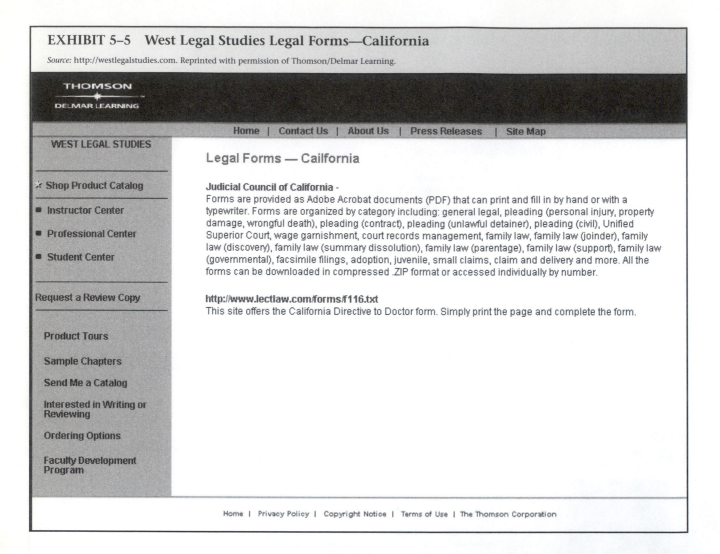

EXHIBIT 5–5   West Legal Studies Legal Forms—California
Source: http://westlegalstudies.com. Reprinted with permission of Thomson/Delmar Learning.

Some states, such as California, are "forms intensive" in that they have many **court forms** that are utilized in lieu of office-typed pleadings and documents. For example, almost all documents required for dissolution of marriage in California are part of a Judicial Council forms packet.

Note that most of the forms on the

http://www.westlegalstudies.com

Web page must be copied and then completed. In most cases they may not be completed on the computer. However, many law offices have software packages that enable you to complete the forms on the computer.

West Publishing Company publishes books of tear-out court forms. These forms books are available for many states.

FEDERAL COURT FORMS

court forms forms developed by the courts that are used instead of office-typed pleadings

Federal court forms are available at

http://www.uscourts.gov/forms

A summons for use in a Federal criminal case is shown in Exhibit 5–7.

EXHIBIT 5–6   California Court Forms

FORMS

- Forms Home
- Browse All Forms
- Using Forms
- Latest Changes
- Viewing and Filling Forms
- Publishers
- Appellate Claim Form
- Judicial Council Reports

C|C
home

Forms

Judicial Council Forms

The Judicial Council and the Administrative Office of the Courts forms presented in the Forms section of the California Courts Web site are current as of January 1, 2007. Submit questions or comments about Judicial Council Forms.

Select a group of forms
Select a form group from the drop down menu below and click the "See Forms" button.

All Forms Listed by Name ▾

See Forms

* Forms marked with an asterisk are adopted for mandatory use by all courts.

Non-Fillable Form	Fillable Form	Date Revised	Description
ADR-101*	ADR-101*	1994	ADR Information Form
PLD-PI-003	PLD-PI-003	1/1/2007	ANSWER-Personal Injury, Property Damage, Wrongful Death
TR-165	TR-165	1/1/2007	Abandonment of Appeal (Infraction)
APP-005	APP-005	1/1/2007	Abandonment of Appeal (Unlimited Civil Case)
EJ-001*	EJ-001*	1/1/2006	Abstract of Judgment—Civil and Small Claims
FL-480*	FL-480*	1/1/2003	Abstract of Support Judgment
JV-129	JV-129	1/1/2007	Abuse of Sibling (§ 300 (i))
JV-129 S		1/1/2007	Abuse of Sibling (§ 300 (i)) - Spanish
EJ-100	EJ-100	1/1/2005	Acknowledgment of Satisfaction of Judgment
JV-101*	JV-101*	1/1/2007	Additional Children Attachment (Juvenile Dependency Petition)
JV-101* S		1/1/2007	Additional Children Attachment (Juvenile Dependency Petition) - Spanish
MC-020	MC-020	1987	Additional Page [to be attached to any form]
SUM-200(A)*	SUM-200(A)*	1/1/2007	Additional Parties Attachment (Attachment to Summons)
FL-341(D)	FL-341(D)	1/1/2005	Additional Provisions-Physical Custody Attachment
ADOPT-210*	ADOPT-210*	1/1/2007	Adoption Agreement
ADOPT-230*	ADOPT-230*	1/1/2007	Adoption Expenses
ADOPT-215*	ADOPT-215*	1/1/2007	Adoption Order

EXHIBIT 5–7   Summons for a Federal Criminal Case

Source: http://www.uscourts.gov

AO83 (Rev. 10/03) Summons in a Criminal Case

UNITED STATES DISTRICT COURT

DISTRICT OF _____

UNITED STATES OF AMERICA
V.

SUMMONS IN A CRIMINAL CASE

Case Number: _____

(Name and Address of Defendant)

YOU ARE HEREBY SUMMONED to appear before the United States District Court at the place, date and time set forth below.

Place	Room
	Date and Time
Before:	

To answer a(n)

☐ Indictment ☐ Information ☐ Complaint ☐ Probation Violation Petition ☐ Supervised Release Violation Petition ☐ Violation Notice

Charging you with a violation of Title _____ United States Code, Section(s) _____

Brief description of offense:

_____

Signature of Issuing Officer   Date

_____

Name and Title of Issuing Officer

continued

Exhibit 5–7   *continued*

AO83 (Rev. 10/03) Summons in a Criminal Case

RETURN OF SERVICE

Date

Service was made by me on:[1]

Check one box below to indicate appropriate method of service

☐ Served personally upon the defendant at:

☐ Left summons at the defendant's dwelling house or usual place of abode with a person of suitable age and discretion then residing therein and mailed a copy of the summons to the defendant's last known address. Name of person with whom the summons was left:

☐ Returned unexecuted:

I declare under penalty of perjury under the laws of the United States of America that the foregoing information contained in the Return of Service is true and correct.

Returned on _____   _____
                          Date   Name of United States Marshal

                                                         _____
                                                         (by) Deputy United States Marshal

Remarks:

[1] As to who may serve a summons, see Rule 4 of the Federal Rules of Criminal Procedure.

A subpoena for use in a federal civil case may be found at

http://www.uscourts.gov/forms/AO088.pdf

It is shown in Exhibit 5–8.

For those cases that go to trial, the federal courts also require a witness list, which may be found at

http://www.uscourts.gov/forms/AO187.pdf

A copy of this form is reproduced in Exhibit 5–9.

E-MAIL

If the purpose of a communication is to disseminate information, e-mail may be used as a substitute for returning telephone calls. It is often faster to compose an e-mail than it would be to play telephone tag. The client may read the e-mail at his leisure and will have a record of the information.

Since e-mail is becoming such a popular method of communication, it is advisable to ask the client's e-mail address at the initial client interview. The address should be noted in the client's file. E-mail is becoming so popular that many businesses and law firms list their e-mail address on their business cards.

Care must be taken when using e-mail for confidential client communications. Many firms have encoding software that translates the e-mail into a code before it is sent to the client. The client must in turn have decoding software on his computer in order to translate the message. Encoding programs protect against e-mail theft and are efficient tools to protect confidential communications.

Internal E-Mail

E-mail has taken the place of the interoffice memorandum in most cases. Law firms, government offices, and corporate law departments usually have their own network so that individuals may send e-mail quickly. It is often more expedient to send someone an internal e-mail than to call on the telephone or write a memorandum. The e-mail arrives at the person's computer almost instantly.

Format of E-Mail

Although the format for e-mails is more informal than for the formal letter, it is appropriate to use the individual's name in the e-mail itself, similar to a salutation. If the e-mail is being sent internally within the law firm or company, or to a personal friend, then no salutation is necessary. Be sure to type the person's e-mail address exactly, using proper spelling, or the recipient will not receive it. Additionally, if the erroneously spelled address actually exists, the e-mail will be sent to that other person. If the e-mail address does not exist, then the e-mail will be returned to you.

If the e-mail is a confidential communication, be sure to indicate the proper designation in the e-mail itself. Always check the e-mail for spelling and grammatical errors. Several Internet providers have

EXHIBIT 5–8   Subpoena in a Civil Case

Source: http://www.uscourts.gov/forms/AO088.pdf

AO88 (Rev. 1/94) Subpoena in a Civil Case

Issued by the
UNITED STATES DISTRICT COURT

DISTRICT OF _____

SUBPOENA IN A CIVIL CASE

V.

Case Number:[1]

TO:

☐   YOU ARE COMMANDED to appear in the United States District court at the place, date, and time specified below to testify in the above case.

PLACE OF TESTIMONY	COURTROOM
	DATE AND TIME

☐   YOU ARE COMMANDED to appear at the place, date, and time specified below to testify at the taking of a deposition in the above case.

PLACE OF DEPOSITION	DATE AND TIME

☐   YOU ARE COMMANDED to produce and permit inspection and copying of the following documents or objects at the place, date, and time specified below (list documents or objects):

PLACE	DATE AND TIME

☐   YOU ARE COMMANDED to permit inspection of the following premises at the date and time specified below.

PREMISES	DATE AND TIME

   Any organization not a party to this suit that is subpoenaed for the taking of a deposition shall designate one or more officers, directors, or managing agents, or other persons who consent to testify on its behalf, and may set forth, for each person designated, the matters on which the person will testify. Federal Rules of Civil Procedure, 30(b)(6).

ISSUING OFFICER'S SIGNATURE AND TITLE (INDICATE IF ATTORNEY FOR PLAINTIFF OR DEFENDANT)	DATE
ISSUING OFFICER'S NAME, ADDRESS AND PHONE NUMBER	

(See Rule 45, Federal Rules of Civil Procedure, Parts C & D on next page)

[1] If action is pending in district other than district of issuance, state district under case number.

continued

Exhibit 5–8 *continued*

AO88 (Rev. 1/94) Subpoena in a Civil Case

PROOF OF SERVICE

	DATE	PLACE
SERVED		

SERVED ON (PRINT NAME)	MANNER OF SERVICE

SERVED BY (PRINT NAME)	TITLE

DECLARATION OF SERVER

I declare under penalty of perjury under the laws of the United States of America that the foregoing information contained in the Proof of Service is true and correct.

Executed on _____
DATE   SIGNATURE OF SERVER

_____
ADDRESS OF SERVER

Rule 45, Federal Rules of Civil Procedure, Parts C & D:

(c) PROTECTION OF PERSONS SUBJECT TO SUBPOENAS.

(1) A party or an attorney responsible for the issuance and service of a subpoena shall take reasonable steps to avoid imposing undue burden or expense on a person subject to that subpoena. The court on behalf of which the subpoena was issued shall enforce this duty and impose upon the party or attorney in breach of this duty an appropriate sanction which may include, but is not limited to, lost earnings and reasonable attorney's fee.

(2) (A) A person commanded to produce and permit inspection and copying of designated books, papers, documents or tangible things, or inspection of premises need not appear in person at the place of production or inspection unless commanded to appear for deposition, hearing or trial.

(B) Subject to paragraph (d) (2) of this rule, a person commanded to produce and permit inspection and copying may, within 14 days after service of subpoena or before the time specified for compliance if such time is less than 14 days after service, serve upon the party or attorney designated in the subpoena written objection to inspection or copying of any or all of the designated materials or of the premises. If objection is made, the party serving the subpoena shall not be entitled to inspect and copy materials or inspect the premises except pursuant to an order of the court by which the subpoena was issued. If objection has been made, the party serving the subpoena may, upon notice to the person commanded to produce, move at any time for an order to compel the production. Such an order to comply production shall protect any person who is not a party or an officer of a party from significant expense resulting from the inspection and copying commanded.

(3) (A) On timely motion, the court by which a subpoena was issued shall quash or modify the subpoena if it

(i) fails to allow reasonable time for compliance,
(ii) requires a person who is not a party or an officer of a party to travel to a place more than 100 miles from the place where that person resides, is employed or regularly transacts business in person, except that, subject to the provisions of clause (c) (3) (B) (iii) of this rule, such a person may in order to attend

trial be commanded to travel from any such place within the state in which the trial is held, or

(iii) requires disclosure of privileged or other protected matter and no exception or waiver applies, or
(iv) subjects a person to undue burden.

(B) If a subpoena

(i) requires disclosure of a trade secret or other confidential research, development, or commercial information, or
(ii) requires disclosure of an unretained expert's opinion or information not describing specific events or occurrences in dispute and resulting from the expert's study made not at the request of any party, or
(iii) requires a person who is not a party or an officer of a party to incur substantial expense to travel more than 100 miles to attend trial, the court may, to protect a person subject to or affected by the subpoena, quash or modify the subpoena, or, if the party in whose behalf the subpoena is issued shows a substantial need for the testimony or material that cannot be otherwise met without undue hardship and assures that the person to whom the subpoena is addressed will be reasonably compensated, the court may order appearance or production only upon specified conditions.

(d) DUTIES IN RESPONDING TO SUBPOENA.

(1) A person responding to a subpoena to produce documents shall produce them as they are kept in the usual course of business or shall organize and label them to correspond with the categories in the demand.

(2) When information subject to a subpoena is withheld on a claim that it is privileged or subject to protection as trial preparation materials, the claim shall be made expressly and shall be supported by a description of the nature of the documents, communications, or things not produced that is sufficient to enable the demanding party to contest the claim.

EXHIBIT 5–9

Source: http://www.uscourts.gov/forms/AO187.pdf

✎AO 187 (Rev. 7/87) Exhibit and Witness List

UNITED STATES DISTRICT COURT

DISTRICT OF

EXHIBIT AND WITNESS LIST

V.

Case Number:

PRESIDING JUDGE				PLAINTIFF'S ATTORNEY	DEFENDANT'S ATTORNEY
TRIAL DATE (S)				COURT REPORTER	COURTROOM DEPUTY

PLF. NO.	DEF. NO.	DATE OFFERED	MARKED	ADMITTED	DESCRIPTION OF EXHIBITS* AND WITNESSES

* Include a notation as to the location of any exhibit not held with the case file or not available because of size.

Page 1 of ____1____ Pages

automatic spell check built into the system. A few providers have a method for an individual to check to see whether the recipient received the e-mail. Other material may be imported into the e-mail, such as reports, documents, graphs, or exhibits if they were prepared on the computer or scanned into the computer's hard drive.

Parts of the E-Mail

The parts of the e-mail are described below, along with the type of information that should be placed in each.

1. **Caption or Heading**

   The caption of your e-mail message resembles that of an interoffice memorandum. It contains the following items:

   TO:

   SUBJECT:

   The date you send the e-mail will appear automatically, as will your name. Usually the time the e-mail is sent also appears. Be sure to key in the individual's exact Internet address, along with the proper subject. In many cases, the ISP automatically places your e-mail address in the "FROM" portion of the e-mail form. If the recipient may not know the designation is your address, you may wish to put your name in the subject portion of the form. For example, suppose your e-mail address is Jdoe@earthlink.com and the recipient is not familiar with your last name. In the subject portion, you may put "From Jane Doe regarding Travel Arrangements to New York."

2. **Copies**

   If you would like to send a copy of the e-mail to another individual, then key in his e-mail address here, in the "cc:" portion of the form. If you would like to send a blind copy (one that the other recipients do not know is being sent), put the person's address in parentheses as follows:(Jdoe@earthlink.com). Only Jdoe and you will know that he received a copy of the message. Be sure to check your own browser's requirements for blind copies.

3. **Body**

   In the "message" portion of the e-mail, it is not always necessary to use the same formal language often used in a letter. You should prepare the e-mail in block style, using a clear and concise writing style. If you want an answer within a certain time period, indicate the due date in the last paragraph of the e-mail, just as you would in a letter. Although it is usually not possible to sign the e-mail, a closing with your name should be included. Some programs allow you to make a signature with a pointing device.

4. **Attachments**

   In some cases you may wish to attach other material to the e-mail. As long as you have this material on your computer in another file, or you have a scanner and can scan it onto your hard drive, you may attach it to your e-mail. Depending on the method used by your provider, you should first find the document and then attach it to the e-mail. You may attach documents, graphics, pictures, or any other item that you have on your computer's hard drive.

PASSWORDS

Password thieves know the most common names to use to try to access another's account. When you create your password, be sure to use something that only you know. Memorize your password and do not write it down and put it next to the computer. A recent after-hours survey of a large corporation revealed that many employees had their passwords on a Post-it note that was attached to the computer. Even if you have a note with one word written on it, it is likely a password.

USING THE INTERNET

Most information that was formerly available only in book form is now obtainable on the Internet. A vast number of Web sites specialize in the legal profession.

Various Web sites exist for making travel arrangements and arranging conferences. Other sites will enable you to make a map to your destination. Online conferences may be set up in chat rooms. Online directories exist to find addresses. Many cities' Yellow Pages may be found on the Internet.

SEARCHING ONLINE

Several search engines are available that enable you to find information. Your Internet service provider, such as AOL or EarthLink, will have its own search engine, or you may prefer to use others as well. Some of the more common are menu driven. That is, they provide a list of categories in which you can search. Others provide a keyword search that enables you to list all keywords in which you are interested. Examples are AOL and Google. The computer will search the Internet and provide you with an abstract of all documents that have your keywords within them. They are listed by percentage of keyword occurrences, with the highest numbers first.

Suppose that you want information about airline travel from New York to Los Angeles. You would type the following words in the search box: **Airlines New York Los Angeles.** This type of search is similar to that with which you may be familiar from using Westlaw. Sometimes the keywords will have to be changed or modified to yield more specific search results. At other times the keywords you choose may be too specific and may have to be made more general. Be prepared for a lengthy search no matter what the subject might be, though, as there is a vast amount of information on the Internet.

Many Web pages display hyperlinks that will connect you to other pages. These take the form of colored and/or underlined titles, similar to those found above on the

Web page. You can click your mouse on the title and be taken directly to the Web page referred to by the hyperlink. Documents are linked to each other over the Web, allowing you to move from one to the other by clicking on the highlighted text.

LINKS WITHIN TEXT

Sometimes when you are reading information on a Web page, you will notice text that is underlined or shown in a different color. This text also represents a link to another Web page. If you click your mouse on that word or group of words, it will take you immediately to another area of the Web. In some cases, you will find Web pages with lists of hypertext links in a given subject area. For instances, some colleges provide hyperlinks on their Web pages to different areas of the college or research materials about given topics.

In the discussion of

http://www.westlegalstudies.com

above, you were introduced to Web pages with hypertext links to other pages. You were able to go from the home page to state sources and to the Web links and forms available for that particular state.

CONDUCTING A SEARCH

The first step in conducting a search is opening your browser. If your computer is turned on, look for the icon that shows your particular browser. Double-click the icon with your mouse. Depending on where you are signing on from, you may need a user name and password to get online. Your school may have a Web page that loads first when the browser opens and acts as the home page when you first go online from your college. The browser may take a few minutes to load, so be patient. When the hourglass shows on the screen, the browser is loading. When the hourglass turns into an arrow, it has fully loaded.

Think of the home page as your home on the Internet. From your home you may visit many other sites, but returning home just takes a click of the mouse on the "home" icon. Using the arrows on the right side of the screen, you may scroll up and down on the home page to become familiar with its contents. If you see an item of interest and it is underlined or in color, click on the link and you will be taken to its site. This may continue for other sites and other links. When you want to return to the home page, just click the "home" icon. If you wish to return to one of the pages you previously visited, you may use the "back" button (or left arrow) on the top of the screen to go back page by page.

The address of the page you are viewing will appear in the box at the top of your screen. If you wish to remember the address to return to the page at a later date, click the heart, "favorites," or "bookmark," depending on which browser you are using. If you are doing research and require the latest information, check the dates on the pages you are viewing to ascertain if the information is current. If it is not, then you may wish to use another page.

Various private Web pages exist for the purpose of providing search capabilities on many topics. One particularly comprehensive page that is very effective for doing general research is located at

http://www.refdesk.com

A picture of the first page of this Web site may be found in Exhibit 5–10.

EXHIBIT 5–10   Refdesk Home Page

Source: Reprinted with permission of Refdesk.com.

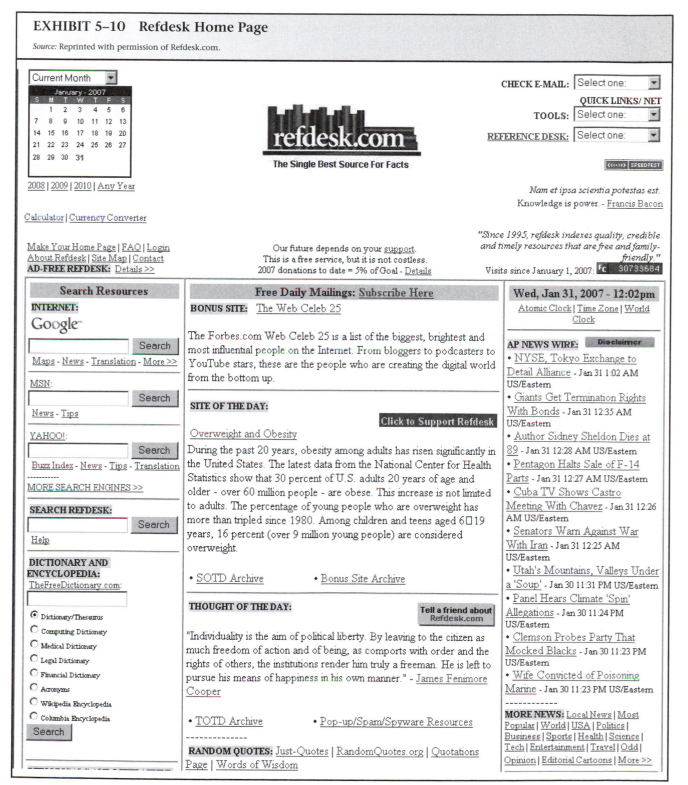

OBSOLETE WEB PAGES

At times you may click on an address in your "bookmarks" or "favorites" and find that the page no longer exists. In that case, you may have to do a new search for its location. Many pages change locations often, and the page you found three months ago may not be there today. Sometimes the new page address is given on the old page; at other times, you may have to do a completely new search to find it. In this case, be sure to delete the obsolete page from your bookmarks and add the new page name.

If many individuals are trying to access a Web page at the same time, you may not be able to get into it. In that case, the page name may not have changed but Internet traffic has made it impossible to access at this time. Wait a few minutes and try again. Usually you will be able to get in the second time.

FINDING A PERSON OR BUSINESS ONLINE

Some ISPs provide their own "white pages" to find people and "yellow pages" to find businesses. Searches may be conducted by name or geographical location. Suppose you have a friend in another state but do not know your friend's postal address. You may search by your friend's name and the state to determine his address and, in some cases, telephone number. Note that some individuals and businesses may not be included in the directories.

If you are looking for a telephone number, area code, or e-mail address, several Web databases may be searched simultaneously by using

http://www.555-1212.com

However, you must register on their home page and pay a fee for this service.

Yellow pages also exist for finding telephone numbers and addresses of businesses. Information on individuals is also available on this site. Door-to-door driving directions may be obtained as well. This service is provided free of charge at

http://www.infospace.com

A copy of the InfoSpace home page is shown in Exhibit 5–11.

ONLINE CONFERENCES

Most of the negative publicity heard about "chat rooms" indicates that they are dangerous places where people use phony names and prey on the unsuspecting. However, the chat room may be used effectively for private meetings of businesses or law firms. Providers that have chat capability also give the subscriber the ability to set up a private chat room and invite only specific individuals to participate.

Endless possibilities exist for holding meetings in chat rooms. An attorney in California may speak online to a client in New York without incurring long distance telephone charges. A lawyer in Washington may set up a meeting in a chat room with members of the same firm

EXHIBIT 5–11   Infospace Home Page

Source: © 2006 InfoSpace, Inc. All rights reserved. Reprinted with permission of InfoSpace, Inc.

InfoSpace® Names. Numbers. Now.™

The easy way to find businesses and people.

What do you want to search?

home ▶
yellow pages
white pages
web search
maps & directions
browse categories
search by phone
near an address
email search
world directories

YELLOW PAGES & WHITE PAGES

Try the new way to find businesses, people, and events

Are you looking for businesses or people?

◉ Find a Business by Type
○ Find a Business by Name
○ Find a Person

Type of Business

City   State* ▾

SEARCH

* Required

Set your Default Location. It's easy and saves you clicks.

Looking for the InfoSpace Corporate Web site?

Free Toolbar
Make Your Homepage
Resources
  Classifieds
  Weather
  Horoscopes
  Public Records
My Lookup History
Bookmark this Page
Help

Find exactly what you need - nearby.

Try it now!

infospace® Find It!

infospace | About InfoSpace | Mobile | Search & Directory | Advertise With Us | Careers | Press | Investor Relations
Privacy Policy | Terms of Use

InfoSpace Network: Dogpile | WebCrawler | MetaCrawler | InfoSpace | Moviso
InfoSpace Resources: Search Engines | Yellow Pages | White Pages | Town Directories | Business Categories | Maps | Ringtones

©2007 InfoSpace, Inc All Rights Reserved.

located in New York. Staff meetings may be conducted with branch offices in other parts of the city, state, or country. Meetings conducted online save firms considerable sums of money in travel time, airline fares, and other travel expenses.

LOCAL TRAVEL

Sometimes meetings are held in other parts of the city or in a nearby location. The attorney may have to drive to attend one of these meetings. Sources for maps and directions from one address to another are

http://www.mapquest.com

http://www.mapblast.com

and

http://www.mapsonus.com

These sites provide directions and maps to all parts of the country. It is advisable to get maps from two sites to compare the directions. It has been the author's experience that occasionally the directions are not accurate on an online site, particularly when dealing with a newly named street or address.

Some traffic information is available on the Internet for various large cities and metropolitan areas. If one route has a lot of traffic, the attorney may wish to take an alternate route to arrive at his destination on time. One Web site that may be useful for this purpose is

http://www.traffic.com

Their home page is shown in Exhibit 5–12. This site shows road closures, accident reports, slowdowns, construction delays, and traffic

EXHIBIT 5–12   Traffic.com Web Site

Source: Reprinted with permission of traffic.com

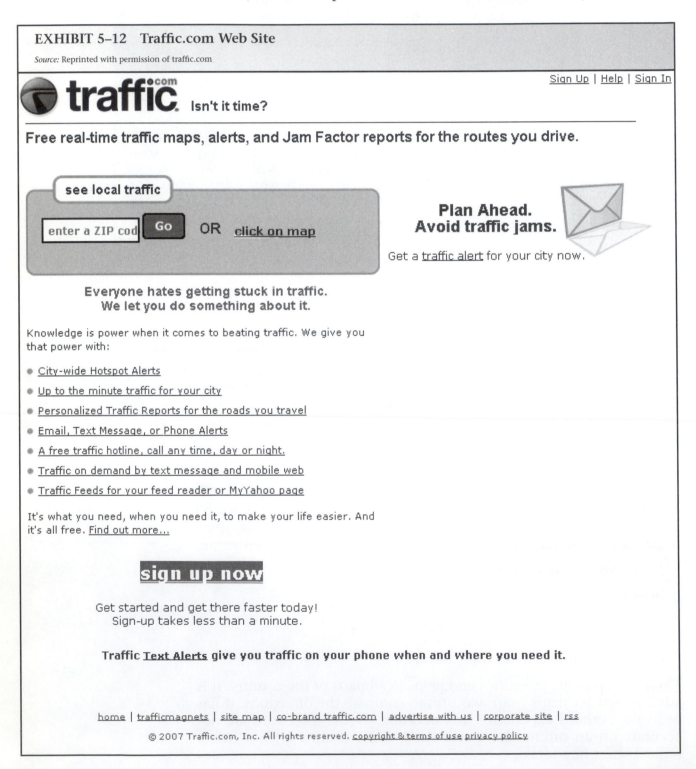

advisories for major cities, including Atlanta, Baltimore, Boston, Chicago, Dallas-Fort Worth, Detroit, Houston, Los Angeles, Miami, Minneapolis, New York, Orlando, Philadelphia, Phoenix, Pittsburgh, Providence, Sacramento, San Diego, San Francisco, Seattle, St. Louis, Tampa, and Washington. If you need traffic information for a city not listed above, conduct your own search by typing "traffic <your city>" to find a site that will give you traffic in your own city.

OUT OF TOWN TRAVEL

Even with the use of chat rooms for online conferences, it often becomes necessary for the attorney to travel to other cities or countries. A considerable amount of information is available on the Internet for this purpose, including weather, hotels, cities, maps, airlines, and travel reservations. You may make all travel reservations online, including transportation, hotels, car rentals, airport limousine services, and even restaurant reservations. If you do not have the particular site address, you may conduct a search using the name of the airline, airport, or restaurant. Sometimes the rates will be less on the airline's own site, so if you know the airline name, conduct a search for that airline's official site. Often the site is just the name of the airline with a .com after it. Some of the airline names are abbreviated. For instance, American Airlines' site may be found at

http://www.aa.com

Most airlines even enable you to choose your seat assignment and check in online.

One site that enables you to make airline reservations as well as hotel and auto rentals is

http://www.cheaptickets.com

Preview Travel/Travelocity provides a means for making flight, hotel, and automobile reservations, and reports on special fares when available. Their Farefinder search engine searches airline databases to find the lowest fares between major United States cities. Their Web site is located at

http://www.previewtravel.com

TRAVEL ABROAD

It is often the legal professional/assistant's responsibility to renew the attorney's passport for travel abroad. As this textbook goes to press, more countries are requiring passports for entry for United States citizens. Check with the State Department prior to taking a trip out of the country to determine whether the particular country requires a passport or visa.

Information about obtaining passports is available on the State Department's home page at

http://www.state.gov/index.html

On the left side of that page, you will find a topic related to Travel. Subheadings include emergencies, passports, and visas. Click on the "passports" heading and you will be taken to a page that gives you a considerable amount of information about obtaining passports and/or passport renewals.

The "travel warnings" section contains information about what countries have had travel warnings issued concerning travel in that particular country. The warnings are issued when the State Department decides to recommend that Americans avoid travel to a particular country. Public announcements disseminate information about terrorist threats and other conditions posing significant risks to the security of American travelers. Such warnings are issued when there is a perceived threat that will include Americans as a particular target group. Some examples of these announcements include short-term coups, bomb threats, violence by terrorists, and anniversary dates of specific terrorist events. This section should always be examined for the particular country to which you are traveling. You may also subscribe to the State Department's e-mail for communication of travel warnings. You will receive an e-mail from the State Department whenever a new travel warning is issued.

Many other sites exist for different aspects of travel abroad. Many cities, states, and countries have their own Web pages for information about those locations. Whenever you plan travel abroad, conduct a search of the information required and other sites will be found.

LAWYER DIRECTORIES

Many private law firms and attorneys have their own Web pages. The best way to find a specific law firm's Web page is to conduct a search using the name of the firm in quotation marks. Using one of the search engines discussed previously, key the name of the law firm within quotation marks into the search box. If that firm has a Web page, its location should show upon the search engine's results page. If you are not certain of the firm's full name, then key in the name as you think it is without the quotation marks. For example, if you know the name of the firm, you might key "Long Law Firm," but if you are not sure of the name of the firm, you would key Long Law Firm.

It is also advisable to indicate the location of the law firm by city and state.

WEST LEGAL DIRECTORY

The *West Legal Directory* has biographical listings of over 800,000 lawyers. Searches are possible by subject, practice area, attributes of the attorney, and location. For example, it would be possible to search for "a German-speaking immigration attorney in Chicago." It is possible to search the following subjects in the *West Legal Directory*, accessible at

http://lawyers.findlaw.com

You may find a lawyer by city and state or by practice area. Another locator service for attorneys may be found at

http://www.attorneyfind.com

This site enables you to search for law firms and lawyers in different states and different specialty areas.

Most individuals who have worked in law offices are familiar with the *Martindale-Hubbell Legal Directory of Attorneys and Law Firms*. This same directory is provided online at

http://www.martindale.com

A copy of this page is included herein as Exhibit 5–13. There are close to a million listings in this directory of law firms and attorneys in the United States and other parts of the world. Searches are possible by name, city, state, country, language, and province. It is also possible to search here for government attorneys and corporate law departments. Individual listings for attorneys include their name, address, telephone number, areas of practice, educational background, professional affiliations, and sometimes representative clients.

PROFESSIONAL ORGANIZATIONS

American Bar Association

The American Bar Association (ABA) maintains its Web site at

http://www.abanet.org

In addition to providing information about the organization for its members, a considerable number of other items are also included on the site, including:

1. membership information.
2. publications of the ABA.
3. continuing legal education issues.
4. the *ABA Journal*.
5. links to law-related sites.
6. information about the legal community.
7. public information about the legal profession.
8. specialty sections and news about their events.
9. paralegal information.

State Bar Organizations

Most state bar organizations have their own Web sites. A search may be conducted to find your own state's bar organization by doing a keyword search. When you go to the search engine, key into the space for keywords "<your state> state bar." Determine the Web address for your state's bar organization and complete the state-specific information box.

EXHIBIT 5–13 Martindale-Hubbell Home Page

Source: Reprinted with permission of LexisNexis. LexisNexis, the Knowledge Burst Logo and Martindale-Hubbell are registered trademarks of Reed Elsevier Properties, Inc. and are used with the permission of LexisNexis.

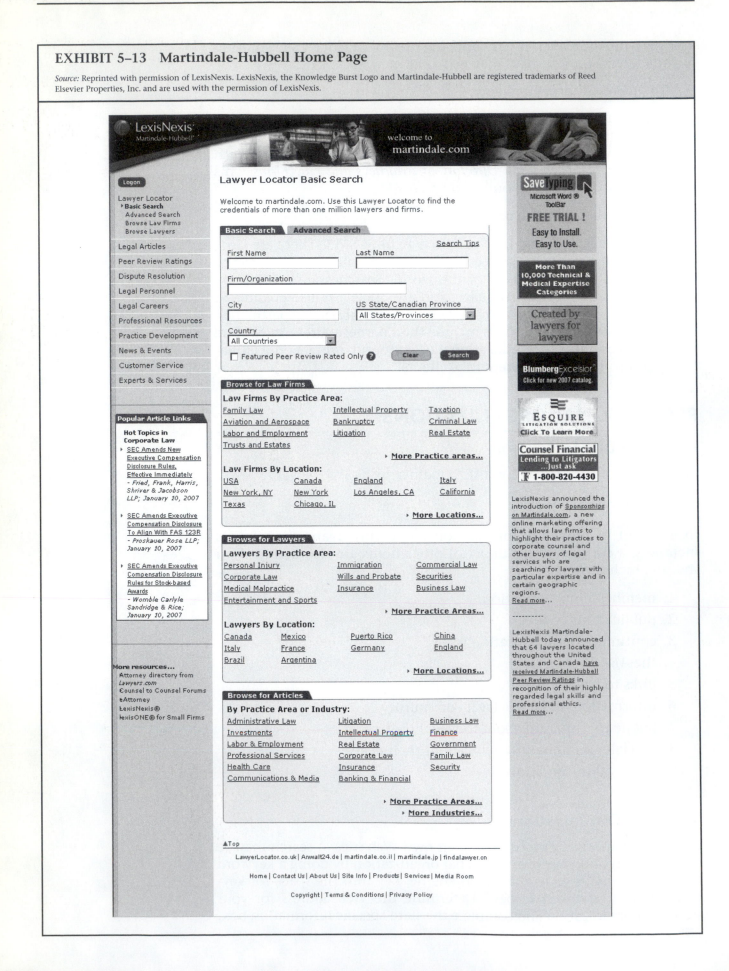

> STATE-SPECIFIC INFORMATION BOX FOR THE STATE OF _____:
>
> The Web address for this state's bar organization's Web site is:
>
> _____

Organization for Legal Professionals

NALS . . . the Association for Legal Professionals maintains chapters throughout the United States. Its Web site is located at

http://www.nals.org

A copy of its Web page may be found in Exhibit 5–14. Its site includes information on membership, education, certification, newsletters, on-line learning, and conferences. Its online forum for legal professionals provides an opportunity to discuss the legal services profession as well as the organization itself.

Paralegal and Legal Assistant Organizations

A number of legal assistant organizations exist both on the local and national level. Probably the largest local organization in the country is the Los Angeles Paralegal Association (LAPA) with over a thousand members in the greater Los Angeles metropolitan region. Its site may be found at

http://www.lapa.org

The organization is dedicated to the development of the legal assistant profession and provides opportunities for professional development and networking. The site maintains information about meetings and upcoming events. Students may join LAPA for a reduced fee.

The National Association of Legal Assistants (NALA) is a leading national professional association for legal assistants. Its site may be found at

http://www.nala.org

The association provides continuing education and professional certification programs for legal assistants. It was incorporated in 1975 and is one of the oldest paralegal organizations in the country. The site contains information about its quarterly journal, along with an online campus of classes and seminars. It provides links to legal vendors and other professional legal organizations.

Another national organization in the paralegal area is the National Federation of Paralegal Associations (NFPA), with a Web site located at

http://www.paralegals.org

Its home page provides links to press releases, surveys, news, legal research sources, products, services, calendar, a career center, articles on

EXHIBIT 5–14 NALS . . . the Association for Legal Professionals Web Page

Source: Reprinted with permission from NALS . . . the Association for Legal Professionals.

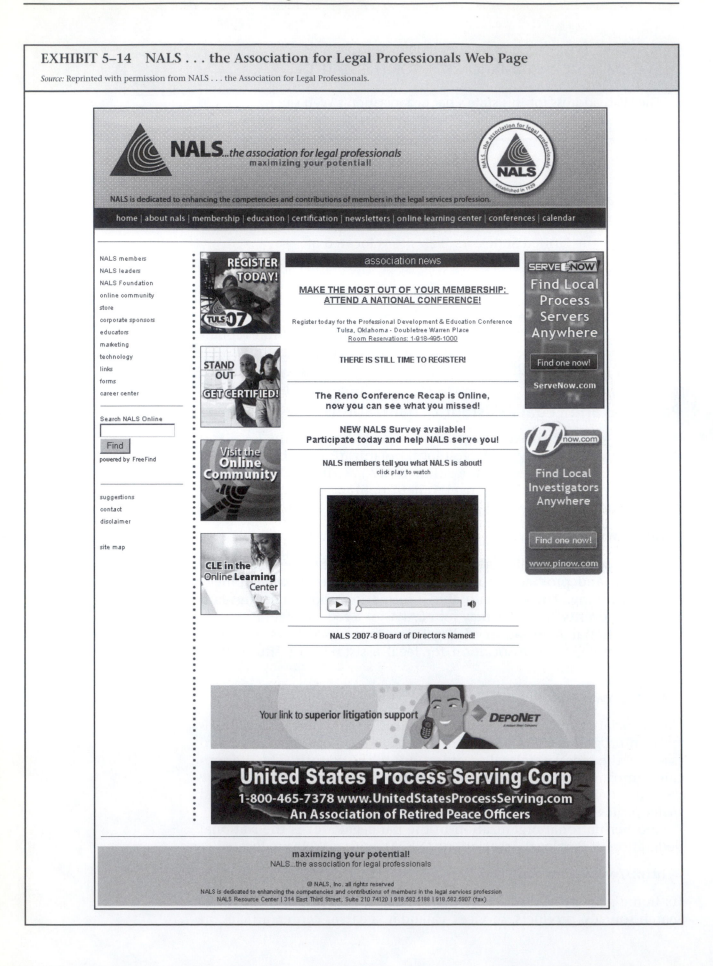

getting started in the profession, membership information, professional development, networking, publications, and opportunities in the field.

The American Association for Paralegal Education (AAfPE) is a national organization that serves paralegal education and institutions offering paralegal programs. Its site is located at

http://www.aafpe.org

and includes information on paralegal programs throughout the country, as well as membership, educational resources, association links, and news for paralegal educators. It contains articles from their journal. The page provides information on how to choose a paralegal program as well as a searchable membership directory with e-mail links to program directors at member colleges and universities.

The Association of Legal Administrators (ALA) has its Web site at

http://www.alanet.org

The group strives to improve the competence and professionalism of legal administrators. Items on the site that are available to members include:

1. links to educational conferences.
2. career information.
3. online discussion group.
4. continuing education.
5. news of the industry.

Many law office employees also become notary publics. The Web site for the National Notary Association is located at

http://www.nationalnotary.org

LIBRARY OF CONGRESS

The Library of Congress maintains a Web page with a catalog of all available publications. Every book that has been published and has an ISBN number may be found. If you were to conduct a search by author using this text's author's name, you would find a list of all books written by me that have been published. Searches may be undertaken by title, keywords, or author. The site for the Library of Congress may be found at

http://www.loc.gov/index.html

A link is provided therein for the Law Library of Congress.

SEARCHES FOR LEGAL SOURCES

One of the more comprehensive Web pages for finding information about different areas of law is available at

http://www.findlaw.com

Links are provided for legal professionals and law students. Many different areas of law are also listed, as well as current legal topics and cases, and state and federal case law. If you are looking for a site on a legal subject and do not know the Web site address, it is often easier to find the site on Findlaw than to do a search on your own. It is especially valuable if you are not sure exactly what topic under which to conduct your keyword search.

In addition to providing a large collection of links to law-related sites, this site provides links to attorneys throughout the country as well as online legal advice:

http://www.legal-pad.com

Customized legal documents are provided at

http://www.legaldocs.com

Some of these documents are free and some are available for a fee. The user may prepare customized documents online from given templates. Documents are available in the areas of wills, trusts, sales, leases, partnerships, employment, business, and real estate. Living wills are available free of charge and may be prepared by completing a questionnaire that is provided on the Web page. Remember to use your own state's documents on the Web page and to review your state's laws to ascertain whether that document is valid in that particular state.

FEDERAL AND STATE GOVERNMENT SOURCES ■

Contacting government agencies by telephone or regular mail is often difficult and time consuming. Spending the necessary time to reach the correct department or person may be an arduous task. Most government agencies and departments have Web sites, where accurate and timely information is provided. The federal courts, codes, and many cases are also available online. Government agencies on the state and federal level have Web sites. Federal agencies and departments are listed alphabetically by name, with a brief description provided for each as well as the Web site address.

Aviation

Two government agencies are primarily responsible for information about airline accidents and incident reports. The National Transportation Safety Board (NTSB), located at

http://www.ntsb.gov

(click on Aviation), provides information helpful for aviation litigation, specifically information about airline crashes and incidents related to certain aircraft. A picture of their Web page appears as Exhibit 5–15. Much of the information found on this page is available because of the Freedom of Information Act (FOIA). However, if requesting information via an FOIA form using regular mail, several weeks may pass before the information arrives. A link is also provided

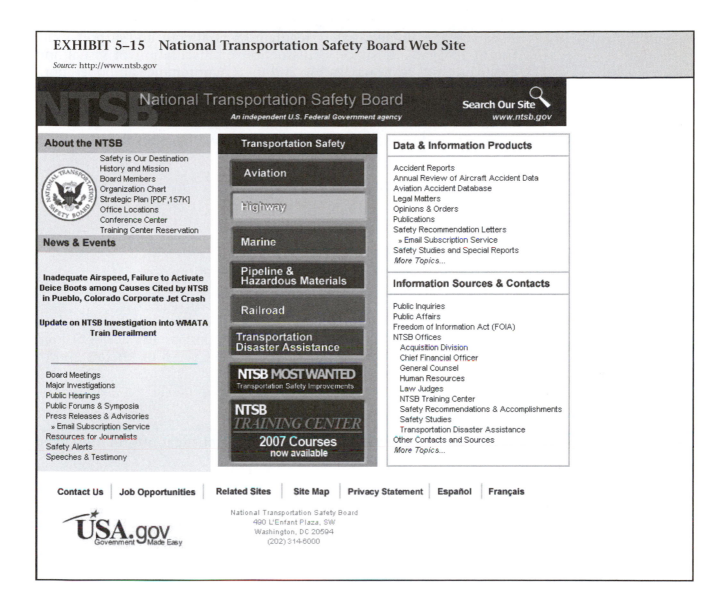

EXHIBIT 5–15   National Transportation Safety Board Web Site

Source: http://www.ntsb.gov

for the Federal Aviation Administration (FAA), whose Web page may be found at

http://www.faa.gov

The FAA is responsible for the safety of civil aviation. As a component of the Department of Transportation, its functions include:

1. regulating civil aviation to promote safety.
2. encouraging the development of air commerce and civil aeronautics.
3. developing and operating air traffic control and navigation systems for both civil and military aircraft.
4. developing and executing programs to control aircraft noise and other environmental effects of civil aviation.
5. regulating commercial space transportation.

Its activities include safety regulations of aircraft and airports, safe use of navigable airspace, construction or installation of visual and electronic aids to air navigation and their maintenance and operation, promotion of aviation safety abroad, regulation of commercial space transportation, and research and development of systems for a safe method of air navigation and air traffic control.

The following additional information is available on the FAA's Web site (see Exhibit 5–16):

1. agency policies
2. regulations
3. air traffic and safety
4. regional offices and site maps
5. commercial space transportation regulations
6. civil aviation security

Both the NTSB's and the FAA's Web sites are particularly helpful for those offices engaged in aviation litigation, particularly accident/incident reports and incidents involving certain types of aircraft and/or certain airlines.

Census Bureau

The United States Census Bureau gathers statistical information from the census. Their Web site, located at

http://www.census.gov

includes census data, financial data for government, economic and population studies, and links to other similar sites.

Central Intelligence Agency

The Director of the CIA heads the agencies that comprise the intelligence community of the United States. They conduct investigations, surveillance, research, and other activities. Their Web site, located at

http://www.cia.gov

describes the function of the agency and provides links to readings about the intelligence community.

Commerce/Patent and Trademark Office

Patent attorneys and paralegals will find this site particularly valuable for obtaining information about trademarks and patents. Forms are provided to register and maintain trademarks and patents. There are links to related sites. This site may be found at

http://www.uspto.gov

and a picture of it appears as Exhibit 5–17.

EXHIBIT 5–16   Federal Aviation Administration Web Site

Source: http://www.faa.gov

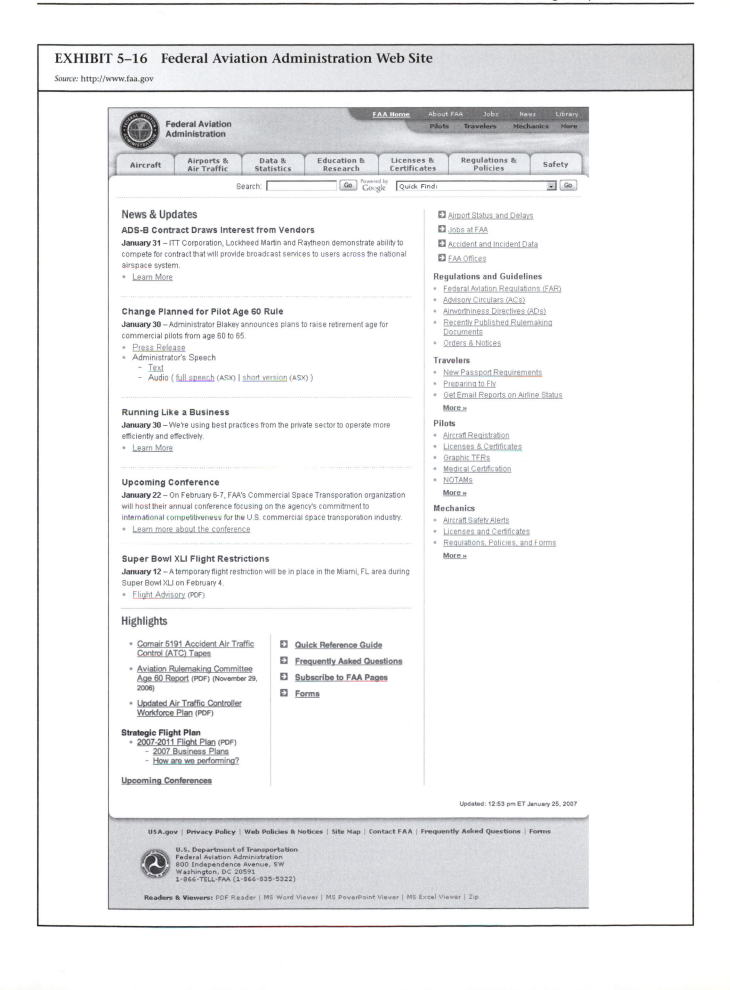

EXHIBIT 5–17   Commerce/Patent and Trademark Office

Source: http://www.uspto.gov

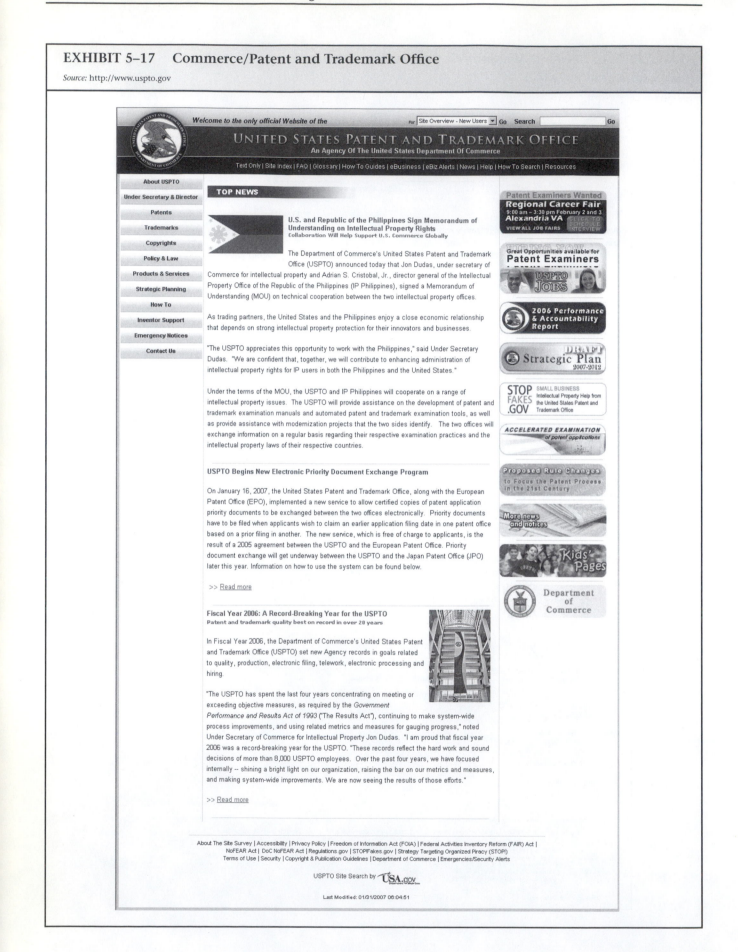

Federal Bureau of Investigation (FBI)

The site for the FBI may be useful for those individuals who work in law offices that specialize in criminal law. Their Web site is located at

http://www.fbi.gov

It includes information about the history of the FBI, programs available, speeches, press releases, chief investigations, the Most Wanted List, the latest e-mail scams, and other related information.

Department of Homeland Security

This department was created after the 9-11 attacks on the United States by terrorists. Its areas of responsibility include security related to emergencies, disasters, travel and transportation, immigration, our borders, threats, and protection. It also includes a section on research and technology. The Web site for this department is located at

http://www.uscis.gov

House of Representatives Library

An extensive law library, particularly valuable for federal sources, is available at the House of Representatives site at

http://www.house.gov

The site also contains text of pending legislation as well as congressional testimony.

Immigration and Naturalization Service (INS)

This organization was formerly an agency of the Department of Justice and is responsible for the admission, naturalization, stopping of illegal entry, and deportation of foreign nationals. However, in 2003 the service and benefit functions of the INS moved into the Department of Homeland Security (DHS) as the United States Citizenship and Immigration Services (USCIS). This organization is responsible for the administration of immigration and naturalization settlement functions and establishing immigration services policies. Their adjudication functions include:

1. immigrant visa petitions.
2. naturalization petitions.
3. asylum and refugee applications.
4. all other adjudications performed by the INS.

Over 15,000 individuals in approximately 250 offices around the world make up the USCIS. Their Appeals Board hears appeals to deportation orders. The Web site is located at

http://www.uscis.gov

Immigration laws change rapidly. Anyone employed in the area of immigration law should consult the INS Web site to obtain the latest rules and regulations. The Web site also contains forms that would be used in this type of specialty practice. It can be found as a link on the above Web site entitled "Immigration."

Various private companies also have Web sites that include downloadable forms for use with the immigration process.

Internal Revenue Service (IRS)

A considerable amount of information about federal taxes is provided at the site for the IRS at

http://www.irs.ustreas.gov

Tax forms may be downloaded from the site. Publications on IRS regulations are also available for downloading.

Department of Justice

The Department of Justice (DOJ) manages the legal business of the United States. All federal law enforcement agencies are within the DOJ. It represents the United States in civil and criminal cases, runs the federal prison system, and has departments responsible for antitrust laws, civil rights laws, the Federal Bureau of Investigation (FBI), the Drug Enforcement Administration (DEA), and a number of other agencies. It is headed by the Attorney General of the United States. The Web site is located at

http://www.usdoj.gov

and includes information about the various agencies within the department, recent case decisions involving the Justice Department, and other information related to the United States legal community. A picture of their Web site appears as Exhibit 5–18.

Department of Labor

The Department of Labor regulates working conditions, manpower development, and labor-management relations. Its Web site contains information on wages, hours of employment, workplace issues, unemployment, pension issues, and running small businesses. It includes federal labor regulations and is located at

http://www.dol.gov

Government Printing Office

Documents available from this office may be obtained from its Web site at

http://www.access.gpo.gov

Information is available on the Web site about the intelligence community, Congress, Office of the Special Counsel, General Accounting

EXHIBIT 5–18

Source: http:.//www.usdoj.gov

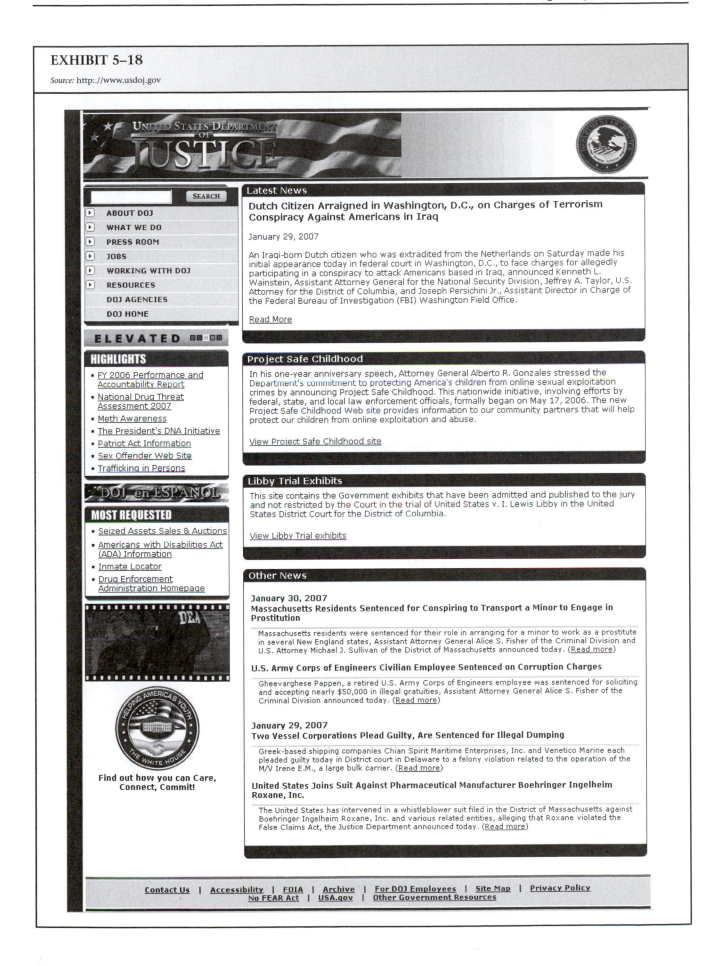

Office, Department of the Interior, Executive Office of the President, and various other departments and agencies.

Securities and Exchange Commission (SEC)

The SEC is responsible for administering the federal and state laws that regulate the sale of securities. The site includes the Securities Act of 1933, which requires the registration of securities to be sold to the public and the disclosure of complete information to possible buyers; the Securities and Exchange Act of 1934, which regulates both stock exchanges and sales of stock over the counter; and a number of other laws related to the purchase and sale of securities the SEC has the responsibility of enforcing. Its Web site is particularly useful for those law offices specializing in corporate law. It is located at

http://www.sec.gov

The Web site provides a method for filing online, information on other corporate filings, a database to search for information on filings, information for small businesses, and current rules and regulations.

Social Security Administration

This Web site provides the opportunity to access your own personal earnings and future benefits estimates. Information is provided about Social Security benefits and Medicare. Explanations are provided for the system's regulations. The site is located at

http://www.ssa.gov

State Department

The Secretary of State is appointed by the President and is the chief foreign affairs adviser for the United States. He oversees the State Department, which is the senior executive department of the United States Government. Some of the activities of the department include:

1. advice on foreign policy.
2. negotiations in foreign affairs.
3. granting and issuing of passports.
4. negotiation, interpretation, and termination of treaties.
5. assuring protection of United States citizens, property and interests in foreign countries.
6. supervising immigration laws abroad.
7. providing information about travel conditions in foreign countries.

Their Web site is located at

http://www.state.gov

A picture of the site appears as Exhibit 5–19.

EXHIBIT 5–19   State Department Web Site

Source: http://www.state.gov

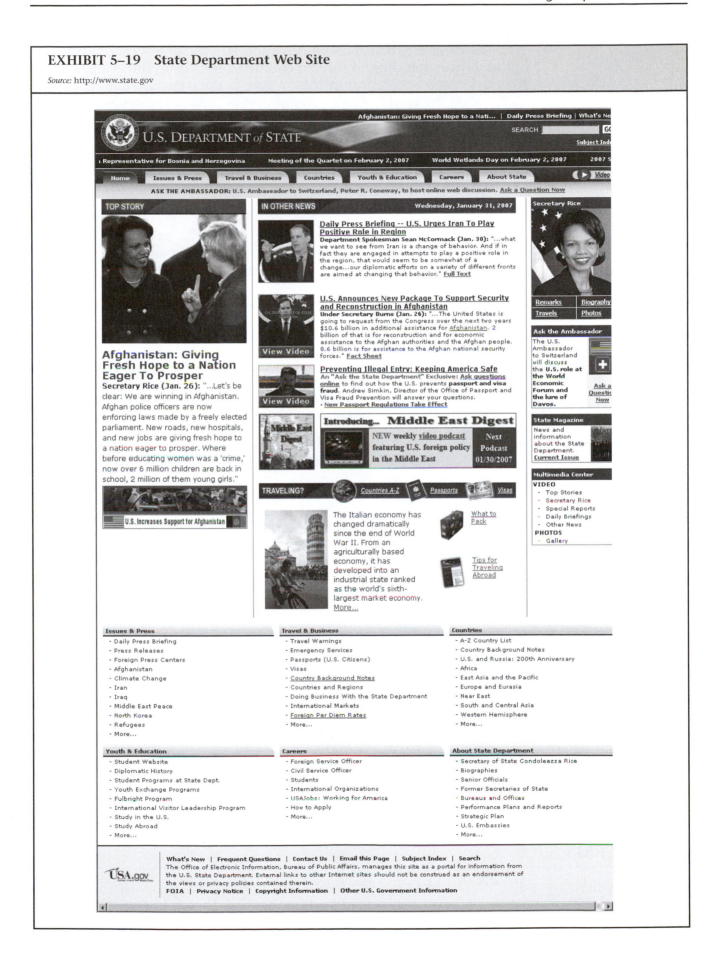

The department also maintains a special page of travel advisories for individuals traveling to foreign countries, including those areas of political unrest or recent uprisings. A link to the page is available at

http://www.travel.state.gov

Consulting this page is particularly useful when traveling to a foreign country. It should always be reviewed before making travel reservations abroad.

Department of Transportation

This federal department governs all transportation agencies of the government, including the FAA. At its Web site, located at

http://www.dot.gov

links are available to the other divisions within the department, including the following:

1. Federal Aviation Agency (FAA)
2. Federal Railroad Administration
3. Federal Transit Administration
4. Maritime Administration
5. National Highway Traffic Safety Administration
6. United States Coast Guard

If your law office has a case that involves safety considerations on a federal highway or waterway, use this site to find information.

The White House

In order to find this site on the Web, use the following address:

http://www.whitehouse.gov

Many of the commercial Internet service providers enable you to reach this site by keying **white house** into the search box. Information available at this site includes data on the President and Vice President, the history of the White House and tour information, a library of press releases, radio addresses, and other related Web pages, summaries of today's press releases, the Constitution, and a considerable amount of material on current events. Cabinet offices and Executive Branch agencies are listed in links on the White House page.

■ KEY TERMS

Caption	Legal cap
Court forms	Pleading

■ SELF TEST

1. Prepare an appropriate caption for a pleading that may be used in your state. File the caption in your notebook after it has been graded.

2. Under what circumstances are court forms used instead of pleadings?

3. List five government offices in your state with Web pages. What are their functions? What are their Web page addresses?

4. Find the Web page for the United States State Department. Describe the duties and responsibilities of the Secretary of State.

■ NOTEBOOK PROJECTS

1. Compile a list of all Web pages that would be useful to you if you were working as a legal professional in your state. Put this into your notebook under "Web Pages."

2. Contact a local law office to obtain copies of forms for your state and include them in your notebook.

3. Prepare a form used in your state and indicate where it was obtained.

For additional resources, visit our Web site at **www.westlegalstudies.com**

LEGAL RESEARCH AND THE COURTS

CHAPTER OUTCOMES

As a result of studying this chapter, the student will learn:

1. the basic principles of legal research.
2. how to distinguish between primary and secondary authority.
3. how to read and write a case citation.
4. how to find cases and statutes for a research project.
5. how to familiar with the structure of the federal and state court systems.

WHAT IS LAW?

The laws of our country are based on the English common law system of **stare decisis**, which means that earlier case decisions set precedents for later cases that the court decides. This type of law is known as case law.

Our laws are based on statutes and case law. The **statutes** are established by the state and federal legislatures and are arranged into **codes** by subject. The state and federal constitutions are also included in the statutory law but take precedence over both statutes and case law.

Each code represents a different type of law, such as civil law, civil procedure, criminal, and probate. As these laws are changed, usually on a yearly basis, the publisher issues **pocket parts** that are inserted in the back of the code books. These pocket parts indicate all changes to the laws that are found in that particular volume since the last volume was printed. Therefore, if you are doing research into a particular code section, it is imperative that you first look in the pocket part to determine whether the law has been changed or repealed. The pocket part will also indicate whether another section of the code deals with this particular law. Some publishers issue supplements in the form of pamphlets or paperback volumes to accompany the original book.

Annotated codes include not only the actual law but also references to cases and other items that referred to that particular law. Therefore, if you are working on a project that deals with a certain law, it is

stare decisis earlier case decisions set precedents for later cases that the court decides

statutes laws established by the state and federal legislatures

codes a compilation of statutes by subject

pocket parts updates to volumes of the annotated codes that are filed in a pocket at the back of each book

advantageous to use the annotated codes so that related reference materials may also be found.

The primary law of the land is the United States Constitution. No state may make a law that conflicts with this document. The order in which laws are considered follows:

1. Constitution
2. Statutes
3. Case law

However, when you are dealing with a case in state court, your own state's laws, including statutes and cases, will be considered by the court in reaching a decision.

Samples of statutes and cases are included as Exhibits 6–1 and 6–2.

PRIMARY AUTHORITY

Primary authority consists of the law itself, and is considered in the following order:

1. Constitution
2. Statutes
3. Cases

However, it is important to note that only your own state's laws are considered to be primary authority in your state. The laws of another state may be used to try to convince the court to rule in your favor, but the court is not obligated to consider these other laws. Therefore, one may conclude that primary authority must be considered in the court's decision while secondary authority is used to convince a court to rule in your favor.

STATUTES AND CONSTITUTIONS

Laws that have been enacted by legislatures of the state or federal government are known as *statutes*. Included in this broad category are the state and federal constitutions, state and federal statutes, local ordinances, and administrative regulations.

The United States Constitution defines the rights of the individual in our society, establishes the power of the federal and state governments, and identifies the association between federal and state governments. A state constitution sets out the rights of the state's residents as well as the powers and limitations placed on the state government.

State and federal statutes are established by the legislatures and define the rights and responsibilities of individuals. *Ordinances* are those local laws that have been passed by particular localities. For instance, a city might have an ordinance that requires a curfew for minors. That same minor may not be covered by a curfew if she were in a different city. However, if a state statute prohibits driving over a certain speed, all drivers in that state are covered by the statute.

primary authority
binding authority that includes statutes, court decisions, administrative regulations, and other similar sources of law rather than interpretive or indirect information from secondary sources

EXHIBIT 6–1   United States Code—Section 1701z

Section 1701z. New technologies in the development of housing for lower income families

(a) Institution of program; assistance to mobile home buyers

In order to encourage the use of new housing technologies in providing decent, safe, and sanitary housing for lower income families; to encourage large-scale experimentation in the use of such technologies; to provide a basis for comparison of such technologies with existing housing technologies in providing such housing; and to evaluate the effect of local housing codes and zoning regulations on the large-scale use of new housing technologies in the provision of such housing, the Secretary of Housing and Urban Development (hereinafter referred to as the "Secretary") shall institute a program under which qualified organizations, public and private, will submit plans for the development of housing for lower income families, using new and advanced technologies, on Federal land which has been made available by the Secretary for the purposes of this section, or on other land where (1) local building regulations permit the construction of experimental housing, or (2) State or local law permits variances from building regulations in the construction of experimental housing for the purpose of testing and developing new building technologies.

(b) Approval of plans utilizing new housing technologies; considerations

The Secretary shall approve not more than five plans utilizing new housing technologies which are submitted to him pursuant to the program referred to in subsection (a) of this section and which he determines are most promising in furtherance of the purposes of this section. In making such determination the Secretary shall consider -

  (1) the potential of the technology employed for producing housing for lower income families on a large scale at a moderate cost;
  (2) the extent to which the plan envisages environmental quality;
  (3) the possibility of mass production of the technology; and
  (4) the financial soundness of the organization submitting the plan, and the ability of such organization, alone or in combination with other organizations, to produce at least one thousand dwelling units a year utilizing the technology proposed.

(c) Number of dwelling units to be constructed for each type of technology; evaluation of projects

In approving projects for mortgage insurance under section 1715x(a)(2) of this title, the Secretary shall seek to achieve the construction of at least one thousand dwelling units a year over a five-year period for each of the various types of technologies proposed in approved plans under subsection (b) of this section. The Secretary shall evaluate each project with respect to which assistance is extended pursuant to this section with a view to determining (1) the detailed cost breakdown per dwelling unit, (2) the environmental quality achieved in each unit, and (3) the effect which local housing codes and zoning regulations have, or would have if applicable, on the cost per dwelling unit.

(d) Transfer of surplus property

Notwithstanding the provisions of the Federal Property and Administrative Services Act of 1949, any land which is excess property within the meaning of such Act and which is determined by the Secretary to be suitable in furtherance of the purposes of this section may be transferred to the Secretary upon his request.

(e) Report of findings; legislative recommendations

The Secretary shall, at the earliest practicable date, report his findings with respect to projects assisted pursuant to this section (including evaluations of each such project in accordance with subsection (c) of this section), together with such recommendations for additional legislation as he determines to be necessary or desirable to expand the available supply of decent, safe, and sanitary housing for lower income families through the use of technologies the efficacy of which has been demonstrated under this section.

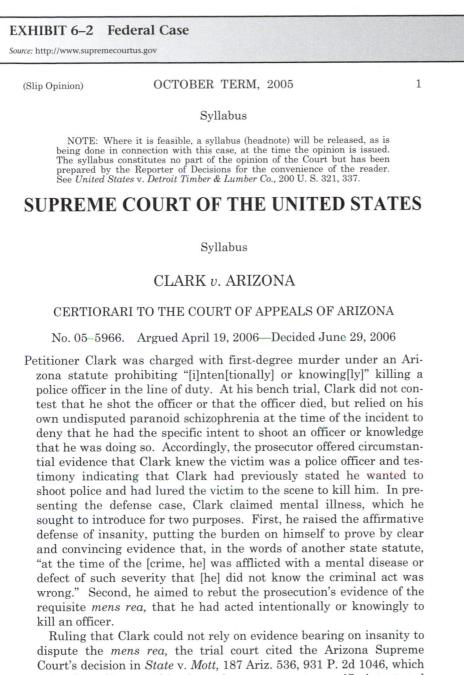

EXHIBIT 6–2 Federal Case

Source: http://www.supremecourtus.gov

(Slip Opinion) OCTOBER TERM, 2005 1

Syllabus

NOTE: Where it is feasible, a syllabus (headnote) will be released, as is being done in connection with this case, at the time the opinion is issued. The syllabus constitutes no part of the opinion of the Court but has been prepared by the Reporter of Decisions for the convenience of the reader. See *United States* v. *Detroit Timber & Lumber Co.,* 200 U. S. 321, 337.

SUPREME COURT OF THE UNITED STATES

Syllabus

CLARK *v.* ARIZONA

CERTIORARI TO THE COURT OF APPEALS OF ARIZONA

No. 05–5966. Argued April 19, 2006—Decided June 29, 2006

Petitioner Clark was charged with first-degree murder under an Arizona statute prohibiting "[i]nten[tionally] or knowing[ly]" killing a police officer in the line of duty. At his bench trial, Clark did not contest that he shot the officer or that the officer died, but relied on his own undisputed paranoid schizophrenia at the time of the incident to deny that he had the specific intent to shoot an officer or knowledge that he was doing so. Accordingly, the prosecutor offered circumstantial evidence that Clark knew the victim was a police officer and testimony indicating that Clark had previously stated he wanted to shoot police and had lured the victim to the scene to kill him. In presenting the defense case, Clark claimed mental illness, which he sought to introduce for two purposes. First, he raised the affirmative defense of insanity, putting the burden on himself to prove by clear and convincing evidence that, in the words of another state statute, "at the time of the [crime, he] was afflicted with a mental disease or defect of such severity that [he] did not know the criminal act was wrong." Second, he aimed to rebut the prosecution's evidence of the requisite *mens rea,* that he had acted intentionally or knowingly to kill an officer.

Ruling that Clark could not rely on evidence bearing on insanity to dispute the *mens rea,* the trial court cited the Arizona Supreme Court's decision in *State* v. *Mott,* 187 Ariz. 536, 931 P. 2d 1046, which refused to allow psychiatric testimony to negate specific intent and held that Arizona does not allow evidence of a mental disorder short of insanity to negate the *mens rea* element of a crime. As to his insanity, then, Clark presented lay testimony describing his increasingly bizarre behavior over the year before the shooting. Other lay and expert testimony indicated, among other things, that Clark thought that "aliens" (some impersonating government agents) were

continued

Exhibit 6–2 *continued*

2   CLARK *v.* ARIZONA

Syllabus

trying to kill him and that bullets were the only way to stop them. A psychiatrist testified that Clark was suffering from paranoid schizophrenia with delusions about "aliens" when he killed the officer, and concluded that Clark was incapable of luring the officer or understanding right from wrong and was thus insane at the time of the killing. In rebuttal, the State's psychiatrist gave his opinion that Clark's paranoid schizophrenia did not keep him from appreciating the wrongfulness of his conduct before and after the shooting. The judge then issued a first-degree murder verdict, finding that in light of that the facts of the crime, the expert evaluations, Clark's actions and behavior both before and after the shooting, and the observations of those who knew him, Clark had not established that his schizophrenia distorted his perception of reality so severely that he did not know his actions were wrong.

Clark moved to vacate the judgment and life sentence, arguing, among other things, that Arizona's insanity test and its *Mott* rule each violate due process. He claimed that the Arizona Legislature had impermissibly narrowed its insanity standard in 1993 when it eliminated the first of the two parts of the traditional *M'Naghten* insanity test. The trial court denied the motion. Affirming, the Arizona Court of Appeals held, among other things, that the State's insanity scheme was consistent with due process. The court read *Mott* as barring the trial court's consideration of evidence of Clark's mental illness and capacity directly on the element of *mens rea.*

Held:

1. Due process does not prohibit Arizona's use of an insanity test stated solely in terms of the capacity to tell whether an act charged as a crime was right or wrong. Pp. 6–15.

(a) The first part of the landmark English rule in *M'Naghten's Case* asks about cognitive capacity: whether a mental defect leaves a defendant unable to understand what he was doing. The second part presents an ostensibly alternative basis for recognizing a defense of insanity understood as a lack of moral capacity: whether a mental disease or defect leaves a defendant unable to understand that his action was wrong. Although the Arizona Legislature at first adopted the full *M'Naghten* statement, it later dropped the cognitive incapacity part. Under current Arizona law, a defendant will not be adjudged insane unless he demonstrates that at the time of the crime, he was afflicted with a mental disease or defect of such severity that he did not know the criminal act was wrong. Pp. 6–7.

(b) Clark insists that the side-by-side *M'Naghten* test represents the minimum that a government must provide, and he argues that eliminating the first part " 'offends [a] principle of justice so rooted in the traditions and conscience of our people as to be ranked as funda-

continued

Exhibit 6–2   *continued*

Cite as: 548 U. S. ____ (2006)   3

Syllabus

mental,' " *Patterson* v. *New York,* 432 U. S. 197, 202. The claim entails no light burden, and Clark does not carry it. History shows no deference to *M'Naghten* that could elevate its formula to the level of fundamental principle, so as to limit the traditional recognition of a State's capacity to define crimes and defenses. See, *e.g., Patterson, supra,* at 210. Even a cursory examination of the traditional Anglo-American approaches to insanity reveals significant differences among them, with four traditional strains variously combined to yield a diversity of American standards. Although 17 States and the Federal Government have adopted recognizable versions of the *M'Naghten* test with both its components, other States have adopted a variety of standards based on all or part of one or more of four variants. The alternatives are multiplied further by variations in the prescribed insanity verdict. This varied background makes clear that no particular formulation has evolved into a baseline for due process, and that the insanity rule, like the conceptualization of criminal offenses, is substantially open to state choice. Pp. 7–12.

(c) Nor does Arizona's abbreviation of the *M'Naghten* statement raise a proper claim that some constitutional minimum has been shortchanged. Although Arizona's former statement of the full *M'Naghten* rule was constitutionally adequate, the abbreviated rule is no less so, for cognitive incapacity is relevant under that statement, just as it was under the more extended formulation, and evidence going to cognitive incapacity has the same significance under the short form as it had under the long. Though Clark is correct that applying the moral incapacity test (telling right from wrong) does not necessarily require evaluation of a defendant's cognitive capacity to appreciate the nature and quality of the acts charged against him, his argument fails to recognize that cognitive incapacity is itself enough to demonstrate moral incapacity, so that evidence bearing on whether the defendant knew the nature and quality of his actions is both relevant and admissible. In practical terms, if a defendant did not know what he was doing when he acted, he could not have known that he was performing the wrongful act charged as a crime. The Arizona appeals court acknowledged as much in this case. Clark adopted this very analysis in the trial court, which apparently agreed when it admitted his cognitive incapacity evidence for consideration under the State's moral incapacity formulation. Clark can point to no evidence bearing on insanity that was excluded. Pp. 12–15.

2. The Arizona Supreme Court's *Mott* rule does not violate due process. Pp. 15–38.

(a) *Mott* held that testimony of a professional psychologist or psychiatrist about a defendant's mental incapacity owing to mental disease or defect was admissible, and could be considered, only for its

continued

Exhibit 6–2 *continued*

4   CLARK *v.* ARIZONA

Syllabus

bearing on an insanity defense, but could not be considered on the element of *mens rea*. Of the three categories of evidence that potentially bear on *mens rea*—(1) everyday "observation evidence" either by lay or expert witnesses of what Clark did or said, which may support the professional diagnoses of disease and in any event is the kind of evidence that can be relevant to show what was on Clark's mind when he fired his gun; (2) "mental-disease evidence," typically from professional psychologists or psychiatrists based on factual reports, professional observations, and tests about Clark's mental disease, with features described by the witness; and (3) "capacity evidence," typically by the same experts, about Clark's capacity for cognition and moral judgment (and ultimately also his capacity to form *mens rea*)—*Mott* imposed no restriction on considering evidence of the first sort, but applies to the latter two. Although the trial court seems to have applied the *Mott* restriction to all three categories of evidence Clark offered for the purpose of showing what he called his inability to form the required *mens rea*, his objection to *Mott*'s application does not turn on the distinction between lay and expert witnesses or the kinds of testimony they were competent to present. Rather, the issue here is Clark's claim that the *Mott* rule violates due process. Pp. 15–25.

(b) Clark's *Mott* challenge turns on the application of the presumption of innocence in criminal cases, the presumption of sanity, and the principle that a criminal defendant is entitled to present relevant and favorable evidence on an element of the offense charged against him. Pp. 25–30.

(i) The presumption of innocence is that a defendant is innocent unless and until the government proves beyond a reasonable doubt each element of the offense changed, including the mental element or *mens rea*. The modern tendency is to describe the *mens rea* required to prove particular offenses in specific terms, as shown in the Arizona statute requiring the State to prove that in acting to kill the victim, Clark intended to kill a law enforcement officer on duty or knew that the victim was such an officer on duty. As applied to *mens rea* (and every other element), the force of the presumption of innocence is measured by the force of the showing needed to overcome it, which is proof beyond a reasonable doubt that a defendant's state of mind was in fact what the charge states. See *In re Winship*, 397 U. S. 358, 361–363. Pp. 25–26.

(ii) The presumption of sanity dispenses with a requirement that the government include as an element of every criminal charge an allegation that the defendant had the capacity to form the *mens rea* necessary for conviction and criminal responsibility. Unlike the presumption of innocence, the presumption of sanity's force varies

continued

Exhibit 6–2   *continued*

Cite as: 548 U. S. ____ (2006)   5

Syllabus

across the many state and federal jurisdictions, and prior law has recognized considerable leeway on the part of the legislative branch in defining the presumption's strength through the kind of evidence and degree of persuasiveness necessary to overcome it, see *Fisher* v. *United States,* 328 U. S. 463, 466–476. There are two points where the sanity or capacity presumption may be placed in issue. First, a State may allow a defendant to introduce (and a factfinder to consider) evidence of mental disease or incapacity for the bearing it can have on the government's burden to show *mens rea.* Second, the sanity presumption's force may be tested in the consideration of an insanity defense raised by a defendant. Insanity rules like *M'Naghten* and the variants noted above are attempts to define or indicate the kinds of mental differences that overcome the presumption of sanity or capacity and therefore excuse a defendant from customary criminal responsibility, see, *e.g., Jones* v. *United States,* 463 U. S. 354, 373, n. 4, even if the prosecution has otherwise overcome the presumption of innocence by convincing the factfinder of all the elements charged beyond a reasonable doubt. The burden a defendant raising the insanity issue must carry defines the strength of the sanity presumption. A State may, for example, place the burden of persuasion on a defendant to prove insanity as the applicable law defines it, whether by a preponderance of the evidence or to some more convincing degree. See, *e.g., Leland* v. *Oregon,* 343 U. S. 790, 798. Pp. 26–29.

(iii) A defendant has a due process right to present evidence favorable to himself on an element that must be proven to convict him. Evidence tending to show that a defendant suffers from mental disease and lacks capacity to form *mens rea* is relevant to rebut evidence that he did in fact form the required *mens rea* at the time in question. Thus, Clark claims a right to require the factfinder in this case to consider testimony about his mental illness and his incapacity directly, when weighing the persuasiveness of other evidence tending to show *mens rea,* which the prosecution has the burden to prove. However, the right to introduce relevant evidence can be curtailed if there is a good reason for doing so. For example, trial judges may "exclude evidence if its probative value is outweighed by certain other factors such as unfair prejudice, confusion of the issues, or potential to mislead the jury." *Holmes* v. *South Carolina,* 547 U. S. ___, ___. And if evidence may be kept out entirely, its consideration may be subject to limitation, which Arizona claims the power to impose here. Under state law, mental-disease and capacity evidence may be considered only for its bearing on the insanity defense, and it will avail a defendant only if it is persuasive enough to satisfy the defendant's burden as defined by the terms of that defense. Such evidence is thus being channeled or restricted to one issue; it is not being excluded en-

continued

Exhibit 6–2 *continued*

6   CLARK *v.* ARIZONA

Syllabus

tirely, and the question is whether reasons for requiring it to be channeled and restricted satisfy due process's fundamental fairness standard. Pp. 29–30.

(c) The reasons supporting the Arizona rule satisfy due process. Pp. 30–38.

(i) The first such reason is Arizona's authority to define its presumption of sanity (or capacity or responsibility) by choosing an insanity definition and placing the burden of persuasion on criminal defendants claiming incapacity as an excuse. Consistent with due process, a State can require defendants to bear that burden, see *Leland, supra,* at 797–799, and Clark does not object to Arizona's decision to require persuasion to a clear and convincing degree before the presumption of sanity and normal responsibility is overcome. If a State is to have this authority in practice as well as in theory, it must be able to deny a defendant the opportunity to displace the sanity presumption more easily when addressing a different issue during the criminal trial. Yet just such an opportunity would be available if expert testimony of mental disease and incapacity could be considered for whatever a factfinder might think it was worth on the *mens rea* issue. The sanity presumption would then be only as strong as the evidence a factfinder would accept as enough to raise a reasonable doubt about *mens rea*; once reasonable doubt was found, acquittal would be required, and the standards established for the insanity defense would go by the boards. What counts for due process is simply that a State wishing to avoid a second avenue for exploring capacity, less stringent for a defendant, has a good reason for confining the consideration of mental disease and incapacity evidence to the insanity defense. Pp. 30–32.

(ii) Arizona's rule also serves to avoid confusion and misunderstanding on the part of jurors. The controversial character of some categories of mental disease, the potential of mental-disease evidence to mislead, and the danger of according greater certainty to capacity evidence than experts claim for it give rise to risks that may reasonably be hedged by channeling the consideration of such evidence to the insanity issue on which, in States like Arizona, a defendant has the burden of persuasion. First, the diagnosis may mask vigorous debate within the psychiatric profession about the very contours of the mental disease itself. See, *e.g., Jones, supra,* at 364–365, n. 13. Though mental-disease evidence is certainly not condemned wholesale, the consequence of this professional ferment is a general caution in treating psychological classifications as predicates for excusing otherwise criminal conduct. Next, there is the potential of mental-disease evidence to mislead jurors (when they are the factfinders) through the power of this kind of evidence to suggest that a defendant suffer-

continued

Exhibit 6–2   *continued*

Cite as: 548 U. S. ____ (2006)   7

Syllabus

ing from a recognized mental disease lacks cognitive, moral, volitional, or other capacity, when that may not be a sound conclusion at all. Even when a category of mental disease is broadly accepted and the assignment of a defendant's behavior to that category is uncontroversial, the classification may suggest something very significant about a defendant's capacity, when in fact the classification tells little or nothing about the defendant's ability to form *mens rea* or to exercise the cognitive, moral, or volitional capacities that define legal sanity. The limits of the utility of a professional disease diagnosis are evident in the dispute between the two testifying experts in this case; they agree that Clark was schizophrenic, but they reach opposite conclusions on whether his mental disease left him bereft of cognitive or moral capacity. Finally, there are particular risks inherent in the opinions of the experts who supplement the mental-disease classifications with opinions on incapacity: on whether the mental disease rendered a particular defendant incapable of the cognition necessary for moral judgment or *mens rea* or otherwise incapable of understanding the wrongfulness of the conduct charged. Unlike observational evidence bearing on *mens rea*, capacity evidence consists of judgment, and judgment is fraught with multiple perils. Although such capacity judgments may be given in the utmost good faith, their potentially tenuous character is indicated by the candor of the defense expert in this very case. He testified that Clark lacked the capacity to appreciate the circumstances realistically and to understand the wrongfulness of what he was doing, but he admitted that no one knew exactly what was on Clark's mind at the time of the shooting. Even when an expert is confident that his understanding of the mind is reliable, judgment addressing the basic categories of capacity requires a leap from the concepts of psychology, which are devised for thinking about treatment, to the concepts of legal sanity, which are devised for thinking about criminal responsibility. Pp. 33–38.

(d) For these reasons, there is also no cause to claim that channeling evidence on mental disease and capacity offends any "'principle of justice so rooted in the traditions and conscience of our people as to be ranked as fundamental,'" *Patterson, supra,* at 202. P. 38.

Affirmed.

SOUTER, J., delivered the opinion of the Court, in which ROBERTS, C. J., and SCALIA, THOMAS, and ALITO, JJ., joined, and in which BREYER, J., joined except as to Parts III–B and III–C and the ultimate disposition. BREYER, J., filed an opinion concurring in part and dissenting in part. KENNEDY, J., filed a dissenting opinion, in which STEVENS and GINSBURG, JJ., joined.

Each administrative agency of the government passes its own regulations to govern the running of that particular agency. Its regulations are more specific than the general statutes because they govern the specific rules for each agency. These laws are known as administrative law and/or administrative regulations.

SAMPLE OF ADMINISTRATIVE AGENCY REGULATIONS

The administrative regulations of many of the federal government agencies are available on the Internet. Exhibit 6–3 shows a page from the Department of Homeland Security's regulations. Note that links are available on this Web page for each of the department's regulations.

CASE LAW (COMMON LAW)

If no statute has been enacted to cover specifically a given area, the courts will use cases to interpret the law, creating **common law.** Case law includes laws created by the courts where no statutes have been enacted as well as the law that is the result of the court's interpretation of the statute as it relates to a particular case. Court decisions that interpret the law may be used in later cases to convince a court to rule in your favor. These decisions establish precedents for future cases.

Only appellate and supreme court cases establish precedents and make new law. Trial court case decisions do not change the law in the

---

EXHIBIT 6–3　Department of Homeland Security Regulation Page

Source: www.access.gpo.gov

Title 6—Homeland Security

Chapter I—Department of Homeland Security, Office of The Secretary

Part 7—Classified National Security Information

7.1	Purpose.
7.2	Scope.
7.3	Definitions.
7.10	Authority of the Chief Security Officer, Office of Security.
7.11	Components' responsibilities.
7.12	Violations of classified information requirements.
7.13	Judicial proceedings.
7.20	Classification and declassification authority.
7.21	Classification of information, limitations.
7.22	Classification pending review.
7.23	Emergency release of classified information.
7.24	Duration of classification.
7.25	Identification and markings.
7.26	Derivative classification.
7.27	Declassification and downgrading.
7.28	Automatic declassification.
7.29	Documents of permanent historical value.
7.30	Classification challenges.
7.31	Mandatory review for declassification requests.

---

common law case law that creates a precedent for future cases

state or federal jurisdiction unless and until these cases are appealed and decided on the appellate or supreme court levels. Note that this system of precedent-setting cases is based on the English common law except in the state of Louisiana, which has established its laws based on the Napoleonic Code. When finding cases that establish precedents, it is important to remember that only cases within your own jurisdiction make law in your jurisdiction. For instance, you would not be able to use a Nevada appellate court case to establish precedent in California. An attorney may wish to use this law to convince a court to change the law in California, but the court is not obligated to use the out-of-state law. Similarly, federal cases establish federal law and should be used for precedent setting on the federal level.

The only binding authority established by these cases is that which relates to issues that have been decided on the trial level and appealed and ruled upon at the appellate or supreme court level. The remainder of the case report is considered "dicta" which may be interesting to read and helpful in determining the manner in which a court might rule on this topic in a future case, but has no bearing on the law for this case.

SECONDARY AUTHORITY

Secondary authority may be thought of as all authority that is not primary authority. That is, any of the sources that a court may rely on in interpreting a case that is not the actual law may be considered to be secondary authority. Some examples of secondary authority follow:

1. **Legal encyclopedias**
   One may depend on the use of a legal encyclopedia to obtain a general understanding of a specific legal area. Some examples of legal encyclopedias include *American Jurisprudence* and *Corpus Juris Secundum* (see Exhibit 6–4). Several states have their own encyclopedia series, such as *California Jurisprudence*. Find the legal encyclopedia for your own state and complete the blanks below.

STATE-SPECIFIC INFORMATION FOR THE STATE OF _____:

The state's legal encyclopedia is called _____

_____.

---

2. **Annotations**
   Most codes are published in additional series known as *annotated codes*. The **annotations** are notes and comments on the law that may be valuable for finding additional information on a given subject area. For instance, the *United States Codes* covers all of the federal statutes, while the *United States Code Annotated* includes both the federal statutes and annotations to cases, law review articles and other related statutes. One series of annotations is

secondary authority persuasive authority that is not actual law; includes various writings about law such as legal encyclopedias and law review articles

annotation a note or commentary explaining the meaning of a passage in a book or document

---

EXHIBIT 6–4 Page from a Legal Dictionary

Source: American Jurisprudence, 2nd ed. Reprinted by permission of Thomson/West.

Westlaw.

```
AMJUR NTSAWD SUM                                              Page 1
NTS Am. Jur. 2d Americans with Disabilities Act Summary


                    American Jurisprudence, Second Edition
                         Database updated May 2006

               Americans with Disabilities Act Analysis and Implications
          Kathy E. Hinck, J.D., C. Angela Van Etten, J.D., John F. Wagner, Jr.,J.D.
Copr. (C) West 2006 No Claim to Orig. U.S. Govt. Works
```

Summary

Scope:

This topic discusses the federal civil rights of individuals with disabilities in the areas of employment, state and local governments, transportation, public accommodations, and telecommunications, as protected by the Americans with Disabilities Act of 1990.

Federal Aspects:

The federal statutes discussed herein include the Americans with Disabilities Act of 1990 (ADA), and the powers, remedies, and procedures incorporated by the ADA from Titles II and VII of the Civil Rights Act of 1964.

Treated Elsewhere:

Equal employment under Title VII of the Civil Rights Act of 1964, see 15 Am. Jur. 2d, Civil Rights

Discrimination in places of public accommodation, see 15 Am. Jur. 2d, Civil Rights

Federal targeted jobs tax credit, see 33, 34 Am. Jur. 2d, Federal Taxation

Agency proceedings under Title VII of the Civil Rights Act of 1964, see 45A Am. Jur. 2d, Job Discrimination

Handicap discrimination, see 45A Am. Jur. 2d, Job Discrimination

Court proceedings under Title II of the Civil Rights Act of 1964, see 45B Am. Jur. 2d, Job Discrimination

Employment rights of veterans (aside from affirmative action programs), see 77 Am. Jur. 2d, Veterans and Veterans' Laws

Research References:

2 USCA § § 1201-1224 (Government Employee Rights Act of 1991)

Primary Authority

42 USCA § 1981a (right to damages under Civil Rights Act of 1991)
42 USCA § § 2000a et seq. (Title II of Civil Rights Act of 1964)
42 USCA § § 2000e et seq. (Title VII of Civil Rights Act of 1964)
42 USCA § § 12101-12189; 47 USCA § § 225, 611 (Americans With Disabilities Act of 1990)
28 CFR Part 35 (Department of Justice)
28 CFR Part 36 (Department of Justice)
49 CFR Part 37 (Department of Transportation)
49 CFR Part 38 and Appx (Department of Transportation)
Appx to 36 CFR Part 1191 (Architectural and Transportation Barriers Compliance Board)
29 CFR Part 1630 (Equal Employment Opportunity Commission)
47 CFR § § 64.601-64.608 Subpart F (Federal Communications Commission)

© 2006 Thomson/West. No Claim to Orig. U.S. Govt. Works.

continued

Exhibit 6–4   *continued*

```
AMJUR NTSAWD SUM                                              Page 2
NTS Am. Jur. 2d Americans with Disabilities Act Summary
```

A.L.R. Library

```
    A.L.R. Digest: Civil Rights
    L. Ed. Digest: Civil Rights §  7.5
    Index to Annotations: Carriers;
    Index to Annotations: Deaf Persons;
    Index to Annotations: Disabled Persons;
    Index to Annotations: Discrimination;
    Index to Annotations: Federal Communications Act and Commission;
    Index to Annotations: Speech Disorders;
    Index to Annotations: Telecommunications
```

Treatises and Practice Aids

```
    Americans with Disabilities: Practice and Compliance Manual, Practice and
Compliance Manual
    Federal Procedure, L. Ed. § §  3:1 et seq.
    Federal Procedure, L. Ed. § §  11:340-11:352;
    Federal Procedure, L. Ed. § §  12:35-12:285;
    Federal Procedure, L. Ed. § §  26:135 et seq., 26:290 et seq., 26:306;
    Federal Procedure, L. Ed. § §  26:356, et seq., 26:509 et seq.;
    Federal Procedure, L. Ed. § §  42:1180 et seq.;
    Federal Procedure, L. Ed. § §  47:1 et seq.;
    Federal Procedure, L. Ed. § §  50:1-50:305;
    Federal Procedure, L. Ed. § §  56:1565 et seq.;
    Federal Procedure, L. Ed. § §  59:256-59:424;
    Federal Procedure, L. Ed. § §  62:20-62:44, 62:61-62:77, 62:397;
    Federal Procedure, L. Ed. § §  65:36-65:39;
    Federal Procedure, L. Ed. § §  72:30, 72:31, 72:271-72:284, 72:308-72:327;
    Federal Procedure, L. Ed. § §  77:225 et seq.
    Pattern Discovery: Employment Discrimination
```

Trial Strategy

```
    Discrimination Against the Obese, 36 Am. Jur. Proof of Facts 2d 249
    Employment Discrimination Action Under Federal Civil Rights Acts, 21 Am. Jur.
Trials 1
```

Forms

```
    2 Am. Jur. Legal Forms 2d, Amusements and Exhibitions §  19:319;
    9A Am. Jur. Legal Forms 2d, Hotels, Motels, and Restaurants §  137:76;
    11 Am. Jur. Legal Forms 2d, Leases of Real Property §  161:421
    5A Am. Jur. Pleading and Practice Forms, Civil Rights, Form 151, 152;
    13A Am. Jur. Pleading and Practice Forms, Hotels, Motels and Restaurants, Form 47
    Federal Procedural Forms, L. Ed. § §  10:271-10:315;
    Federal Procedural Forms, L. Ed. § §  45:1-45:215
```

Additional References

```
    Employment Coordinator
    Employment Discrimination Coordinator
```

© 2006 Thomson/West

AMJUR NTSAWD SUM

END OF DOCUMENT

the *American Law Reports,* which contains selected cases with explanations of the issues raised in the case. The annotations will give the reader an analysis of the particular issues and also assist in finding additional cases dealing with this issue.

3. **Restatements of the Law**
   The American Law Institute publishes restatements of different areas of law that discuss the law as well as commentary on each one. The restatements are written by experts in the various areas of the law, such as contracts and torts.

4. **Legal Dictionaries**
   Definitions of legal terms are provided in legal dictionaries. The official dictionary of the courts is *Black's Law Dictionary*. If the definition of a particular term is at issue, this dictionary is used by the court to determine the proper definition. Several other legal dictionaries are useful for the student, including *Oran's Dictionary of Law*, which explains legal terms in language suitable for a lay person's understanding.

5. **Law Reviews**
   Each law school publishes its own law review with articles on timely legal topics. Discussions of legal issues are very comprehensive and may include detailed explanations as well as references to cases and statutes on a given topic. They are generally written by law school professors, practicing attorneys, judges, and law school students.

6. **Treatises**
   Experts in specific legal areas write treatises on their area of expertise. These volumes are valuable tools for a very detailed description of the law in a given area. Statutes and related cases are referenced.

CITATIONS

The proper reference for a particular legal authority and where it is found is known as a **citation.** In general, a citation is comprised of three identifying features. The first is the volume where the material is found, the second is the name of the series, and the third is the page number or section number where the material may be found. After the identifying material, the date of publication will be given in parentheses. *The Bluebook: A Uniform System of Citations* contains the proper method for writing citations to different types of legal publications. The various types of citations will be described below.

1. **Statutes**
   A. **Federal**
      Federal statutes include the code's title number, the abbreviated name of the code, the section number, and the year of the code. For example, 22 U.S.C.A. §. 1234 (1982) refers to Volume 22 of the United States Code Annotated, Section 1234, adopted in 1982.

citation a reference for a particular legal authority and where it is found, such as a case citation

B. **State**

The various states vary in their method of listing citations. One should always cite from the official state statutory code. Some examples follow:

    Colo. Rev. Stat. §. 55-22-3333 (2004)
    Ill. Rev. Stat. ch. 433, para. 99/5 (2001)

2. **Federal administrative regulations**

The citation should include the title number, the abbreviation CFR (for Code of Federal Regulations), the section number, and the year of publication in parentheses. For example, 22 C.F.R. §. 499 (2004) refers to Volume 22 of the Code of Federal Regulations, Section 499, published in 2004.

3. **Case citations**

Most case citations are listed in two different publications, one of which is the official publication and the other of which is the unofficial one. The official citation should always be given first. Included in the case citation is the name of the case, the official citation, the unofficial citation, and the year of the decision. Following is an example of a case citation from the United States Supreme Court:

John Doe v. Superior Court, 233 U.S. 35 (1981), 102 S. Ct. 23 (1981).

Federal appellate court decisions' citations include the case name, circuit court where the decision was rendered, and the date, as follows:

United States v. Lang, 22 F.2d 595 (9th Cir. 1977)

which is a case taken from the Federal Reporter, second series. The Federal District Court decisions are found in the Federal Supplement and are written as follows:

State v. Jones, 222 F.Supp. 55 (S.D. Ohio 1970)

which is a case from the southern district of Ohio in 1970.

State court citations are written based on the names of the reporter series in the particular state. Find the manner in which case citations are written for your own state and write an explanation below.

STATE-SPECIFIC INFORMATION FOR THE STATE OF _____:

Case citations for this state are written as follows:

_____. An

explanation of each part of the citation follows: _____

_____.

A full explanation of the various types of citations and the proper manner to write each of them may be found in *Citation-at-a-Glance, Citations for Use in Legal Memoranda and Documents (rev. ed)*, (Clifton Park, NY: West Legal Studies/Thomson Learning, 1999). Another comprehensive guide to writing citations is *The Bluebook: A Uniform System of Citation.*

FEDERAL COURTS

The federal courts are divided into the following general court systems: the United States Supreme Court, the Circuit Courts of Appeals, and the **U.S. District Courts.**

United States Supreme Court

The **United States Supreme Court** is the highest court in the country. It is located in Washington, D.C., and is in session from the first Monday in October until the end of May. Nine justices sit on the court, one of whom is the Chief Justice and presides over the court. All decisions of the Federal Circuit Courts of Appeal may be appealed to the Supreme Court. It may also hear cases where the highest state court has issued a decision that challenges the validity of a federal law. Generally, the Supreme Court only hears cases that raise significant issues, and declines to hear the majority of cases referred to it. Their Web site is

http://www.supremecourtus.gov

Information included on this Web site includes:

1. general information about the Court.
2. the Court's automated docket case tracking system. It contains information about the status of cases for both the current and the prior term of the court.
3. oral arguments and briefs.
4. court rules.
5. the proper forms to apply for admission to the Supreme Court bar.
6. guides to filing cases before the Supreme Court.
7. Supreme Court decisions.
8. court orders and cases list.
9. visitor services.
10. public information.
11. career opportunities and internships

U.S. District Court trial court on the federal level

United States Supreme Court highest court in the United States

Circuit Courts of Appeal intermediate court that hears appeals from the federal district court

Circuit Courts of Appeal

The **Circuit Courts of Appeal** hear cases appealed from the United States District Courts, which are the trial courts on the federal level. There are 13 circuits that each represents several states, along with the federal system. Twelve of these regional circuits represent intermediate courts of appeal and hear appeals from the United States District

Courts in each state, including the Bankruptcy Courts, the Tax Court, and the Administrative Agency Tribunal.

The United States Court of Appeals for the Federal Circuit represents federal appeals from the various courts with special jurisdiction, including Court of Claims, Court of International Trade, Court of Veterans Appeals, Patents and Trademarks, and others. A general source for all circuits may be found at

http://www.uscourts.gov/courtlinks/index.cfm

This Web page includes links to each of the 13 circuit courts, state-specific information, court links, and a link to the library that includes the following:

1. publications and reports
2. periodicals
3. policy manuals
4. statistical reports
5. forms
6. court fees
7. Web resources

The home page of the United States Courts Web site is shown in Exhibit 6–5. The link to the U.S. Courts of Appeals Web site is shown in Exhibit 6–6.

The opinions of Federal courts may be found in the **Pacer** Service Center's system. This system is the federal judiciary's centralized registration, billing, and technical support center, and provides electronic access to federal district, bankruptcy, and appellate court records. Written opinions of the court may also be accessed from this Web site.

http://pacer.psc.uscourts.gov

Exhibit 6–7 shows a copy of their home page.

The individual circuit courts may also have their own Web sites that provide libraries of appellate court opinions within individual districts. You may conduct a search for the appropriate Web site for your own state. List your search results in the state-specific information box below.

STATE-SPECIFIC INFORMATION FOR THE STATE OF _____:

The _____ Circuit Court of Appeals Web site is located at:

_____. You may access the following information at this site:

_____

_____

_____

_____

_____.

Pacer   system that provides court opinions of the federal courts

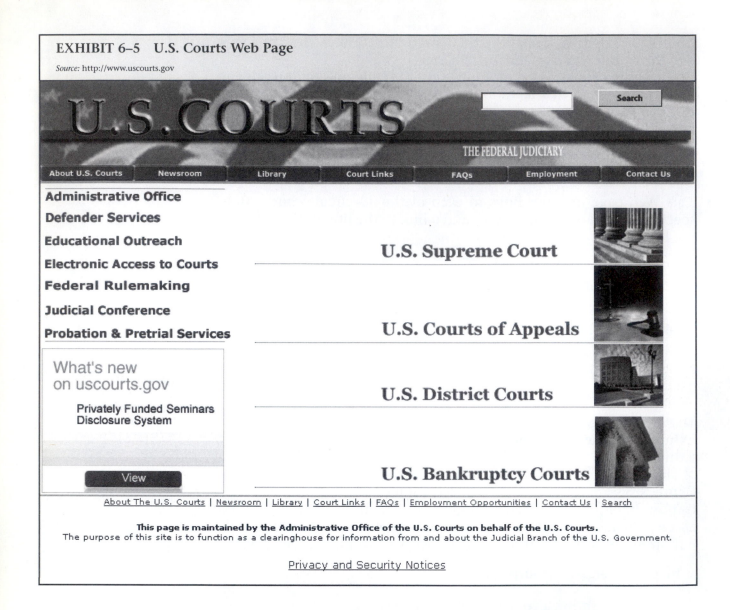

EXHIBIT 6–5   U.S. Courts Web Page

Source: http://www.uscourts.gov

U.S. District Courts

A link to the United States Federal District Courts may be found in Exhibit 6–5. This link provides information about the trial courts on the federal level. There are 94 federal judicial districts with at least one in each state. Larger and heavily populated states may have several districts. Most cases heard in these courts involve questions of federal law, such as statutes, treaties, or the Constitution. Cases against the United States government, cases involving diversity of citizenship (where the plaintiff and defendant reside in different states and the amount in controversy meets the required minimum), and cases in specialized areas such as customs and admiralty also come under the original jurisdiction of the district courts. Federal crimes, such as racketeering, securities fraud, mail fraud, bank robbery, kidnapping, and certain drug-related crimes are also heard in these courts. The general Web page for the Federal courts is found at

http://www.uscourts.gov

EXHIBIT 6–6   U.S. Courts of Appeal Web Page

Source: http://www.uscourts.gov

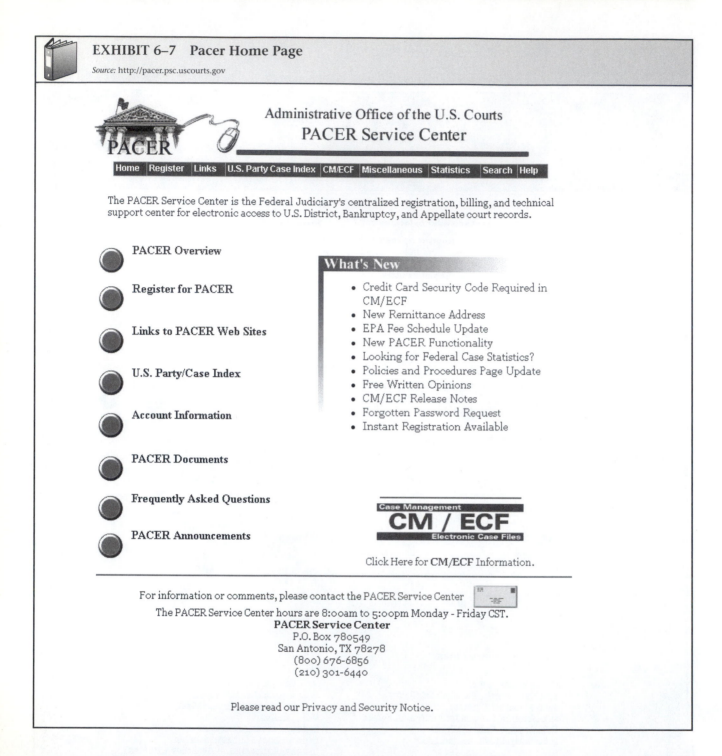

EXHIBIT 6–7 Pacer Home Page

Source: http://pacer.psc.uscourts.gov

Administrative Office of the U.S. Courts
PACER Service Center

| Home | Register | Links | U.S. Party Case Index | CM/ECF | Miscellaneous | Statistics | Search | Help |

The PACER Service Center is the Federal Judiciary's centralized registration, billing, and technical support center for electronic access to U.S. District, Bankruptcy, and Appellate court records.

- PACER Overview
- Register for PACER
- Links to PACER Web Sites
- U.S. Party/Case Index
- Account Information
- PACER Documents
- Frequently Asked Questions
- PACER Announcements

What's New

- Credit Card Security Code Required in CM/ECF
- New Remittance Address
- EPA Fee Schedule Update
- New PACER Functionality
- Looking for Federal Case Statistics?
- Policies and Procedures Page Update
- Free Written Opinions
- CM/ECF Release Notes
- Forgotten Password Request
- Instant Registration Available

Case Management
CM / ECF
Electronic Case Files

Click Here for **CM/ECF** Information.

For information or comments, please contact the PACER Service Center

The PACER Service Center hours are 8:00am to 5:00pm Monday - Friday CST.
PACER Service Center
P.O. Box 780549
San Antonio, TX 78278
(800) 676-6856
(210) 301-6440

Please read our Privacy and Security Notice.

FEDERAL STATUTES

Federal Court rules are found in the United States Code. The Appendix to Title 28 contains the Federal Rules of Evidence, Appellate Procedure, and Civil Procedure. The appendix to Title 18 contains the Federal Rules of Criminal Procedure. These statutes set out the procedural rules that must be followed in the federal courts.

Links to federal and state statutes may be found at

http:// www.law.cornell.edu

EXHIBIT 6–8   Constitutions, Statutes, and Codes

Source: http://www.law.cornell.edu. Reprinted with permission of Cornell Law School.

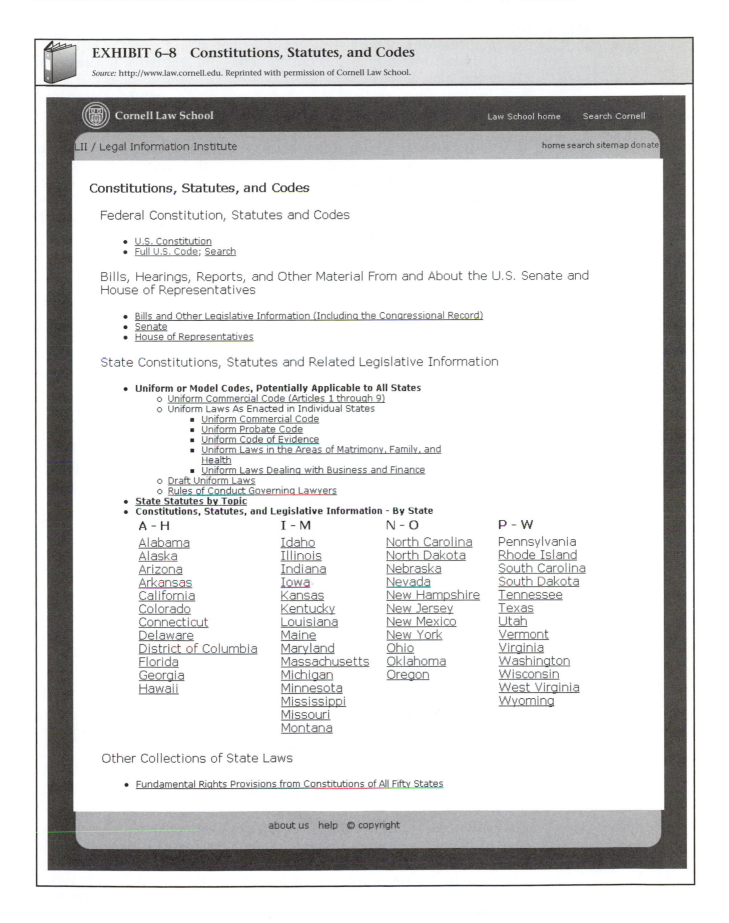

Cornell Law School

Law School home   Search Cornell

LII / Legal Information Institute

home search sitemap donate

Constitutions, Statutes, and Codes

Federal Constitution, Statutes and Codes

- U.S. Constitution
- Full U.S. Code; Search

Bills, Hearings, Reports, and Other Material From and About the U.S. Senate and House of Representatives

- Bills and Other Legislative Information (Including the Congressional Record)
- Senate
- House of Representatives

State Constitutions, Statutes and Related Legislative Information

- **Uniform or Model Codes, Potentially Applicable to All States**
  - Uniform Commercial Code (Articles 1 through 9)
  - Uniform Laws As Enacted in Individual States
    - Uniform Commercial Code
    - Uniform Probate Code
    - Uniform Code of Evidence
    - Uniform Laws in the Areas of Matrimony, Family, and Health
    - Uniform Laws Dealing with Business and Finance
  - Draft Uniform Laws
  - Rules of Conduct Governing Lawyers
- **State Statutes by Topic**
- **Constitutions, Statutes, and Legislative Information - By State**

A - H	I - M	N - O	P - W
Alabama	Idaho	North Carolina	Pennsylvania
Alaska	Illinois	North Dakota	Rhode Island
Arizona	Indiana	Nebraska	South Carolina
Arkansas	Iowa	Nevada	South Dakota
California	Kansas	New Hampshire	Tennessee
Colorado	Kentucky	New Jersey	Texas
Connecticut	Louisiana	New Mexico	Utah
Delaware	Maine	New York	Vermont
District of Columbia	Maryland	Ohio	Virginia
Florida	Massachusetts	Oklahoma	Washington
Georgia	Michigan	Oregon	Wisconsin
Hawaii	Minnesota		West Virginia
	Mississippi		Wyoming
	Missouri		
	Montana		

Other Collections of State Laws

- Fundamental Rights Provisions from Constitutions of All Fifty States

about us   help   © copyright

A picture of the home page is included herein as Exhibit 6–8. It contains links to state statutes, constitutions, and legislative information for each state.

Under the link to "Full U.S. Code," you may search for the federal court rules, Federal Rules of Civil Procedure, and federal cases. The U.S. Code is arranged in titles, beginning with the general provisions (Title I) and continuing alphabetically to the last title, which is War and National Defense (Title 50.) Each code title is further divided into sections and chapters. Updating of the codes and rules may not be accomplished in a timely fashion, so if you require the latest section, be sure to check the advance sheets and your computerized legal research system, such as Westlaw.

STATE GOVERNMENT SOURCES

A vast number of Web sites exist with information on state government offices. Instead of providing Web page addresses for all fifty states, the Web pages that provide links to the different states are included below. These particular links supply information about state government offices and also statutes, law reviews, publishers, and other material. One of the most comprehensive sites for this purpose is

http://www.findlaw.com

which provides a great number of sources for legal research, including federal government sources, legal news, law reviews, statutes, cases, and international legal sources.

Many states have their own Web sites for government departments, statutes and cases, and the courts. One source that provides a method of linking to most state and federal law sources is

http://www.lawsonline.com

In order to conduct a search for these sources, provide the following information in the search box:

1. name of state
2. type of information requested

For instance, you might wish to find Alabama statutes. Type "Alabama statutes" in the search box and you will be provided with a list of places where these statutes can be found.

The West Legal Studies Web site, located at

http://www.westlegalstudies.com

provides links to both state and federal sources. On their home page, click the link to "Professional Center" on the left of the page; on the next page, click the box on the bottom for "state specific sources" and you will be taken to a page listing links to all states as well as the forms utilized in these states. Exhibits 6–9, 6–10, and 6–11 show the steps in this search.

EXHIBIT 6–9   West Legal Studies Home Page

Source: http://www.westlegalstudies.com. Reprinted with permission of Thomson/Delmar Learning.

WESTLAW AND LEXIS

These all-encompassing computerized legal research systems are available online for a fee. They may be accessed on the Internet via their respective Web pages. You must enter your password to gain access to the database. Your time using the database is computed automatically. These systems are available at

http://www.westlaw.com

EXHIBIT 6–10   West Legal Studies Professional Center Web Page

Source: http://www.westlegalstudies.com. Reprinted with permission of Thomson/Delmar Learning.

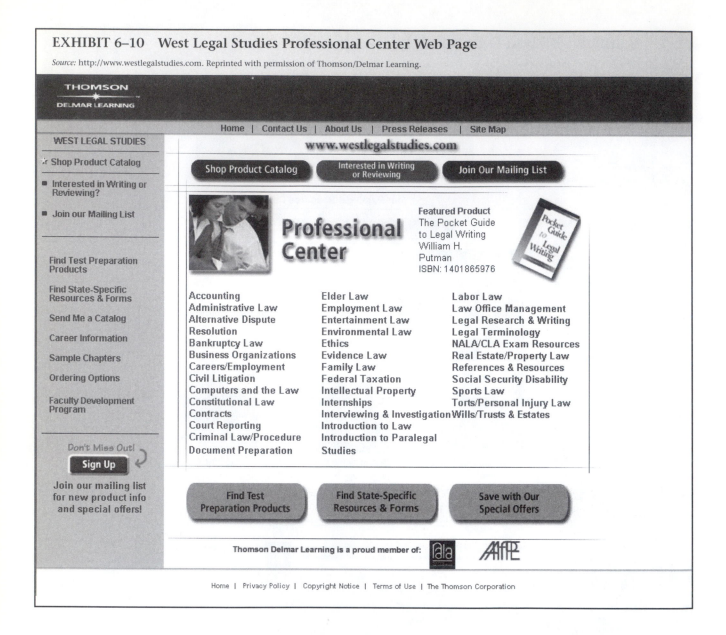

and

> http://www.lexis.com

Additional resources are also available on these Web pages. For instance, West's Legal Directory of Attorneys may be accessed through the address for Westlaw above. Note that these are subscription services and cannot be accessed without membership. Most law offices will have a membership to one of these services.

DOCUMENTS AND FORMS

A number of different sites make forms and documents available on the Web. In addition, many attorneys who have their own Web pages provide documents and forms, some free and some for a fee. The

EXHIBIT 6–11   West Legal Studies–State Sources

Source: http://www.westlegalstudies.com. Reprinted with permission of Thomson/Delmar Learning.

THOMSON
DELMAR LEARNING

Home | Contact Us | About Us | Press Releases | Site Map

WEST LEGAL STUDIES

- Shop Product Catalog

- Instructor Center

- Professional Center

- Student Center

Request a Review Copy

Product Tours

Sample Chapters

Send Me a Catalog

Interested in Writing or
Reviewing

Ordering Options

Faculty Development
Program

FACULTY DEVELOPMENT
PROGRAM

SIGN UP FOR A FREE TRIAL

Don't Miss Out!
Sign Up

Join our mailing list
for new product info
and special offers!

State Resources - By State

For each state you will find "Web Links" and "Legal Forms".
"**Web Links**" are links to state-specific sites which may be of interest to legal and paralegal instructors,
students, and professionals.
"**Legal Forms** " are links to state-specific sites which offer a variety of legal forms online.

Alabama - Web Links - Legal Forms	Alaska - Web Links - Legal Forms	Arizona - Web Links - Legal Forms	Arkansas - Web Links - Legal Forms
California - Web Links - Legal Forms	Colorado - Legal Forms	Connecticut - Web Links - Legal Forms	Delaware - Web Links - Legal Forms
Florida - Web Links - Legal Forms	Georgia - Web Links - Legal Forms	Hawaii - Web Links - Legal Forms	Idaho - Web Links - Legal Forms
Illinois - Web Links - Legal Forms	Indiana - Web Links - Legal Forms	Iowa - Web Links - Legal Forms	Kansas - Web Links - Legal Forms
Kentucky - Web Links - Legal Forms	Louisiana - Web Links - Legal Forms	Maine - Web Links - Legal Forms	Maryland - Web Links - Legal Forms
Massachusetts - Web Links - Legal Forms	Michigan - Web Links - Legal Forms	Minnesota - Web Links - Legal Forms	Mississippi - Web Links - Legal Forms
Missouri - Web Links - Legal Forms	Montana - Web Links - Legal Forms	Nebraska - Web Links - Legal Forms	Nevada - Web Links - Legal Forms
New Hampshire - Web Links - Legal Forms	New Jersey - Web Links - Legal Forms	New Mexico - Web Links - Legal Forms	New York - Web Links - Legal Forms
North Carolina - Web Links - Legal Forms	North Dakota - Web Links - Legal Forms	Ohio - Web Links - Legal Forms	Oklahoma - Web Links - Legal Forms
Oregon - Web Links - Legal Forms	Pennsylvania - Web Links - Legal Forms	Rhode Island - Web Links - Legal Forms	South Carolina - Web Links - Legal Forms
South Dakota - Web Links - Legal Forms	Tennessee - Web Links - Legal Forms	Texas - Web Links - Legal Forms	Utah - Web Links - Legal Forms
Vermont - Web Links - Legal Forms	Virginia - Web Links - Legal Forms	Washington - Web Links - Legal Forms	West Virginia - Web Links - Legal Forms
Wisconsin - Web Links - Legal Forms	Wyoming - Web Links - Legal Forms		

District of Columbia
- Web Links
- Legal Forms

Home | Privacy Policy | Copyright Notice | Terms of Use | The Thomson Corporation

Westlaw site described above provides some forms. The West Legal
Studies site described above

http://westlegalstudies.com

also offers a link to court forms for each state on their State Resources
page (see Exhibit 6–7). Find the state in which you are located and click
on the link for legal forms under that state.

Several general legal sites provide links to legal forms. They include

http://www.washlaw.edu

and

http://www.findlaw.com

■ KEY TERMS

Annotation	Pocket parts
Circuit Courts of Appeal	Primary authority
Citation	Secondary authority
Codes	*Stare decisis*
Common law	Statutes
U.S. District Court	United States Supreme Court
Pacer	

■ SELF TEST

1. Explain the meaning of the following citation: 48 U.S. 322.

2. List the sources of federal law and state law.

3. Explain the difference between primary and secondary authority.

4. Find the codes for your state and indicate their Internet addresses.

5. Are the court decisions from the appellate and supreme courts of your state included on the Web? If so, indicate their addresses.

■ NOTEBOOK PROJECTS

1. Find a case from your state dealing with murder and write a summary for your instructor. Use the following format: *CASE NAME*, and CITATION

Facts:	Summarize the facts of the case
Issue:	What issue is being decided in this case?
Rule:	What rule of law did the court use in reaching its decision?
Application:	Apply the rule of law to the facts of the case and discuss the rationale of the court in reaching its decision.
Conclusion:	How did the court rule and why?

NOTE: Use this format for writing case briefs throughout your legal career.

2. Find the statute for drunk driving in your state and write a summary of it.

3. List those volumes for your own state that contain both primary and secondary authority.

4. Does your state recognize capital punishment? If so, under what circumstances? In addition to the answers, indicate the Web page where the information was found.

For additional resources, visit our Web site at **www.westlegalstudies.com**

RESEARCH DUTIES

CHAPTER OUTCOMES

As a result of studying this chapter, the student will learn:

1. how to perform basic legal research tasks.
2. the use of primary and secondary sources.
3. how to write citations.
4. how to use form books.
5. the principles of updating law books with inserts and pocket parts.
6. how to perform legal research on the Internet.

INTRODUCTION

Learning legal research is similar to learning a sport. To perform the task proficiently, one must practice, practice, practice. The more often you perform a research task, the better and more efficient you will become at executing the proper results. The student may not understand the basic concepts of legal research by reading a textbook, but the manner in which the task is performed will become clearer as more research projects are undertaken. Do not be discouraged if the principles are not understood well at the initial reading of the chapter. You will find that the more research you perform, the clearer the methods will appear to you.

The first time the attorney asks a legal professional to perform a research assignment in the law office, it may not be performed effectively and may take considerably longer than was originally anticipated. The first time one sees a law library can be quite overpowering and intimidating. Spending some time perusing the titles of the books in the library as well as looking at the headings of the various topics included therein will assist the student in learning how to maneuver around the library.

This chapter provides an introduction for the student in the methods of performing legal research tasks by utilizing the books available in the law library. The previous chapter afforded the opportunity to learn how to complete research tasks by using the Internet. Both of these methods will be used in the law office, depending on the individual task to be accomplished. Most important in the performance of any type of legal research is a clear understanding of what is expected. New legal professionals may be given limited research assignments; therefore, it is imperative that the individual know exactly what the attorney expects to be done. For instance, finding a case is a much less complicated task than writing a summary of the case for the attorney.

Be sure that the scope and limitations of the research are explained clearly by the attorney, as well as the possible research sources and prior research conducted on the topic. Each research project should be carefully filed in your notebook so that the you can use it as a source for future research on the same topic.

All research conducted should be precise and up to date. On a field trip to the California Supreme Court, the author heard an attorney arguing his case based on that court's decision in another earlier case. Upon the completion of his argument, one of the Justices asked the attorney if he had "Shepardized" (updated) the case. The Justice then explained that if the attorney had done so, he would have found that the case had been overruled by a later case decided by that same court. In other words, the attorney was arguing "bad law" to convince the California Supreme Court to rule in his favor. In reality, whoever did the research on the case had not found the most recent case on the topic. It is likely that this case was lost on the Supreme Court level because of a simple error that could have been avoided by more diligent research. If you learn nothing else from this chapter, it is imperative that you learn that all research conducted must be accurate and that it must include the most recent information available.

LOCAL LAWS

Statutes also exist on the county and local levels and are called ordinances and codes. These local statutes must be consistent with state and federal law. The state and federal administrative and regulatory agencies establish their own rules and regulations.

LEGISLATIVE HISTORY

If a research project requires that you find the legislative history of a particular law, it can be found in the Statutes at Large, which are published at the end of each session of Congress. The laws are shown chronologically, and each volume includes the laws passed during that particular session of Congress. To find the proper law in the Statutes at Large, you must first find the law in the appropriate code section, where you will find reference to the Statutes at Large number.

CODES

Since statutes are numbered chronologically and not by subject, the codes have been established to enable one to find the various laws more easily. The codes are arranged by topics for the laws passed within a jurisdiction. As new laws are passed on that subject, revisions are made to the codes in the form of "pocket parts." These are placed in a pocket in the back of each code volume so that the researcher may readily find the latest law on that topic. When performing legal research using a particular code, always look in the pocket part to determine whether that particular law has been changed or repealed.

ONE METHOD OF PERFORMING RESEARCH

Various volumes available for performing legal research have been described in the previous chapter. The methods of conducting this research will be discussed here. The most important part of any research assignment is the identification of what is expected in relation to the parameters of the assignment and any time constraints involved. Once these items are clearly understood, an outline of the steps to reach a solution should be written. The general steps to conducting a research project follow:

1. **Preparation**
   Obtain all preliminary information and material that is available in relation to this project. Read the file thoroughly to determine the facts of the case.

2. Use the IRAC system for the solution of your research problem. This method is taught in law school and includes:

   A. **Issue**
      What is the major issue of the case?

   B. **Rule of law**
      What law applies to this particular issue?

   C. **Application**
      How does this rule of law apply to this particular issue?

   D. **Conclusion**
      Summarize the analysis described in A–C and reach a conclusion based on your analysis.

3. **Research Memorandum**
   After completing your research, the results must be reported to the attorney who gave you the research assignment. Each office has a slightly different format for its memoranda; therefore, you should peruse the file to determine this office's layout for the report. Some offices use the IRAC format described above, while others use a variation of this setup.

MINOR RESEARCH PROJECTS

The most extensive research project that the legal professional will encounter has been described above. However, the attorney will often have less complex assignments. It is imperative that sufficient inquiries are made to know the complexity of the assignment. If not, the legal professional may spend many hours performing an extensive research assignment, only to find that the actual task was much less complicated.

FINDING A CASE

If the attorney gives the citation to a case to the legal professional and asks him to find a certain case, he should find the appropriate series, then the volume, and then the case itself. For example, suppose the attorney asks for a case that is found at 22 U.S. 555. The legal professional would find Volume 22 of the United States Reports and then find page 555 of that volume. If the case is found under Westlaw or another computerized research service, a copy of the case should be made for the attorney. If the case is found in a bound volume, it may be sufficient to bookmark the page in the volume where the case starts and give the volume to the attorney.

The legal professional may be asked to go one step further and determine whether the case is still valid. With a computerized system, this may be accomplished by clicking the appropriate code. A portion of a United States Supreme court decision may be found at Exhibit 7–1.

If the legal professional is performing the research in book volumes, then the first volume of *Shepard's* must be found for your case series (i.e., California Reporter.) Then the case must be found to determine whether it has been overruled. A small "o" will appear in the reference to the case where other later cases are listed. Find the case that has overruled the original case to determine whether it was overruled on a different issue. Be sure to look up the case number in all subsequent volumes of *Shepard's* by keeping a list of the dates encompassed in each later volume. The research will include a bound volume, and later paper bound volumes with red and yellow covers.

FINDING A STATUTE

At times, the assignment may be to find a particular statute by its number. In this case, the legal professional would go to the appropriate named code and look up the appropriate section number. For instance, suppose the attorney has asked to find the United States Code Annotated section on "ransom money in a kidnapping." The code would be found in Title 18, section 1202. The annotated code for that section defines "ransom money" and lists the statute history and official comments. It also lists the amendments to this section as well as sentencing guidelines and the section of *American Law Reports* that includes the topic.

Exhibit 7–2 shows an example of the above code section taken from the United States Code Annotated from Westlaw.

POCKET PARTS

The volumes of the codes are updated with pocket parts that are filed in a pocket at the back of each book. Any changes, revisions, and new information are placed in a paper leaflet that is part of the pocket part. Pocket parts are prepared after the individual volume is printed to indicate any changes to that particular volume.

EXHIBIT 7–1   United States Case—*Gideon v. Wainwright*

Source: Reprinted with permission from West, a Thomson business.

83 S.Ct. 792

372 U.S. 335, 83 S.Ct. 792, 9 L.Ed.2d 799, 93 A.L.R.2d 733, 23 O.O.2d 258
(Cite as: 372 U.S. 335, 83 S.Ct. 792)

Supreme Court of the United States
Clarence Earl GIDEON, Petitioner,
v.
Louie L. WAINWRIGHT, Director, Division of
Corrections.
No. 155.

Argued Jan. 15, 1963.
Decided March 18, 1963.

The petitioner brought habeas corpus proceedings against the Director of the Division of Corrections. The Florida Supreme Court, 135 So.2d. 746, denied all relief, and the petitioner brought certiorari. The United States Supreme Court, Mr. Justice Black, held that the Sixth Amendment to the federal Constitution providing that in all criminal prosecutions the accused shall enjoy right to assistance of counsel for his defense is made obligatory on the states by the Fourteenth Amendment, and that an indigent defendant in a criminal prosecution in a state court has the right to have counsel appointed for him.

Judgment reversed and cause remanded to Florida Supreme Court for further action.

Mr. Justice BLACK delivered the opinion of the Court.

Petitioner was charged in a Florida state court with having broken and entered a poolroom with intent to commit a misdemeanor. This offense is a felony under Florida law. Appearing in court without funds and without a lawyer, petitioner asked the court to appoint counsel for him, whereupon the following colloquy took place:

'The COURT: Mr. Gideon, I am sorry, but I cannot appoint Counsel to represent you in this case. Under the laws of the State of Florida, the only time the Court can appoint Counsel to represent a Defendant is when that person is charged with a capital offense. I am sorry, but I will have to deny your request to appoint Counsel to defend you in this case.

'The DEFENDANT: The United States Supreme Court says I am entitled to be represented by Counsel.'

Put to trial before a jury, Gideon conducted his defense about as well as could be expected from a layman. He made an opening statement to the jury, cross-examined the State's witnesses, presented witnesses in his own defense, declined to testify himself, and made a short argument 'emphasizing his innocence to the charge contained in the Information filed in this case.' The jury returned a verdict of guilty, and petitioner was sentenced to serve five years in the state prison. Later, petitioner filed in the Florida Supreme Court this habeas corpus petition attacking his conviction and sentence on the ground that the trial court's refusal to appoint counsel for him denied him rights 'guaranteed by the Constitution and the Bill of Rights by the United States Government.[1][FN1] Treating the petition for habeas corpus as

continued

Exhibit 7–1   *continued*

properly before it, the State Supreme Court, 'upon consideration thereof' but without an opinion, denied all relief. Since 1942, when Betts v. Brady, 316 U.S. 455 , was decided by a divided Court, the problem of a defendant's federal constitutional right to counsel in a state court has been a continuing source of controversy and litigation in both state and federal courts.[FN2] To give this problem another review here, we granted certiorari. 370 U.S. 908. Since Gideon was proceeding in forma pauperis, we appointed counsel to represent him and requested both sides to discuss in their briefs and oral arguments the following: 'Should this Court's holding in Betts v. Brady, 316 U.S. 455, be reconsidered?'

The facts upon which Betts claimed that he had been unconstitutionally denied the right to have counsel appointed to assist him are strikingly like the facts upon which Gideon here bases his federal constitutional claim. Betts was indicated for robbery in a Maryland state court. On arraignment, he told the trial judge of his lack of funds to hire a lawyer and asked the court to appoint one for him. Betts was advised that it was not the practice in that county to appoint counsel for indigent defendants except in murder and rape cases. He then pleaded not guilty, had witnesses summoned, cross-examined the State's witnesses, examined his own, and chose not to testify himself. He was found guilty by the judge, sitting without a jury, and sentenced to eight years in prison. Like Gideon, Betts sought release by habeas corpus, alleging that he had been denied the right to assistance of counsel in violation of the Fourteenth Amendment. Betts was denied any relief, and on review this Court affirmed. It was held that a refusal to appoint counsel for an indigent defendant charged with a felony did not necessarily violate the Due Process Clause of the Fourteenth Amendment, which for reasons given the Court deemed to be the only applicable federal constitutional provision. The Court said: 'Asserted denial (of due process) is to be tested by an appraisal of the totality of facts in a given case. That which may, in one setting, constitute a denial of fundamental fairness, shocking to the universal sense of justice, may, in other circumstances, and in the light of other considerations, fall short of such denial.' 316 U.S., at 462 .

Treating due process as 'a concept less rigid and more fluid than those envisaged in other specific and particular provisions of the Bill of Rights,' the Court held that refusal to appoint counsel under the particular facts and circumstances in the Betts case was not so 'offensive to the common and fundamental ideas of fairness' as to amount to a denial of due process. Since the facts and circumstances of the two cases are so nearly indistinguishable, we think the Betts v. Brady holding if left standing would require us to reject Gideon's claim that the Constitution guarantees him the assistance of counsel.

Upon full reconsideration we conclude that Betts v. Brady should be overruled.

Pocket parts are published on a yearly basis. In some offices, the legal professional will have the responsibility of putting the pocket parts in their appropriate volumes. They should be filed as soon after they are received as is practicable. Be sure to file the appropriate pocket part in the correct volume by checking the name and number of the volume before inserting the pocket part.

PROCEDURAL RULES

Each state, as well as the federal government, maintains rules for conducting civil and criminal cases under its rules of civil procedure and rules of criminal procedure. In most states, these rules are part of the

> **EXHIBIT 7–2   18 United States Code Annotated. Section 1202—Ransom Money**
>
> *Source:* Reprinted with permission from West, a Thomson business.

18 U.S.C.A. § 1202

Effective: [See Text Amendments]

United States Code Annotated Currentness
  Title 18. Crimes and Criminal Procedure (Refs & Annos)
    Part I. Crimes
      Chapter 55. Kidnapping (Refs & Annos)

→ **§ 1202. Ransom money**

(a) Whoever receives, possesses, or disposes of any money or other property, or any portion thereof, which has at any time been delivered as ransom or reward in connection with a violation of section 1201 of this title, knowing the same to be money or property which has been at any time delivered as such ransom or reward, shall be fined under this title or imprisoned not more than ten years, or both.

(b) A person who transports, transmits, or transfers in interstate or foreign commerce any proceeds of a kidnapping punishable under State law by imprisonment for more than 1 year, or receives, possesses, conceals, or disposes of any such proceeds after they have crossed a State or United States boundary, knowing the proceeds to have been unlawfully obtained, shall be imprisoned not more than 10 years, fined under this title, or both.

(c) For purposes of this section, the term "State" has the meaning set forth in section 245(d) of this title.

CREDIT(S)

(June 25, 1948, c. 645, 62 Stat. 760; Sept. 13, 1994, Pub.L. 103-322, Title XXXII, § 320601(b), Title XXXIII, § 330016(1)(L), 108 Stat. 2115, 2147.)

HISTORICAL AND STATUTORY NOTES

Revision Notes and Legislative Reports

1948 Acts. Based on Title 18, U.S.C., 1940 ed., § 408c-1 (June 22, 1932, c. 271, § 4, as added Jan. 24, 1936, c. 29, 49 Stat. 1099).

Words "in the penitentiary" after "imprisoned" were omitted in view of section 4082 of this title committing prisoners to the custody of the Attorney General. (See reviser's note under section 1 of this title.)

Minor changes were made in phraseology.

1994 Acts. House Report Nos. 103-324 and 103-489, and House Conference Report No. 103-711, see 1994 U.S. Code Cong. and Adm. News, p. 1801.

Amendments

1994 Amendments. Subsec. (a). Pub.L. 103-322, § 320601(b)(1), designated existing provisions as subsec. (a).

Pub.L. 103-322, § 330016)1)(L), substituted "under this title" for "not more than $10,000".

Subsecs. (b), (c). Pub.L. 102-322, § 320601(b)(2), added subsecs. (b) and (c).

FEDERAL SENTENCING GUIDELINES

  See Federal Sentencing Guidelines § 2A4.2, 18 USCA.

LIBRARY REFERENCES

American Digest System

  Kidnapping ⚷ 1.

RESEARCH REFERENCES

continued

Exhibit 7–2 *continued*

ALR Library

123 ALR, Fed. 397, What Constitutes Three Previous Convictions for Offenses Committed on Occasions Different from One Another for Purpose of Sentence Enhancement Under Armed Career Criminal Act...

119 ALR, Fed. 319, What Constitutes "Violent Felony" for Purpose of Sentence Enhancement Under Armed Career Criminal Act (18 U.S.C.A. § 924(E)(1)).

107 ALR, Fed. 309, Recovery of Damages for Infliction of Emotional Distress Under Federal Tort Claims Act (28 U.S.C.A. § § 2671-2680).

103 ALR, Fed. 422, Propriety, Under 18 U.S.C.A. § 2517(5), of Interception or Use of Communications Relating to Federal Offenses Which Were Not Specified in Original Wiretap Order.

74 ALR, Fed. 486, What Constitutes Receipt of Firearm, Under 18 U.S.C.A. § 922(H), Prohibiting Certain Persons from Receiving Any Firearm Which Has Been Shipped or Transported in Interstate or Foreign Commerce.

62 ALR, Fed. 829, Receipt, Possession, or Transportation of Multiple Firearms as Single or Multiple Offense Under 18 U.S.C.A. App. 1 § 1202(A)(1), Making it Federal Offense for Convicted Felon to Receive, Possess, or Transport Any...

57 ALR, Fed. 234, Seizure and Forfeiture of Firearms or Ammunition Under 18 U.S.C.A. § 924(D).

55 ALR, Fed. 633, Propriety of Imposing Consecutive Sentences Upon Convictions, Under Federal Statutes, of Unlawful Receipt, Transportation, or Making and Possession of Same Firearm.

44 ALR, Fed. 692, State Pardon as Affecting "Convicted" Status of One Accused of Violation of Gun Control Act of 1968 (18 U.S.C.A. § § 921 et seq.).

31 ALR, Fed. 916, What Constitutes Violation of 18 U.S.C.A. § 1202, Prohibiting Receipt, Possession, or Disposition of Ransom Money.

32 ALR, Fed. 946, What Constitutes Unlawful "Dealing in Firearms or Ammunition" Under 18 U.S.C.A. § 922(A)(1).

13 ALR, Fed. 103, Validity, Construction, and Application of Provision of Omnibus Crime Control and Safe Streets Act of 1968 (18 U.S.C.A. App. 1 § 1202(A)(1)) Making it Federal Offense for Convicted Felon to Possess...

37 ALR 4th 1179, Sufficiency of Evidence as to Nature of Firearm in Prosecution Under State Statute Prohibiting Persons Under Indictment For, or Convicted Of, Crime from Acquiring, Having, Carrying, or Using Firearms.

Encyclopedias

Am. Jur. 2d Abduction and Kidnapping § 20, Conduct Regarding Ransom Money.

Am. Jur. 2d Abduction and Kidnapping § 34, Prohibited Conduct Regarding Ransom Money.

Am. Jur. 2d Abduction and Kidnapping § 42, Jurisdiction.

Am. Jur. 2d Abduction and Kidnapping § 59, Federal Kidnapping Statute.

Am. Jur. 2d Aliens and Citizens § 2309, Conviction of Aggravated Felony.

Am. Jur. 2d Criminal Law § 306, Manner of Raising and Determining Question.

Treatises and Practice Aids

Handbook of Federal Evidence (3d Ed.) § 609:6, Rule 609(A) and (B): Method of Establishing Convictions; Preserving Error for Appeal; Timing of Ruling; Limiting Instructions; the "Mere Fact Method".

continued

Exhibit 7–2   *continued*

Immigration Law and Business § 6:66, Criminal-Based Grounds.

Immigration Law and Crimes § 7:22, Definition of Aggravated Felony.

Immigration Law Service 2d § 13:35, Definition Under IIRIRA.

Immigration Law Service 2d PSD INA § 101, Definitions.

U.S. Citizenship and Naturalization Handbook § 8:12, Aggravated Felonies — Current Statutory Definition.

Wright & Miller: Federal Prac. & Proc. § 527, Sentences on Multiple Counts.

Wright & Miller: Federal Prac. & Proc. § 5239, Other Crimes, Wrongs, or Acts-General Rule.

NOTES OF DECISIONS

1. Delivery

Where defendant picked up money which was intended as kidnap ransom but had been left in wrong place and, after learning that it was intended to be ransom money, continued to keep it, defendant was guilty of possession of ransom money, notwithstanding contention that there had been no "delivery," in purview of this section which defined offense as possession of money "which has at any time been delivered as ransom." U. S. v. Ortega, C.A.3 (N.J.) 1975, 517 F.2d 1006. Kidnapping ⚷ 1

2. Interstate commerce

To establish violation of this section prohibiting possession of ransom money there was no requirement that defendant be connected with interstate commerce element of primary kidnapping offense under section 1201 of this title. U. S. v. Ortega, C.A.3 (N.J.) 1975, 517 F.2d 1006. Kidnapping ⚷ 1

3. Indictment or information

Indictment charging in several counts conspiracy to commit offenses under this section and sections 875 and 1202 of this title and charging substantive offense of kidnapping and three separate offenses of transmitting communications in interstate commerce demanding ransom money and charging receiving, possessing and disposing of ransom money charged separate offenses and was not duplicitous. Amsler v. U. S., C.A.9 (Cal.) 1967, 381 F.2d 37. Indictment And Information ⚷ 125(2)

4. Instructions

In prosecution for possession of ransom money and making false statements to grand jury, trial court did not err in refusing to charge that defendant could be acquitted if he had relied upon advice of Federal Bureau of Investigation agents in attempting to return money anonymously, where such advice occurred a week after defendant had made his false statements to grand jury and no attempt was ever made to return money in manner suggested. U. S. v. Ortega, C.A.3 (N.J.) 1975, 517 F.2d 1006. Criminal Law ⚷ 772(6)

In prosecution under former section 408c-1 of this title accused could not complain of instruction that receipt of ransom money was criminal offense, where court instructed as to what constituted a conspiracy, and that unless jury found accused became part of conspiracy there should be acquittal, and that if accused entered conspiracy jury should further find that accused accepted ransom money knowing it was such, or aided owners in exchanging it. Laska v. U.S., C.C.A.10 (Okla.) 1936, 82 F.2d 672, certiorari denied 56 S.Ct. 957, 298 U.S. 689, 80 L.Ed. 1407. Criminal Law ⚷ 823(16)

18 U.S.C.A. § 1202, **18 USCA § 1202**

Current through P.L. 109-482 (End) approved 01-15-07

codes and may be represented by separate volumes dealing with the civil and criminal cases.

Each state also maintains local rules of court that may be available in the law office. The rules of court are generally accessible via a subscription service with looseleaf volumes. Updates are provided to insert into the loose leaf, with instructions stating which sections should be removed and which new sections should be inserted in their place. It is imperative that close attention be paid to placing the appropriate materials in the proper section in order to maintain a smooth-flowing volume of the current rules. At one time, the author had a new secretary who inserted the wrong pages into the wrong places, to the point where one complete volume of court rules had to be destroyed and a new one had to be purchased. If the directions for taking out pages and inserting pages are followed explicitly, errors of this type will not be made.

Federal court rules may be found at the United States Courts Web site at

http://www.uscourts.gov

The regulations for subpoenas adopted by the Judicial Conference are included as Exhibit 7–3.

LOOSELEAF SERVICES

Some specialty areas have looseleaf services available so that updates to the law may be readily made. If the law office has any of these services, the changes should be filed in a timely manner. Check the name of the series to be sure the proper material is being inserted. The updates will have a page of instructions accompanying the insertion pages. Directions should be followed carefully to be sure that the correct pages are being removed and the new ones are being inserted in their proper place.

RESEARCH FILE

Each time a research project is completed, a copy should be filed in the notebook or in a special research file that has been categorized by subject. Most law offices practice specified legal specialties and may have similar research projects in the future. Therefore, often it is easier to update the research previously performed than it would be to start from the beginning and perform the research over again.

Card files may also be kept of those cases used in the research memoranda. File these cases under the name of the case with a cross reference to the subject. This method also enables the legal professional to find related cases more quickly when he is working on a similar research project. In many offices, this function is now being performed on the computer with a software package developed for this purpose.

EXHIBIT 7–3   Subpoena Regulations—Federal

Source: From http://www.uscourts.com

Subpoena Regulations Adopted by United States Judicial Conference

At its March 2003 meeting, the Judicial Conference endorsed regulations governing responses to subpoenas issued to federal judges and employees. By establishing procedures for litigants to follow to obtain documents or testimony from offices within the judicial branch, as well as the procedures judges and employees would follow if they receive subpoenas, these regulations accomplish three goals:

- they establish an administrative process for subpoena requests;
- they impose general limitations on the nature of responses; and
- they direct agency employees not to comply with subpoenas that are not approved through the administrative process.

The regulations are principally procedural in nature, and do not interfere with substantive decisions by individual courts and officers as to the availability of official documents and testimony. For example, the regulations provide that for a subpoena directed to a judge or a member of a judge's personal staff, that judge would be the official authorized to determine the proper substantive response to the subpoena. For a subpoena directed to a court unit or office, the determination would be assigned to the head of the unit or office, in consultation with the chief judge of the court, when appropriate.

Thus, the only real change that these regulations accomplish is to provide the "determining officer" with well-recognized procedural and substantive grounds to respond to a subpoena. The following is the full text of the subpoena regulations, as adopted by the Judicial Conference in March 2003.

Testimony of Judiciary Personnel and Production of Judiciary Records in Legal Proceedings

As adopted by the Judicial Conference of the United States in March 2003

Section 1. Purpose.

(a) These regulations establish policy, assign responsibilities and prescribe procedures with respect to: (1) the production or disclosure of official information or records by the federal judiciary, and (2) the testimony of present or former judiciary personnel relating to any official information acquired by any such individual as part of that individual's performance of official duties, or by virtue of that individual's official status, in federal, state, or other legal proceedings covered by these regulations.

(b) The purpose of these regulations is, among other things, to: (1) conserve the time of federal judicial personnel for conducting official business; (2) minimize the involvement of the federal judiciary in issues unrelated to its mission; (3) maintain the impartiality of the federal judiciary in disputes between private litigants; (4) avoid spending the time and money of the United States for private purposes; and (5) protect confidential and sensitive information and the deliberative processes of the federal judiciary.

Section 2. Authority.

These regulations are promulgated under the authority granted the Director of the Administrative Office of the United States Courts, under the supervision and direction of the Judicial Conference of the United States, to "[s]upervise all administrative matters relating to the offices of clerks and other clerical and administrative personnel of the courts," 28 U.S.C. § 604(a)(1); to "[p]erform such other duties as may be assigned to him by . . . the Judicial Conference of the United States," 28 U.S.C. § 604(a)(24); to "make, promulgate, issue, rescind, and amend rules and regulations . . . as may be necessary to carry out the Director's functions, powers, duties, and authority," 28 U.S.C. § 604(f); and to "delegate any of the Director's functions, powers, duties, and authority . . . to such officers and employees of the judicial branch of Government as the Director may designate," 28 U.S.C. § 602(d).

Section 3. Definitions.

(a) **Request.** An order, subpoena, or other demand of a court, or administrative or other authority, of competent jurisdiction, under color of law, or any other request by whatever method, for the

continued

Exhibit 7–3 *continued*

production, disclosure, or release of information or records by the federal judiciary, or for the appearance and testimony of federal judicial personnel as witnesses as to matters arising out of the performance of their official duties, in legal proceedings. This definition includes requests for voluntary production or testimony in the absence of any legal process.

(b) **Judicial personnel.** All present and former officers and employees of the federal judiciary and any other individuals who are or have been appointed by, or subject to the supervision, jurisdiction, or control of, the federal judiciary, including individuals hired through contractual agreements by or on behalf of the federal judiciary, or performing services under such agreements for the federal judiciary, such as consultants, contractors, subcontractors, and their employees and personnel. This phrase also includes alternative dispute resolution neutrals or mediators, special masters, individuals who have served and are serving on any advisory committee or in any advisory capacity, and any similar personnel performing services for the federal judiciary.

(c) **Legal proceedings.** All pretrial, trial, and post-trial stages of all existing or anticipated judicial or administrative actions, hearings, investigations, cases, controversies, or similar proceedings, including grand jury proceedings, before courts, agencies, commissions, boards or other tribunals, foreign and domestic, or all legislative proceedings pending before any state or local body or agency, other than those specified in section 4(b).

(d) **Information or records.** All information, records, documents, or materials of any kind, however stored, that are in the custody or control of the federal judiciary or were acquired by federal judicial personnel in the performance of their official duties or because of their official status.

(e) **Testimony.** Any written or oral statement in any form by a witness arising out of the performance of the witness' official duties, including personal appearances and statements in court or at a hearing or trial, depositions, answers to interrogatories, affidavits, declarations, interviews, telephonic, televised, or videotaped remarks, or any other response during discovery or similar proceedings that would involve more than production of documents.

Section 4. Applicability.

(a) These regulations apply to:
   (1) All components of the federal judiciary and their personnel, except the Supreme Court of the United States, the Federal Judicial Center, and the United States Sentencing Commission, and their personnel.

(b) These regulations do not apply to:
   (1) Legal proceedings in which the federal judiciary or a court or office of the federal judiciary is a party.
   (2) Legal proceedings, arising out of the performance of official duties by federal judicial personnel, in which federal judicial personnel are parties.
   (3) Legal proceedings in which federal judicial personnel are to testify while in leave or off-duty status as to matters that do not arise out of the performance of official duties. These regulations do not seek to deny federal judicial personnel access to the courts as citizens in their private capacities on off-duty time.
   (4) Congressional requests for testimony or documents.
   (5) Requests governed by the Regulations for Garnishment of Pay of Officers and Employees of the Federal Judiciary, Guide to Judiciary Policies and Procedures, Vol. I-C, Chap. XI, Part A.
   (6) Proceedings conducted under the Judicial Conduct and Disability Act, 28 U.S.C. § 372(c), under the authority conferred on the judicial councils of the respective federal judicial circuits by 28 U.S.C. § 332, or under the authority conferred on the Judicial Conference of the United States by 28 U.S.C. § 331.
   (7) Requests by members of the public, when properly made through the procedures established by a court for that purpose, for records or documents, such as court files or dockets, routinely made available to members of the public for inspection or copying.

continued

Exhibit 7–3 *continued*

Section 5. Policy.

(a) Federal judicial personnel may not provide testimony or produce records in legal proceedings except as authorized in accordance with these regulations.

(b) Testimony may be taken from federal judicial personnel only at the federal judicial personnel's place of business, or at any other place authorized by the determining officer designated in section 7(b). Additional conditions may be specified by the determining officer. The time for such testimony shall be reasonably fixed so as to avoid substantial interference with the performance of official duties by federal judicial personnel.

(c) Nothing in these regulations shall restrict in any way any defenses, objections, or privileges that may be asserted by federal judicial personnel in response to a request.

(d) These regulations are not intended to, and do not:

(1) Waive the sovereign immunity of the United States; or
(2) Infringe upon or displace the responsibilities committed to the Department of Justice in conducting litigation on behalf of the United States in appropriate cases.

(e) These regulations are intended only to govern the internal operation of the federal judiciary and are not intended to create, do not create, and may not be relied upon to create any right or benefit, substantive or procedural, enforceable in law or equity against the United States or against the federal judiciary or any court, office, or personnel of the federal judiciary.

Section 6. Contents and timeliness of a request.

(a) The request for testimony or production of records shall set forth, or shall be accompanied by an affidavit setting forth, a written statement by the party seeking the testimony or production of records, or by counsel for the party, containing an explanation of the nature of the testimony or records sought, the relevance of the testimony or records sought to the legal proceedings, and the reasons why the testimony or records sought, or the information contained therein, are not readily available from other sources or by other means. This explanation shall contain sufficient information for the determining officer designated in section 7(b) to determine whether or not federal judicial personnel should be allowed to testify or the records should be produced. Where the request does not contain an explanation sufficient for this purpose, the determining officer may deny the request or may ask the requester to provide additional information.

(b) The request for testimony or production of records, including the written statement required by section 6(a), shall be provided to the federal judicial personnel from whom testimony or production of records is sought at least fifteen (15) working days in advance of the time by which the testimony or production of records is to be required. Failure to meet this requirement shall provide a sufficient basis for denial of the request.

(c) The determining officer designated in section 7(b) has the authority to waive the requirements of this section (6) in the event of an emergency under conditions which the requester could not reasonably have anticipated and which demonstrate a good faith attempt to comply with the requirements of these regulations. In no circumstance, however, shall a requester be entitled to consideration of an oral or untimely request; to the contrary, whether to permit such an exceptional procedure is a decision within the sole discretion of the determining officer.

Section 7. Identity of determining officer.

(a) Federal judicial personnel shall not, in response to a request for testimony or the production of records in legal proceedings, comment, testify, or produce records without the prior approval of the determining officer designated in section 7(b).

(b) The determining officer authorized to make determinations under these regulations shall be as follows:

(1) In the case of a request directed to a federal court of appeals judge, district judge, Court of International Trade judge, Court of Federal Claims judge, bankruptcy judge, or magistrate judge, or directed to a current or former member of such a judge's personal staff (such as a judge's

continued

Exhibit 7–3 *continued*

secretary, law clerk, or courtroom deputy clerk), the determining officer shall be the federal court of appeals judge, district judge, Court of International Trade judge, Court of Federal Claims judge, bankruptcy judge, or magistrate judge himself or herself.

(2) In the case of a request directed to a former federal court of appeals judge, district judge, Court of International Trade judge, Court of Federal Claims judge, bankruptcy judge, or magistrate judge, or directed to a former member of a former judge's personal staff who is no longer a court employee and thus is not covered by sections 7(b)(1) or (3), the determining officer shall be the chief judge of the court on which the former judge previously served.

(3) In the case of a request directed to an employee or former employee of a court office (other than an employee or former employee covered by section 7(b)(1)), such as the office of the clerk of court, the office of the circuit executive, the staff attorneys' and/or preargument attorneys' office, the probation and/or pretrial services office, and the office of the Federal Public Defender, the determining officer shall be the unit head of the particular office, such as the clerk of court, the circuit executive, the senior staff attorney, the chief probation officer, the chief pretrial services officer, or the Federal Public Defender. In these instances, the determining officer (except the Federal Public Defender, as provided below) shall, as provided by local rule or order, consult with the chief judge of the court served by the particular office regarding the proper response to a request. The Federal Public Defender, in the case of a request related to the defender office's administrative function (but not requests related to the defender office's provision of representation pursuant to the Criminal Justice Act, 18 U.S.C. 3006A, and related statutes), shall, as provided by local rule or order, consult with the chief judge of the court of appeals that appoints the Federal Public Defender regarding the proper response to such a request.

(4) In the case of a request directed to an employee or former employee of the Administrative Office of the United States Courts, the determining officer shall be the General Counsel of the Administrative Office.

(5) In the case of a request not specified in subsections (1) through (4) above (such as, for example, a request made to federal judicial personnel as defined by section 3(b) above who are not current or former judges or their staff, employees of a court office, or employees of the Administrative Office), the determining officer shall be the officer designated to serve as the determining officer by the chief judge of the court served by the recipient of the request. In these instances, the determining officer (if someone other than the chief judge of the relevant court) shall, as provided by local rule or order, consult with the chief judge of the relevant court regarding the proper response to a request.

Section 8. Procedure when request is made.

(a) In response to a request for testimony or the production of records by federal judicial personnel in legal proceedings covered by these regulations, the determining officer may determine whether the federal judicial personnel may be interviewed, contacted, or used as witnesses, including as expert witnesses, and whether federal judicial records may be produced, and what, if any conditions will be imposed upon such interview, contact, testimony, or production of records. The determining officer may deny a request if the request does not meet any requirement imposed by these regulations. In determining whether or not to authorize the disclosure of federal judicial information or records or the testimony of federal judicial personnel, the determining officer will consider, based on the following factors, the effect in the particular case, as well as in future cases generally, which testifying or producing records will have on the ability of the federal judiciary or federal judicial personnel to perform their official duties.

(1) The need to avoid spending the resources of the United States for private purposes, to conserve the time of federal judicial personnel for the performance of official duties, and to minimize the federal judiciary's involvement in issues unrelated to its mission.

(2) Whether the testimony or production of records would assist the federal judiciary in the performance of official duties.

(3) Whether the testimony or production of records is necessary to prevent the perpetration of fraud or injustice in the case or matter in question.

(4) Whether the request is unduly burdensome or is inappropriate under applicable court or administrative rules.

continued

Exhibit 7–3   *continued*

(5) Whether the testimony or production of records is appropriate or necessary under the rules of procedure governing the case or matter in which the request arises, or under the relevant substantive law of privilege.

(6) Whether the request is within the proper authority of the party making it.

(7) Whether the request meets the requirements of these regulations.

(8) Whether the request was properly served under applicable court, administrative, or other rules.

(9) Whether the testimony or production of records would violate a statute, regulation, or ethical rule.

(10) Whether the testimony or production of records would disclose information regarding the exercise of judicial or quasi-judicial responsibilities by federal judicial personnel in the decisional or deliberative process.

(11) Whether the testimony or production of records would disclose confidential information from or pertaining to a pre-sentence investigation report or pertaining to an individual's probation, parole, or supervised release, or would disclose any other information that is confidential under any applicable statute or regulation.

(12) Whether the testimony or production of records reasonably could be expected to result in the appearance of the federal judiciary favoring one litigant over another, or endorsing or supporting a position advocated by a litigant.

(13) Whether the request seeks testimony, records or documents available from other sources.

(14) Whether the request seeks testimony of federal judicial personnel as expert witnesses.

(15) Whether the request seeks personnel files, records or documents pertaining to a current or former federal judicial officer or employee, and (1) the personnel files, records or documents sought by the request may be obtained from the current or former federal judicial officer or employee in question, or (2) the personnel files, records or documents sought by the request would be made available to the requester with the written consent or authorization of the current or former federal judicial officer or employee in question.

(16) Any other consideration that the determining officer designated in section 7(b) may consider germane to the decision.

(b) Federal judicial personnel upon whom a request for testimony or the production of records in legal proceedings is made shall promptly notify the determining officer designated in section 7(b). If the determining officer determines, upon consideration of the requirements of these regulations and the factors listed in section 8(a), that the federal judicial personnel upon whom the request was made should not comply with the request, the federal judicial personnel upon whom the request was made shall notify the requester of these regulations and shall respectfully decline to comply with the request. In appropriate circumstances federal judicial personnel may—through the Department of Justice, or with the assistance of retained legal counsel if the Department of Justice is unavailable—file a motion, before the appropriate court or other authority, to quash such a request or to obtain other appropriate relief.

(c) If, after federal judicial personnel have received a request in a legal proceeding and have notified the determining officer in accordance with this section, a response to the request is required before instructions from the determining officer are received, federal judicial personnel shall notify the requester of these regulations and inform the requester that the request is under review pursuant to these regulations. If necessary, federal judicial personnel may—through the Department of Justice, or with the assistance of retained legal counsel if the Department of Justice is unavailable—seek a stay of the request pending a final determination by the determining officer, or seek other appropriate relief.

(d) If, in response to action taken under section 8(c), a court of competent jurisdiction or other appropriate authority declines to stay the effect of a request pending a determination by the determining officer, or if such court or other authority orders that the request be complied with notwithstanding the final decision of the determining officer, the federal judicial personnel upon whom the request was made shall notify the determining officer and shall comply with the determining officer's instructions regarding compliance with the order or request. Unless and until otherwise instructed by the determining officer, however, the federal judicial personnel upon whom the request was made shall respectfully decline to comply with the order or request. See United States ex rel. Touhy v. Ragen, 340 U.S. 462 (1951).

LEGAL RESEARCH SOURCES ON THE INTERNET ■

A number of excellent sources exist on the Internet for assisting in the performance of legal research projects. Many firms subscribe to either the Westlaw or Lexis/Nexis service online. If the firm uses one of these services, training programs will be made available for learning how to use the service.

Note that the Web site addresses are current as of the writing of this textbook. However, if the site is not available at the address given, conduct a search using your own Internet search engine by typing the name of the Web site in the search box to determine its current Web address. For instance, if you were searching for the Library of Congress Web site, type "Library of Congress" in the search box.

The Library of Congress maintains a Web page that provides a catalog of all available publications. The legal professional can search for any book that has been published and has an ISBN number. Searches may be undertaken by title, key words, or author. The site for the Library of Congress is located at

http://www.lcweb.loc.gov

and appears as Exhibit 7–4.

EXHIBIT 7–4   Library of Congress Web Site

Source: http://www.lcweb.loc.gov

One of the best sites for finding legal resources is located at

http://www.findlaw.com

which provides links to state cases and statutes, as well as to the following:

1. consumer law.
2. United States Supreme court cases.
3. law schools.
4. legal subject indexes.
5. state law resources.
6. state court rules and administrative regulations.
7. foreign and international resources.
8. law firms and legal organizations.
9. government directories.

If you are searching for a site on a legal subject and the Web site address is not known, it is often easier to find the site on FindLaw than to do a search on your own. It is especially valuable if you are not sure exactly what topic under which to conduct the key word search. Exhibit 7–5 displays the FindLaw home page.

The American Bar Association maintains a legal research Web page that enables the researcher to connect to different government branches as well as the various courts, Judicial Council, law school libraries, and a number of other legal reference sources. It is located at

http://www.abanet.org

A Web page that enables the user to prepare customized documents online from given templates is located at

http://www.legaldocs.com

Some of these documents are free and others require a small payment. Documents may be found in the areas of wills, trusts, sales, leases, partnerships, employment, business, and real estate. Since these documents are generic in nature, state laws should always be reviewed for the state in which the document is being prepared and filed to ascertain whether that document is valid in that particular state.

Many federal government agencies have Web sites. Because contacting them by telephone or regular mail is often difficult and time consuming, it is usually beneficial to find the Web site and send an inquiry to the appropriate source of information available on that site.

The major federal agencies with Web sites may be found in Table 7–1, along with their individual functions.

If the government agency in which you are interested is not listed in the above table, conduct a search by typing the name of the agency in your browser's search box. For example, if you were looking for the Interstate Commerce Commission, type "Interstate Commerce Commission" in the search box.

EXHIBIT 7–5   FindLaw Web Site

Source: Reprinted with permission of FindLaw, a Thomson business.

TABLE 7–1	Federal Government Agencies Web Sites	
Department	**Agency**	**URL**
AVIATION	Federal Aviation Administration (FAA)	http://www.faa.gov
	National Transportation Safety Board (NTSB)	http://www.ntsb.gov
CENSUS	United States Census Bureau	http://www.census.gov
CIA	Central Intelligence Agency	http://www.cia.gov
COURTS	Federal Courts	http://www.uscourts.gov
INTERNAL REV.	Internal Revenue Service (IRS)	http://www.irs.gov
JUSTICE	Department of Justice	http://www.usdoj.gov
LABOR	Department of Labor	http://www.dol.gov
LIBRARY	House of Representatives Library	http://www.house.gov
PATENT	Department of Commerce/Patent and Trademark Office	http://www.uspto.gov
PPRINTING	Government Printing Office	http://www.access.gpo.gov
SECURITIES	Securities & Exchange Commission (SEC)	http://www.sec.gov
SOCIAL SEC.	Social Security Administration	http://www.ssa.gov
STATE	State Department	http://www.state.gov
	State—Travel Warnings	http://www.state.gov travel_warnings
TRANSPORTATION	Department of Transportation (DOT)	http://www.dot.gov

One site that provides a considerable number of links to other legal sites may be found at

http://www.westlegalstudies.com

This site provides links to all state Web sites as well as to the various forms and documents used in those states.

Many other sites are available to assist in your legal research. For a more comprehensive listing of legal related Web sites, consult *Legal Research Using the Internet* by Judy A. Long (West/Thomson Learning, 2000).

SOLVING A COMPLEX RESEARCH PROBLEM

A number of questions should be asked before attempting to solve a complex legal research problem. An entry-level legal professional may find all legal research problems to be difficult and complex. However, by breaking down the questions to be answered into simple terms, the project will be easier to complete.

1. What is the problem and/or subject of the research?
2. What is the specific question that the attorney wants answered?
3. What sources will be used to find the answer?
4. What legal issues are involved?

5. Find the appropriate cases and statutes to answer the question.

6. Expand the search to include adverse authority.

7. Update to find the latest law.

8. Write a report to the attorney.

Although this method works best for complex legal problems, the legal professional may mentally perform these same steps conducting a simple research task for the attorney.

1. **Subject of the research**

   In most cases this will be a simple topic, particularly for a new legal assistant. The topics will become more complex as the individual learns more about the process of legal research. In a complex legal problem, the researcher must analyze the facts of the case to determine the objective of the client and the desired result.

2. **Specific question**

   While the subject of the research may be very broad, the attorney may require the answer to a very specific question related to that particular subject. If a complex legal question is involved, the legal professional may be required to determine the statutes or codes related to this particular question. It is important to also determine which court has primary jurisdiction in the case.

3. **Sources**

   Make a list of those sources to be used in finding the answer. If one of the computerized legal research systems is being utilized, a list of the key words to be used should be made. If the legal professional is unfamiliar with the particular area of law, it would be beneficial to read a treatise or other secondary authority to become familiar with the particular legal area. Primary authority may also be found using this method. In this manner, the legal professional will be able to find cases and statutes that relate to that particular issue. Be sure to check the pocket parts of the statutes and update the cases to be sure the law is still relevant.

4. **Update ("Shepardize")**

   Shepard's Citations may be used to find the latest statutes or judicial opinions. Read the updated cases and statutes to be sure they have the same issues as the case at hand. Make a notation of the dates the cases were decided and the dates the statutes were enacted to determine whether they were in effect on the pertinent dates for the case at hand. In addition to using the bound volumes of *Shepard's,* be sure to see the subsequent paper bound volumes as well as the advance sheets. If using a computerized legal research system, you should be able to find the latest cases more easily. Research the law or case from the current date back to the date of the original cause of action.

5. **Report to attorney**

   Many attorneys have been critical of the reporting ability of legal assistants in preparing legal research memoranda. One should be concise but include all pertinent material. Report the positive

Shepardize updating a case by finding the citation in *Shepard's Citations*

results as well as the negative research that will be found by the opposing side. Use only the case's report on the issues being addressed and not the information found in the headnotes, which is merely a description of the issues to be decided in the case itself. If the case is not understood, reread it until the scenario becomes clear. Find past legal research reports in your office on the same topic. Check with the attorney if any aspect of the research project is not clear. Read past legal research reports to the attorney to determine the degree of content and writing style preferred. Do not expend considerable effort in explaining the steps required to find the material. The end result is what is required.

USING PAST RESEARCH

Many law offices have computer files of past research conducted on different topics. The legal professional should become familiar with the file and the system used for finding special subjects. If this type of file is not available in the law firm, start a file of this type that will be used for future research. You should establish a file of this type in your notebook prior to obtaining a legal position.

A record should be kept of all case citations used by their topics. In this manner, when you undertake research on a given topic, a reference point at which to begin the research will be available. The file of case citations may be compiled in a similar fashion as a bibliography. A card file, a computer file, or another method may be used.

SECONDARY AUTHORITY

Many beginning researchers find it easier to begin their research using secondary authority, which includes writings that set forth the author's interpretation of the law. It might include restatements of the law, legal encyclopedias, annotations of statutes and cases, form books, treatises, and law review articles. While this information may not be cited as authority, it can be a useful tool for finding primary authority and for developing a basic understanding of the topic at hand.

On some occasions, the researcher may be unfamiliar with the issue at hand and might have to use a legal dictionary to find its meaning. *Black's Law Dictionary* represents the official dictionary of the court. However, unless the specific definition is at issue and being used as a question in the case, some of the other legal dictionaries may be easier to read and understand for the beginning legal professional. Your instructor may have already required you to purchase a legal dictionary for this class. If not, find legal dictionaries in the library, read some definitions, and determine whether you are able to understand them. While one may not use the dictionary as primary authority, it is often helpful for finding other primary sources.

Legal Encyclopedias

Legal encyclopedias are often the best place to begin your legal research. Each legal topic provides the elements of that area of law, background data on the law, and definitions for legal terms used. Citations are given to cases and statutes. In particular, the beginning researcher may find the legal encyclopedia the best source for the start of the legal research project. As with a regular encyclopedia, the legal encyclopedia is arranged alphabetically by subject area. Be sure to look up the cases and statutes whose references are found here because encyclopedia articles are not considered to be primary authority. Updates to the encyclopedias may be found in their pocket parts. Be sure to check the pocket parts on any area of law being researched since they will contain the latest information obtainable on that topic.

Legal Textbooks

Legal textbooks have been written on many different subjects of law. The bibliographies in your own textbooks and a subject index in a law library are good sources for finding secondary source textbooks, which are available on many different legal areas.

Restatements

Restatements have been prepared to clarify the laws of contracts and torts. The American Law Institute has compiled a restatement of the law that provides a persuasive arrangement of what judges, professors at law schools, and attorneys believe the law should be. These volumes provide a comprehensive explanation of the various aspects of tort and contract law as well as a source for finding the primary sources for those laws.

Law Reviews

Law reviews are published by all law schools and contain articles written by law professors and law students on timely controversies in the law in different areas. These articles provide very detailed analyses of the subject area, as well as extensive footnotes of the sources used in the article, such as cases, statutes, and other law review articles.

Legal Newspapers

Legal newspapers are devoted to timely news in the legal profession. They also may include copies of the latest cases as they are decided by the appellate and supreme courts before they are published in the case reports. *The Los Angeles Daily Journal*, for instance, provides an insert with each journal of the appellate and supreme cases that are decided each day.

restatements
comprehensive explanations of the law authored by judges, law school professors, and attorneys; restatements are available for contracts and tort law

law reviews   published by law schools; a compilation of articles on current legal issues

USING PRIMARY AUTHORITY

Primary authority consists of statutory law and case law in the jurisdiction in which the case is being heard. The statutes and cases may be on the state or federal level.

Case Law

In most cases, law office staff will be involved in researching state law. Each state has its own system of case reports and/or reporters. Some states have an official and unofficial series of cases. In those states, the researcher must use the citations for the official series and may also use the unofficial series. In most cases, the series entitled "reports" will be official and the series entitled "reporter" will be unofficial.

Make a note below of your own state's requirements.

THE STATE OF _____ HAS THE FOLLOWING
SERIES OF REPORTING FOR CASE LAW:

_____

_____

This series is the _____ official _____ unofficial version.
The other version (if available) is _____.

On the federal level, the United States Supreme Court cases are reported in both the United States Reports and the Supreme Court Reporter. (See Exhibit 7–1.) The Federal cases are reported in the Federal Reports and Federal Reporter. The Federal Court Rules establishes rules of procedure on the federal courts. West's Federal Rules Decisions contains cases interpreting the rules. In most law offices, the legal professional will not be involved with research on the federal level.

UPDATING CASES AND STATUTES ■

Shepard's publishes a system for updating both state and federal cases and statutes. The processing of using these volumes is called "Shepardizing." When you have a case citation that you wish to "Shepardize," find the volume of *Shepard's* that contains that particular series, such as the Supreme Court Reporter. The volume covered will be shown in the upper right corner of the page. Go to the volume required, and then go through the pages until you find the appropriate page number, set out in the middle of each column. Under the appropriate volume and page number, you will find later cases that used your case. Be particularly watchful of the small "o" after the case reference because that indicates that your case was overruled by the subject case reference. It would be appropriate to look up the later case to determine whether it actually overruled the issue being argued in your case.

If a computerized legal research system is being used, Shepardizing may take a few seconds. If using a manual system, it may take an hour since you will have to look up each issue of *Shepard's* published after the case you are using. This might include a bound volume, several paper bound volumes, and some advance sheets as well.

RULES OF COURT

Most state court systems publish volumes that provide rules for the various state courts. In California, for example, the Rules of Court are published in a looseleaf binder, with separators for the various counties in California. Updates should be inserted as soon as they are received to be sure the attorney knows the current rules. Each time the attorney is required to practice in a different county, the legal professional should refer to the rules of that county to determine whether there are any differences from the general rules of the state. Similarly, there are Federal rules of court that should be referenced when the attorney will be in Federal court.

CITATIONS

The case citation is the title of the case. *The Blue Book: A Uniform System of Citations* publishes the official manner in which all citations should be referenced. West publishes a handy guide called *Cite-Mate Citation Guide* that illustrates the proper style for citations.

Case names should be typed in italics.

Example: *Roy v. Allen*

When a case name is written within a document, it may be separated by a comma. The comma is not set in italic. Thus, in the preceding example:

In *Roy v. Allen,* the court held: . . . . .

Although business names should be written out in their entirety, individual names should not include the first names. Note the above example for an individual name. For a company name:

John Smith Manufacturing Co. v. Selena Fabrics

In a case citation, the name of the case should always be followed by its location and date published. However, only the names of the parties are italic:

Roy v. Allen, 55 U.S. 222 (1955)

In most cases, do not put a space between the volume reference, such as U.S. above. Exceptions to this rule exist, so it is always desirable to check the *Bluebook* when typing different citations.

Case citations for federal cases are shown here:

1. United States Supreme Court: *John v. Doe,* 425 U.S. 111 (1992)
2. U.S. Court of Appeals: *John v. Doe,* 255 F.2d 888 (3d Cir. 1985)
3. U.S. District Court: *John v. Doe,* 222 F. Supp. 44 (S.D.N.Y.)

STATE COURT CITATIONS

Citations of state court decisions must include both the official and unofficial citation of the case. Determine your state's official and unofficial version and insert the appropriate abbreviations:

> STATE-SPECIFIC INFORMATION FOR THE STATE OF _____:
>
> Citations for the state of _____ should be written as follows:
>
> _____
>
> _____ .

For the appropriate style for citations from other sources, the student is encouraged to obtain one of the reference books described in this chapter.

FORM BOOKS AND PROGRAMS

A number of the documents produced in the legal office are repetitive. Once a certain document has been developed for use in a case, it may be adapted for utilization in other cases. An office file of documents may be prepared to enable all legal assistants to use this file for the same type of documents.

Various software programs are available for the writing of documents in different types of cases. Generally, the law office will have the appropriate programs for use in their particular type of practice.

Form books are also available in the law library for use in different types of cases. Templates may also be available in these books for the various pleadings and documents used in a law firm.

Most law offices use one of the online subscription services available for a fee for their legal research. Both primary and secondary authority may be found in these systems, as well as a large amount of other legal information. The main Web sites are:

1. Westlaw **http://www.westlaw.com**

2. Lexis **http://www.lexis.com**

Loislaw is another comprehensive legal research service that is available online for a fee at

http://www.loislaw.com

In addition to providing primary and secondary legal sources, Loislaw has a large database of documents and pleadings for the many specialty areas of law.

Forms for the various states and the federal government may be found at

http://www.westlegalstudies.com

These forms are available for each state and the federal government.

The notebook will provide the student with a forms book for both state and federal forms. It may be appropriate for you to develop a separate notebook of forms, documents, and pleadings, separated by tabs with subject headings. They may be used to develop templates for the computer.

The law office may have its own database of documents, pleadings, and forms used in that particular office for the area of law practiced. Be sure to make use of these templates for the documents being produced. Additionally, Microsoft Office has its own general legal templates that may be adapted for use in the law office.

■ KEY TERMS

Law reviews   Shepardize
Restatement

■ SELF TEST

1. What is the statute in your state that prohibits drunk driving?

2. Explain the statute.

3. Find a case in your state that relates to drunk driving. What is the case citation?

4. Shepardize the case in #3 above. Is it still "good law" in your state?

5. Write a memorandum to your instructor explaining the information you found in #1–3 above.

■ NOTEBOOK PROJECTS

1. Find three Web pages that contain legal resources for your own state.

2. List the Web pages for the state courts in your own state. If possible, make a copy of these pages and insert them in your notebook.

3. Find a computerized legal research system that is used in a local law office. Write a memorandum to your instructor discussing the advantages and disadvantages of this particular system.

For additional resources, visit our Web site at **www.westlegalstudies.com**

FILING AND RECORDS MANAGEMENT

CHAPTER OUTCOMES

As a result of studying this chapter, the student will learn:

1. the different types of filing systems.
2. how to set up a filing system.
3. the filing systems most commonly used in a law office.
4. the principles of file management.
5. about the ethical considerations in setting up filing systems.

FILING SYSTEMS

Most law firms will have a specific type of filing system that has been customized to that particular firm's requirements. A considerable number of records are now kept on a computer and backed up onto a zip drive, CDs, or some other type of backup system. Although the advent of computers assured us that the paperless office was the way of the future, the computer has instead made it easier to produce more detailed documents and more paperwork has resulted. Computers generate paperwork very swiftly and make it easier to create long and complicated correspondence, pleadings, and reports.

CENTRALIZED FILES

Most large firms, corporate law departments, and government law offices provide a **centralized filing system** where all files are located in the "file room" that is run by the file room manager. File clerks work in the file room retrieving material and placing items in the files. In general, file requests must be made to the person in charge of the file room, and one of the file clerks will retrieve the item requested. It is often difficult, if not impossible, to remove a file from the file room without authorization from the person in charge. Firms vary as to the amount of time a file may be kept outside of the file room. "Out cards" are prepared when files are removed.

The usual procedure used for this type of system is that each person working in the Law Department, law firm, or government law office has an "out" box on her desk specifically designed for outgoing files. Periodically throughout the day, a file clerk will go to each office to

centralized files central filing system where all files are located in a central file room

pick up any material in the file "out box." She will take the material to the file room, and it will be filed in the proper folders.

In this type of arrangement, it is imperative that the legal professional refer to the subject of the file where the copy of any correspondence or document must be placed. File clerks are not familiar with the cases in the office and might not know where to file paperwork unless the file's subject is given. Since law office correspondence utilizes "RE:" lines, use that line for the proper name for the file. Some offices use numerical filing systems. In those cases, be sure the number is correct on each piece of paper that is being filed.

One of the advantages of this type of filing system is that it is easier to just place a piece of paper in a box than it would be to prepare a file and file each piece of paper individually. Additionally, the central file room may have other material on a particular case that would be beneficial to read. If each legal professional kept her own files, others in the office who worked on the same case would also have files, and it would be difficult to find all of the information on a particular case or topic. However, there are disadvantages, which relate to misfiling or missing files. Sometimes items are misfiled into the wrong file and are not easy to find. Perhaps a whole file is misfiled and may be difficult to find. In some cases, the attorney or legal professional may wish to use a particular file that is being used by another person in the firm.

Computer Filing Systems

Various software programs are available for automating the filing system. These systems will categorize files and assign numbers (if utilizing a numerical system). It is often easier to find files when a computerized system is used. In these cases, however, it is imperative that a backup of all files be kept by the legal professional in the event a computer virus is contracted or the computer system crashes. Even with virus protection programs, it is possible to obtain a virus on the hard drive. Various methods are employed for backing up files, and the firm should have a system in place.

Decentralized or Local Filing Systems

Small firms generally use a **decentralized** or **local filing system** located in the legal professional's office. The legal professional will be responsible for the keeping of these files. Even those firms that use centralized filing systems will often have individual duplicate files that are used frequently in each attorney's office.

Computerized filing systems software programs used for automating the filing system.

decentralized or **local filing system** a local filing system located in the legal professional's office and generally used in small law offices

CLIENT CONFIDENTIALITY ■

In order to preserve client confidentiality, it is advantageous to use a numerical filing system that is cross-referenced to clients' names. The cross-reference file should be kept confidential. No one should have access to these files except the attorney, legal professional, and anyone who is working on a particular case.

Whenever files are removed from the file cabinet, they should not be left open on a desk, table, or anywhere else where someone might be able to read the information contained therein. If an individual is working on a particular file, extreme care must be taken so that the file is not accessible to someone who might be in the office. At all times the client's confidence must be preserved.

THE CHRONOLOGICAL FILE

Some law offices require that a **chronological file** be kept of all outgoing correspondence. It is helpful when looking for a particular letter or memorandum that was sent out on a certain date, particularly in those offices that use centralized files. For example, if a letter was sent out on June 25, 2006, it may be found easily in the chronological file ("chron file.") Chron files are kept in chronological order with the most recent correspondence on top. They are generally kept for about six months to one year and then discarded by careful shredding so that no confidential information is readable. Copies of all correspondence are also kept in the regular files.

FILE SUBJECTS

Individual files are kept for each client in the law office. Other files may include specialty areas of law, by subject. Some law offices keep individual files of all research projects under their subject matter. Other offices keep a card file of cases used in performing legal research, with information about the particular case. In most instances, the filing system will have already been set up and the legal professional must perform the file functions within the parameters of the given system.

The best way to become familiar with the files is to read them. Some firms allow a new employee to spend the first day "on the job" reading the files.

ALPHABETICAL FILING SYSTEMS

Smaller law firms generally use some type of **alphabetical filing system.** Client files are arranged alphabetically with last name (surname) first. Nonclient files relating to the business of the law firm are arranged by subject, also in alphabetical order. Some examples of a firm's subject files include billing, timekeeping, management, human relations, accounting, pensions, benefits, and insurance. The subjects will vary by the size of the firm and the type of law practiced.

The system used for alphabetical filing is the same as that which is used in the telephone book. First consider the first letter of the surname, then the second letter, and so on. If there are two clients with the same first and last name, then use their middle initials to separate their files. The same names without initials go first; then names with initials, which are alphabetized; and then first names with middle names. For example, the proper method of arranging the following names follows:

> Long, Bill
> Long, Billy

chronological file   file of outgoing correspondence kept by date with most recent date on top

alphabetical filing system   client files are arranged alphabetically with last name (surname) first; generally used by smaller law firms

Long, Carol
Long, Carol B.
Long, Carol C.
Long, Carol Marie

When a name starts with a number, it is filed before other names. Numbers are filed first, numerically, followed by letters. For example:

21 Jump Street Company
555 Fifth Avenue Restaurant
Jonathan Clubs
Lewis Law Corporation

Some law firms arrange their files by the names of the cases. In those situations, use the surnames first, then the first names, of each party. The plaintiff's name always precedes the defendant's name, such as:

Adams, Eve v. Arnold, John W.
Barrister, L. v. Williams, J.
Rodriguez, S. v. Allen, J. T.
Stark, Diana W. v. Michaels, N.

Some firms prefer to file the case names with their own clients' names first, even when the client is the defendant. The legal professional should learn the system used in the firm and follow it. She should never attempt to completely redo the file system unless specifically instructed to do so by the attorney.

NUMERICAL FILING SYSTEMS

Numerical filing systems are generally used in law firms to protect the client's confidence. A number of different numerical systems may be used, including sequential numbering and case number. In sequential numbering, the files start at 1 and go upwards. Case numbers are usually four or five digits preceded by letters that denote the type of case. For instance, PI-4231 might refer to a personal injury case.

COLOR CODING

Strips of color at the top of the file folders indicate that the firm uses some type of color-coding system. Sometimes the colors are used to indicate a certain type of case. Other times the colors indicate which lawyer in the office is handling the case. Colored stickers may be added to indicate the court in which the case is filed. Some firms even use color coding within a file to indicate the type of correspondence or document.

numerical filing systems
files are numbered sequentially with cross-reference lists kept separately from the name of the client

REMOVING FILES

It is imperative that the firm has a system for retrieving files that have been removed. Most firms use an "out" card. The individual who removes the file replaces it with the "out" card with her signature and the date it was removed. The last name written on the "out" card will generally be the person who has the file.

Sometimes the "out" card is actually a file folder that is placed in the space from which the file folder was removed. This is usually done in the centralized file room where the file clerks will be inserting material into the folder until the actual file is returned.

COMPUTERIZED FILES

Many law firms are progressing to the use of the computer for their files, employing the use of **computer filing systems.** Each attorney in the firm inputs information and data into the file, which is accessible to other members of the firm. Different members of the firm will have information about a given topic available almost instantly. Confidentiality may be protected by having certain files "password protected." That is, only those parties who are working on a particular file will have the password to access the material therein. In this manner, several members of the case team will have access to the same material at the same time, whereas with paper files, only one person may review the file at one time.

In addition to the time saved, these files save considerable space in the office. In large metropolitan areas office space is at a premium and is very expensive. The firm will be able to have a smaller file room and pay less rent in a building when the files are computerized.

Documents may be scanned into the computer. One clerk may spend some time scanning all documents involved in a case into the computer at the same time. What might take up a room full of file cabinets will be accessible in a computer system that takes up considerably less space.

It is not uncommon for large firms involved in multiparty cases and/or class action cases to have to rent additional office space to accommodate the additional files, as well as hire additional personnel to manage these files. Although many of the pleadings and documents in a case must be preserved by having the original on paper, a large number of additional items may be preserved on a computer system. Files are easier to maintain and to locate when they are maintained in a computerized filing system.

One former student of the author was hired to develop a filing system for a large multiparty case. When she began working at the firm, her attorney/employer escorted her into a room filled with miscellaneous papers, and she was asked to organize them into a file for the case. She developed a computerized filing system that was easily accessible to all members of the firm who were working on the case. She received a promotion as a result of her diligence.

UTILIZING COMPUTERIZED FILING SYSTEMS

As an example of how computerized filing systems work in a legal setting, a system called "Legal Files" found at

http://www.legalfiles.com

computer filing systems software programs used for automating the filing system; categorize files and assign numbers if utilizing a numerical system will be discussed. Legal Files software provides the ability to keep track of one's time and provides litigation support. Documents may be assembled and managed. The office calendar and pending matters may be integrated into the system. Documents that were written in Word or other word-processing programs may be saved into the legal filing system.

To preserve confidentiality, users of the system may not have access to case documents unless they have access to the case file itself. If an individual is not assigned to the case, she may not gain access to that case file on the computer. An additional level of security allows access to the case and allows one to read the case materials but not make copies or changes to them.

ETHICS ISSUES

Many of the ethical considerations inherent in dealing with client files have been discussed above. It is important to remember that the most important ethical concern is protecting the client's confidence. Be aware of this concern when developing files and reviewing files.

Never place files in a place where others may read them. Do not leave open files on the desk and leave the office. Files should be put away when a visitor is present and when the office is not occupied. If working on a case in the office and many open files are scattered around the desk, a client interview should be conducted in a conference room or another office. Clients know that if they can read others' files on the desk, the next person interviewed will be able to read their file as well.

If the legal professional works in a large firm where only a few attorneys and legal assistants are working on a case, a password-protected file should be used for the case. The password should be given to only the members of the firm who are working on the case. General research files may usually be made available to others in the firm, however. Be sure that there is no confidential information in the material before it is placed into a general file accessible to everyone in the firm.

A database file should be maintained of all clients' names as well as other parties who have been involved in the firm's cases. Each time a prospective client wishes to hire the law firm, this database should be checked to be sure that the firm did not represent an adverse party in a prior suit against the client or the adverse party in the present case. Either scenario creates a conflict of interest situation that must be fully explained to the prospective client. If the client still chooses to hire the firm, a written agreement indicating that the client is aware of the prior conflict must be drafted by the attorney and signed by the client and the attorney.

The requirement for a writing varies by state. The student should research the requirements in her own state and complete the state-specific information box below.

> STATE-SPECIFIC INFORMATION BOX FOR THE STATE OF _____:
>
> This state _____ requires _____ does not require a written agreement with the client in a potential or prior conflict of interest situation.
>
> _____

OPENING THE FILE

Once it has been ascertained that no conflict of interest situation exists, the client's file will be opened. Some firms have standardized procedures for opening the file, and many of them are automated. Some systems will guide the legal professional to enter certain information about the file into the computer. These systems guide the maker through the whole file process by asking key questions such as the following:

1. Is there a potential conflict of interest? (Previously or at this time, check the database of clients and cases in which the firm is involved to determine whether there is a conflict of interest situation.)

   If yes, notify the attorney.

   If no, proceed with opening the file.

2. What is the statute of limitations for this case? (The legal professional should be familiar with the statute of limitations for the type of cases in which the firm is engaged.)

   Insert this information into the file and into your office's docket control and tickler systems.

3. What is the date that the file is being opened? (Use today's date.)

4. Did another client recommend this client to the firm? (Note that if this is the case, a "thank you" letter may be sent, depending on the attorney's policies.)

The maker of the file then proceeds to enter certain information pertinent to the case into the file, which includes the following:

1. Client's name, address, telephone number, fax number, and e-mail address.

2. Same information as in #1 for the opposing party and her attorney.

3. Names of all members of the firm who are working on the case, along with the type of billing used for each individual. For example, is the attorney working on this case hourly or on a

contingency basis? This information will be used by the billing department when reproducing bills for the client.

4. Type of case and a brief paragraph about the facts of the case.

5. List of witnesses or potential witnesses, along with their addresses, telephone numbers, fax numbers, and e-mail addresses. (This information may usually be obtained from the client.)

The above information will serve as a cover sheet for the file and should be placed immediately inside the file folder. Some firms may keep a separate notebook of the cover sheets for each client's file.

Files in law offices are usually arranged so that the correspondence goes on the right side of the inside of the folder and the pleadings and legal documents go on the left. Each pleading and document will have a small tab on the bottom that indicates its name. If there are multiple parties in the case, there may either be separate folders for each party or separate tabs in the folder for each party. Remember that a folder may be a paper folder or a folder in the computer in an automated system. In a large case with numerous documents and pleadings, there may be separate file folders for correspondence, pleadings, and discovery documents.

Many companies sell organizers for case files. Organizers for a civil case may be found in Exhibit 8–1. Organizers for a criminal case are found in Exhibit 8–2. These organizers assist the file's maker in organizing the file. Software packages are also available for this purpose.

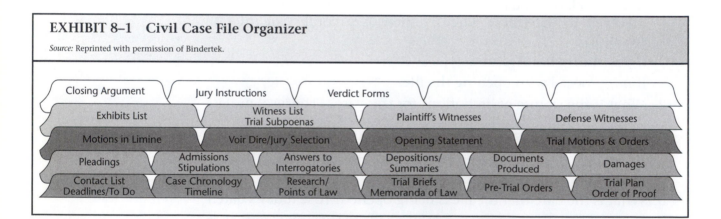

EXHIBIT 8–1   Civil Case File Organizer

Source: Reprinted with permission of Bindertek.

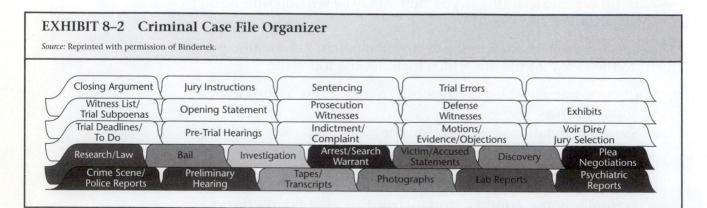

EXHIBIT 8–2   Criminal Case File Organizer

Source: Reprinted with permission of Bindertek.

■ KEY TERMS

Alphabetical filing systems   Computer filing system
Centralized file   Decentralized or local filing system
Chronological file   Numerical filing system

■ SELF TEST

1. List two ethical considerations when opening a file.

2. What are the advantages and disadvantages of a centralized filing system?

3. Which type of filing system is usually used in a small law office?

4. What information is included when opening a new case file?

■ NOTEBOOK PROJECTS

1. Research a computerized filing system on the Internet. Obtain information about the system and include it in your notebook.

2. Prepare a list of topics to be included in a subject file for a civil litigation law firm.

3. Make a list of computerized document control systems that have Web sites along with their Web addresses.

For additional resources, visit our Web site at **www.westlegalstudies.com**

COMMUNICATIONS

CHAPTER OUTCOMES

As a result of studying this chapter, the student will learn:

1. the proper way to address various individuals.
2. the format of e-mail and letters.
3. how to write different types of letters and e-mail.
4. how to answer the telephone.
5. the correct approach to oral communications.

E-MAIL

Since **e-mail** is so much faster than regular mail ("snail mail"), more individuals are utilizing this method of written communication. It is not unusual to receive 40 to 50 e-mails a day. Attorneys typically receive about 50 e-mails a day.

Although e-mail is a more informal method of written communication than letters, it is important to remember that one should always be professional in his approach to writing e-mail. Some offices use a memorandum format for e-mail and leave out the **salutation** and **closing** portions. Other offices eliminate an inside address and use the salutation and closing. Before sending e-mail in your office, check the files to determine the proper method to use. Exhibit 9–1 contains some typical approaches to writing e-mail.

E-mail is generally more informal than a letter. However, any e-mail sent out from the law office should be professionally written. Therefore, avoid contractions, slang expressions, and the type of informal language you might use for an e-mail to a friend. The salutation "Hi Dee," may be used to address a friend, but for a professional e-mail from a law office, the salutation would be "Dear Ms. Jackson:" A comma may be used after a salutation to a friend ("Hi Susie,") but a colon should be used on a business e-mail ("Dear Mr. Samuels:").

One should be careful what is sent from an office computer because most employers will monitor e-mail as well as Internet activity. The Federal Electronic Communications Privacy Act (ECPA) has given employers the right to examine all e-mail and Internet activity emanating from their computers. Several companies have been forced to produce

e-mail electronic mail sent on the computer via the Internet

salutation greeting at the beginning of correspondence

closing line before the signature line used in formal communications

---

EXHIBIT 9–1   Typical Approaches to Writing E-Mail

1. **No salutation or closing**

Heading: To: X

From: Y

Subject: Case No. XXW

Begin your e-mail here after the subject line. Do not put in a salutation.
You may wish to put your name and title at the end of the e-mail, such as:

Susie Smith
Legal Professional

2. **With salutation and closing**

Heading: To: X

From: Y

Subject: Case No. XXX

Dear Mr. Jones:

The e-mail goes here after the salutation. The closing goes at the end.

Sincerely yours,*
Jack Smith
Legal Assistant

*If the e-mail is to a business associate that is not also a friend, then the proper closing would
be "Very truly yours,". Your firm's confidentiality statement should accompany e-mail under
the signature.

---

e-mail by the courts, and many companies have defended sexual
harassment suits because of their employees' e-mails and/or Internet
activity. Many employers feel that they may reduce their legal responsibility or liability if they closely monitor the Internet activity and
e-mail of their employees.

A good virus protection program is essential if e-mail or the Internet
is being used on a regular basis. Some virus protection programs will
scan all e-mails to be sure they do not contain a virus. If an e-mail is

received from an unfamiliar source, it should be deleted if there is any possibility that it may contain a virus. At one time, the author opened an e-mail from an unfamiliar source and received a virus that destroyed all material on the hard drive of her computer. All files had to be reloaded, and items that were not backed up were lost forever.

Netiquette

E-mail has its own form of etiquette, which governs the manner in which the sender conducts himself when communicating by e-mail. It is considered rude to violate the general rules of conduct for e-mail. Here are a few generally accepted rules for communicating by e-mail:

1. Do not use all capital letters within the e-mail; this is taken to be shouting at the recipient and is frowned upon.

2. Only one subject should be used in each e-mail.

3. Do not send private information by e-mail. Remember that it takes a few clicks of the keys to forward your e-mail to another individual, and your e-mail may be read by the administrator of the system.

4. Never give your password or user ID to another individual. If someone else were to send e-mail using your user ID and password, a recipient would believe the communication came from you.

5. E-mail should be short and to the point.

6. Do not make derogatory remarks in an e-mail. The e-mail may be easily forwarded and could start a "flame war" where individuals angrily respond to each other's derogatory e-mails. Nothing is accomplished by the use of this type of e-mail.

7. Be sure that the recipient of the e-mail has been informed of your name and status. Most people will not open mail from names they do not recognize because of the fear of obtaining a virus or worm that could damage their computer or erase their hard drive.

8. If your system has this capability, request a return receipt that indicates when the recipient has read your message. Keep the receipts if the e-mail is related to a case.

9. Use spell check for e-mails and other methods of written communication.

10. Check for incoming e-mails at least twice a day: once the first thing in the morning and again in the early afternoon. You may also wish to check a third time in the late afternoon.

11. Set aside a certain time of day to answer e-mails.

12. Do not use emoticons in business e-mail. (Emoticons are faces that are smiling, happy, sad, and so on.) For instance, ☺ means "happy."; These expressions should be reserved for your personal e-mails.

Maintaining Confidentiality with E-Mail

As discussed earlier, it is often difficult to maintain privacy when using e-mail. This is particularly problematic when someone sends a confidential communication to a client via e-mail. In most cases, the courts have held that a lawyer must take reasonable precautions to protect the attorney-client privilege in the use of e-mail communications. Some firms have encryption software so that messages are sent out in code. However, most encryption software must be used by both the law office and the client to preserve its coding capabilities. Many firms have standard confidentiality statements that are affixed to all outgoing e-mails and other correspondence.

The state bars of many states have considered the problem of using e-mail for privileged communications. The rules vary by state. Some states require that clients sign a document verifying that they understand the dangers of sending confidential information via e-mail. Others have stated that there is a reasonable expectation of privacy when using e-mail. Find the rules for your own state and list them below.

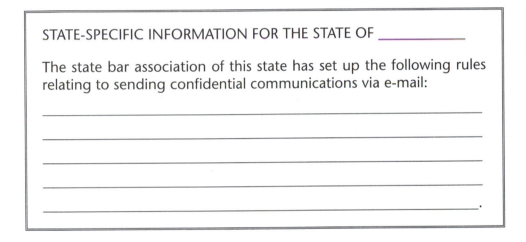

STATE-SPECIFIC INFORMATION FOR THE STATE OF _____

The state bar association of this state has set up the following rules relating to sending confidential communications via e-mail:

_____

_____

_____

_____

_____ .

Filing E-mail

Imagine the filing problem if you receive 50 e-mails each day. Many of these communications could be "junk mail" such as advertisements and unsolicited requests. Others may contain objectionable material that has been sent to a large number of addresses.

Some computers have filters for e-mail that automatically delete questionable e-mails or those containing objectionable material. Some e-mail may be kept for a certain period of time, and others may be archived on your computer and/or copied for your files.

WRITING LETTERS

Fewer letters are being sent by law firms since the advent of e-mail. However, some clients may not have e-mail capability. Letters may also be used for more formal communications. To determine the style of letter used in your office, review the files for letter format. The most common letter formats are block and modified block. An illustration of each may be found in Exhibits 9–2 and 9–3.

EXHIBIT 9–2 Sample Letter Using Modified Block Format

(Firm Letterhead)

Today's Date

Name of recipient
Address
City, State ZIP Code

Re: Subject of the letter; usually the case name or client name

Dear Ms. Client:

{The body of the letter goes here.)

Very truly yours,
James A. Roberts
Attorney at Law

JAR:urs

EXHIBIT 9–3 Sample Letter Using Block Format

(Firm Letterhead)

Today's date

Name of Recipient
Address
City, State ZIP Code

Re: Subject of the letter; usually the case name or client name

Dear Ms. Client:

{The body of the letter goes here, flush with the left margin.)

Very truly yours,
Jane L. Sanchez
Attorney at Law

JLS:urs

Titles

Clients are usually addressed by their titles (Mr., Ms., Dr., and so on) and surnames (last names) when writing a letter. Listed below are some proper forms for address:

1. Mr. James A. Roberts
2. Ms. Jane A. Bell
3. Dr. Alice Coop   (medical doctor or PhD)
4. Judge Harry Adams   (trial court judge)
5. Justice James Roberts   (appellate or supreme court justice)
6. Reverend Ann Smith   (clergy)
7. Father Hugh Curran   (priest)

Templates

Whenever the same type of letter has been written several times to different individuals, a template should be made of the letter using a word-processing program. This letter may be reused each time a different person is addressed by merely filling in the blanks. For instance, a letter of confirmation regarding a meeting with a client should always be sent to the client. With a template of this type letter, the legal professional only needs to change the name and address, and the date and time, instead of having to retype the letter every time an appointment is being confirmed.

INTERNAL MEMORANDA

Several different formats are used by firms when sending out memoranda to other members of the firm. Sometimes these memoranda are sent via e-mail. One format for a memorandum is shown in Exhibit 9–4.

In most cases, memoranda are initialed by the sender. Some firms require a full signature on internal correspondence. The **research memorandum** may have a slightly different format. Exhibit 9–5 shows the format for a typical research memorandum.

EXHIBIT 9–4   Internal Memorandum

                                                          Date

MEMORANDUM TO: (Recipient)

FROM: (Sender)

RE: Subject

(Body text)

---

research memorandum informal memorandum sent to a member of the law firm answering a legal question

---

EXHIBIT 9–5   Research Memorandum

Date

MEMORANDUM TO: Recipient

FROM: Sender

RE: Issue to be addressed (This section, referred to as the *subject line*, is usually phrased in the form of a question)

BACKGROUND INFORMATION / FACTS
(write the background information/facts)

LEGAL ISSUES ADDRESSED
(write the legal issues)

APPLICATION OF LAW TO FACTS
(write the application of law to facts)

CONCLUSION
(write the conclusion)

Some firms prefer that the conclusion be given after the subject line, which contains the issue to be addressed. Others use the same format as is used for the case brief, with the following subject headings:

1. Issue addressed
2. Rule of law applied
3. Application of law to the facts
4. Conclusion

Be sure to consult the attorney's files to determine the proper format for writing research memoranda. Since this type of correspondence is usually quite extensive, it is important to include the relevant issues and explanations only. Perhaps 10 other cases were found that did not relate to the case before finding the one that applied. In that case, discuss only the case that applies to the facts of the initial case and do not spend several pages discussing the cases found that were irrelevant.

FOLLOW-UP

Whenever a legal professional sends out a letter, e-mail, or memorandum that requires the recipient to respond, he should place a copy of the correspondence in the tickler file under a date that is a few days before the answer is due. On that date, either call or write to the recipient asking them for their response.

Some due dates are especially critical, particularly those that require a filing with the court or a court appearance. In those cases, be sure the recipient understands the gravity of making a timely response. In your original correspondence, ask for a response about a week before your response is due with the court. Some situations may require that an earlier due date is given to the individual, such as when the document being filed with the court is particularly complicated and lengthy.

If the original correspondence was for the purpose of setting up a meeting or an interview, call the recipients to determine whether or not they will attend the conference. In general, the same people will respond late each time they have a due date. In those cases, give them a slightly earlier due date to make up for their late responses.

ORAL COMMUNICATIONS

Oral Communications with the Attorney

On a day-to-day basis, most **oral communications** will be with the attorney. The most common problems encountered in this regard are that the attorney may be under a degree of stress due to pressures imposed by deadlines, and the attorney may have unfair expectations of the legal professional's abilities.

One of the most important rules to remember when working with an attorney is that the primary job is to save time for the lawyer so that he is free to perform other tasks. All tasks should be accomplished accurately and in a timely fashion. If it is impossible to complete a job on time, tell the attorney or office manager before the deadline so that assistance can be obtained.

The following is a list of the more common expectations and requirements an attorney has for a legal professional:

1. **Receive and understand instructions for each assignment.**
   Remember that attorneys are often very busy and may assume that their instructions are understood even when they are unclear. All instructions should be written down by the legal professional. Repeat any instructions that are unclear back to the attorney for clarification. Never begin an assignment until it is known exactly what is expected. It may take several hours to complete what is interpreted as what the attorney wants, only to find that what he really wanted would have taken a much shorter period of time. The most important consideration with any assignment is its due date. It is helpful to receive the client's file at the same time as the assignment is received so that background information can be found, such as names, spellings, and other key information that might be needed for the accomplishment of the task.

2. **Communicate limitations.**
   If given an assignment that you are not capable of completing, be sure to indicate this to the attorney at the outset. If you are a new legal professional, the attorney may not be familiar with your capabilities. However, if you can obtain guidance on how to complete the assignment by doing a minimal amount of research, try

oral communications
communicating via your voice by telephone or in person

to accomplish the task before admitting defeat. The attorney may become impatient when the assistant makes the same mistakes over and over again, so all work should be checked and proofread carefully.

3. **Be willing to accept responsibility.**
Approach new tasks with a smile and enthusiastically. Be ready to accept added responsibility. If the legal professional grudgingly accepts a new assignment with a scowl, he may be relegated to the more mundane tasks, which can make the job very boring.

4. **Take notes.**
Never enter the attorney's office without a pen and notebook in your hand. Expect instructions each time you see the attorney and don't expect to remember them on your own. Write everything down. Keep the instructions in a notebook even after the assignment is completed. Date the notebook at the beginning of each day so that the date the assignment was given is available for future reference. Note its due date.

5. **Listen carefully.**
One of the major causes of errors in assignments is not listening carefully. Listen to every word the attorney says and take good notes. Do not expect to remember instructions without writing them down. If the instructions are not clear, ask questions.

6. **Record instructions for later use.**
If a particular type of task is being completed for the first time, type up the instructions and put them in a notebook of completed projects for future reference. When the attorney has a similar assignment, the instructions may be found easily in the Notebook.

7. **Review the files.**
If time permits, review the client's file to obtain background information on the assignment. If you are asked to do a type of project that you have not done before, ask the attorney if a sample can be obtained from another client's file. Make copies of each sample for the Notebook.

8. **Review the assignment.**
Read through the instructions before starting the assignment to determine whether it is clear what has to be done. If there are further questions, make a list and ask the attorney all of them (ideally, when he has time to give good explanations). Never ask several different questions at dissimilar times if it is possible to ask them all at the same time.

9. **Do the work in a timely fashion.**
Keep in mind the assignment's deadline. Work efficiently and accurately. Check and recheck the work. Remember that using spell check is not enough because the wrong word may be written, and it will not be noted because it is an actual word. For example, writing "there" for "their" would not be noted by spell check.

10. **Prioritize projects.**
Prioritizing projects is particularly important when working for more than one attorney. Know which job is the most important

and should be completed first. If unsure, ask both attorneys or the office manager.

11. **Assemble the finished product neatly.**
Complete the project accurately and be sure there are no smudges on the document. Correct any errors in grammar, sentence structure, and spelling. Staple multiple pages in the upper left corner. Reread the document one last time to be sure there are no errors. Depending on the attorney's preference, put the finished project in a folder, an "in box," or another place preferred by that attorney. If the project requires the attorney's signature, be sure that he will be in the office on the date the job is completed.

Oral Communications with Other Law Firm Employees

Maintain the same positive attitude when dealing with all employees of the firm. Remember that individuals will protect their territories and domains, so always follow proper procedures when taking books from the library, taking files from the file room, or removing materials that are supervised by another individual.

Avoid office gossip. The confidentiality issue makes this particularly sensitive in the law office environment.

As a new member of the law office team, do not attempt to make changes in procedures. Never use the expression, "But they did it this way at the last firm where I worked." After the legal professional has been with the firm for some time, he may attempt to establish new procedures, but should do so very carefully and sensitively. Others are usually not receptive to criticism.

Requests

From time to time, the legal professional will be required to request information or items from other individuals or law firms. The manner in which this is accomplished will predict whether the request will be met in a timely manner. Be polite and courteous in making the request, and give the recipient of the request plenty of time to comply. If the items needed must be received by a certain date, ask for the information several days ahead of time. One important point to remember: one's deadlines are irrelevant to others. Therefore, be especially courteous when asking for any information that must be received by a certain date.

After the items have been received, be sure to write a "thank you" letter to the individual who provided the material to you. Remember that the appreciative person is more likely to receive a prompt response the next time information or material is sought.

Telephone Calls To The Court

It is often difficult to reach the court clerk's office to ask for information about a case. Be sure to have the case number any time information is requested. Some courts have become so overburdened that they will only answer requests about cases in person. Call the local courthouse where the attorney you work with practices and ask if they allow telephone inquiries about cases; if not, ask whether an appearance in person is required to make a request. Also ask them if they have an e-mail address and/or Web site for requests for information or forms or court documents.

Face-To-Face Communications

When you are introduced to someone for the first time, extend your hand and display a firm handshake. A firm handshake is very positive body language. However, be sure the handshake is not so firm that it injures the recipient.

If at a meeting or a large gathering, you may be required to introduce yourself to someone. In that case, walk up to the person, offer your hand, and identify yourself.

Keep a polite smile on your face and look at the person as they speak. It is annoying to have a conversation with someone who is looking everywhere else but at you while you are speaking. Do not interrupt the other person; wait until they finish their sentence and then make a comment, answer a question, or respond appropriately.

If meeting a trial court judge, the proper method of addressing him is by "Judge Johnson." An appellate court or supreme court justice should be addressed "Justice Johnson." Never address an attorney or judge by his first name unless he specifically requests that he be addressed in that manner.

■ KEY TERMS

Closing	Research memorandum
E-mail	Salutation
Oral communications	

■ SELF TEST

1. List the methods of addressing the following individuals:

   (a) the attorney for whom you work

   (b) Ms. Jones, the attorney for the adverse party

   (c) John Sanchez, your client

   (d) Jeffrey Gallo, the local trial judge

   (e) Danielle Maris, an appellate justice

2. List five items to remember when you are receiving instructions from the attorney.

3. Write an e-mail to your instructor asking a question about this chapter.

■ NOTEBOOK PROJECTS

1. Call the local courthouse where the attorney you work with practices and ask if they allow telephone inquiries about cases and, if not, whether you have to appear in person to make a request. Also ask them if they have an e-mail address and/or Web site for requests for information or forms or court documents. Record this information in your notebook.

2. Prepare a letter to your client informing him of an upcoming court date two weeks from today at 10:00 a.m. at the local trial court. Be sure to include the address of the court. Your client's name and address are: Nicole Rodriguez, 459 Thimble Lane, Your City, Your State. The name of the case is *Rodriguez v. Campbell,* Case No. PI-44455.

For additional resources, visit our Web site at **www.westlegalstudies.com**

MAIL AND DOCKET CONTROL SYSTEMS

CHAPTER OUTCOMES

As a result of studying this chapter, the student will learn:

1. how to create an incoming mail log.
2. how to keep track of incoming mail.
3. how to prepare outgoing mail and e-mail.
4. how to route mail to appropriate individuals.
5. how to determine deadlines from incoming and outgoing mail.
6. about the calendar deadlines.
7. how to answer routine correspondence for the attorney.

INCOMING MAIL LOG

Most law offices receive a large amount of mail each day. The efficient legal assistant will keep track of the mail by using an **incoming mail log.** This log will indicate the date of the mail, the date received, the sender, the recipient, the subject, and the disposition. Any disposition that must be followed up, such as routing to another individual to answer, should be written in red to alert the legal assistant that action is required. A typical outline for an incoming mail log is shown in Exhibit 10–1. This sample log is made for one individual attorney. If the legal professional is maintaining the log for more than one attorney, then either separate logs should be kept or a separate column after the dates should be headed "to" with the recipient's name or initials noted.

The legal professional should review the log every few days to determine whether or not those items requiring action have been handled. If the mail states a deadline, court date, or appointment date, the date and time should be recorded on the calendar or in the tickler file. Deadlines are critical in a law office, and the legal professional must be certain that they are met.

Incoming mail logs may be kept in a notebook with entries made by hand, or on the computer.

incoming mail log a notebook or other type of log that will indicate the date of the incoming mail, the date received, the sender, the recipient, the subject, and the disposition.

INCOMING CORRESPONDENCE

Incoming correspondence should be stamped with the date and time it was received, logged into the mail log promptly, and given to the attorney.

EXHIBIT 10-1   Incoming Mail Log Headings

FOR: Jeffrey W. Daniels, Attorney

From

Dated

Date recd

Subject

Disposition

In some cases, the legal professional will forward the correspondence to another member of the law firm for a response. These instances should be noted in the mail log.

If the legal professional is able to answer the questions asked in a piece of correspondence, she should prepare a draft answer and include it with the original correspondence sent to the attorney. In this manner, the attorney may merely make appropriate revisions to the answering correspondence instead of being required to prepare a complete answer. However, the first few times this method is used, the answering correspondence should be labeled "Draft" or the attorney may feel that the assistant is being presumptuous to think that she can answer the attorney's letters.

In most cases, the attorney will not want to see "junk mail" such as advertisements. Some attorneys will require the legal professional to handle certain items on her own. For example, if a letter arrives from the court with a due date for a certain document or pleading, some attorneys would prefer that the legal professional merely make a notation of the date in the tickler file and file the correspondence itself. The due date should also be noted about a week ahead of time and three days ahead of time to give the attorney time to prepare the document.

Some attorneys, however, may wish to see all correspondence and will note the due dates in their own tickler files. The legal professional in those cases should always keep her own tickler file in which the due dates are noted so that she may remind the attorney of pending deadlines.

Personal correspondence should never be opened by the legal assistant without the permission of the attorney. This mail will be stamped "Personal," "Personal and Confidential," or "Confidential" on the envelope. Log this mail in and write "personal," "personal and confidential," or "confidential" in the subject heading in the mail log.

INCOMING MAIL FOLDER

Because most correspondence that arrives in the law office is related to a client's case, it is considered to be a privileged communication and its contents should be protected. Therefore, all incoming correspondence should be placed in a folder that is labeled "INCOMING MAIL FOLDER FOR <NAME>" and placed in the attorney's in-box.

If the attorney is out of town or will be out of the office for a period of time, the assistant should keep the folder of incoming mail locked in her desk. Generally, attorneys who are out of the office will call in to get their telephone messages and important mail, or will designate another attorney in the office to handle their cases. If another attorney is handling the attorney's business while she is out of the office, the mail should be routed to her for handling. Make a copy of the mail in the event it is inadvertently misplaced. Note the name of the individual who receives the mail in the mail log.

Some law firms require that all incoming first-class mail that pertains to a client's file be copied for the attorney while the original is retained for the files. This practice alleviates the time it takes to search for an item that has come into the office and become lost in piles of papers.

OUTGOING MAIL

All correspondence that is sent out of the office reflects on the proficiency of the law firm. If the mail contains typographical errors and misspelled words, the recipient will have a poor opinion of the law firm. Therefore, it is imperative that all outgoing mail be proofread carefully for misspellings, grammatical errors, transposed numbers, or errors in numbers. Even though your computer will have a method for checking spelling, you must still proofread all outgoing mail because the spell check feature will not distinguish between words that are spelled correctly but used in the wrong context. For instance, if you use "their" when you should have used "there," the computer will not indicate that an error exists.

In many firms, the attorney will type her own correspondence and documents and e-mail them directly to the clients. In some cases, the mail may not be formatted properly or proofread. The legal professional should urge the attorney to allow her to review correspondence and documents before they have been disseminated to correct errors in format, spelling, or grammar.

CHRONOLOGICAL FILE

In many cases, it is desirable to keep a chronological file of all outgoing correspondence. This file, called a "chron file" for short, is arranged chronologically with the most recent correspondence on top. The chron file contains an additional copy of the outgoing correspondence, which is therefore sometimes easier to find if it was sent out in the last day or two. This method is particularly valuable when the files are kept in a centralized location and most requests are for recent outgoing mail. In some firms, this file is referred to as a "reading file."

For example, suppose the attorney asks for a letter that was sent out yesterday in a certain case. It may be faster and easier to look in the chronological file under yesterday's correspondence than to walk to the file room to find the correspondence in the regular files. By keeping both a mail log and extra copy of incoming correspondence and a chronological file of outgoing correspondence, it will be difficult to misplace a letter.

ROUTING MAIL

In a large law firm where you are working for an attorney who supervises several other attorneys and paralegals, the legal professional may be required to route mail to several individuals. In general, any legal newspapers, magazines, periodicals, and cases are routed by means of routing slips with the names or initials of all attorneys and/or paralegals who are supervised by your attorney. In some cases, the supervising attorney may wish to see the periodical before it is routed.

As the legal professional becomes more familiar with the manner in which the law firm operates, she will become aware of which individuals you should route certain items to. For instance, one of the attorneys on the attorney's team may be involved in civil litigation. The local legal newspaper may have a new case on that topic that would be of interest to that particular attorney, so the newspaper would be routed to her first.

If the firm does not have a special routing stamp or routing slip to use when circulating material to all members of the office team, the legal professional might either suggest the purchase of a stamp or make up a routing slip and make copies on your printer.

CALENDARING DEADLINES

Many deadlines involving cases in the office are found in the incoming mail. Different offices have different systems for calendaring these deadlines. One of the most efficient methods is by use of a computer program that is accessible to the legal professional and the attorney. One former student worked in a law office where the office deadlines for each day appeared on each staff member's computer every morning when the computer was accessed. Several different programs are available for calendaring purposes.

When the incoming mail arrives in the office, log it into the mail log and read it to determine whether a deadline or due date is included in the correspondence. If so, note the date on the calendar as well as a few days ahead of time. If the due date is for a complicated project, note it several days ahead, three days ahead, and on the actual due date. It may also be necessary to make a copy of the calendar each morning and place it in the attorney's in-box.

TICKLER FILES

A number of different methods exist for scheduling the lawyer's commitments, from the simple desk calendar to the complex document control system. Many computer software packages are available for these purposes. Overlooking a deadline in a law office can be extremely critical. In some cases, if the attorney neglects to file a document with the court by the due date, her client may be barred from continuing the lawsuit. This could result in sanctions from the court as well as a malpractice suit by the client. Recent studies have shown that most legal malpractice cases are filed because of missed deadlines. Therefore, the tickler file used in the office must ensure that all deadlines are met and that work has been allocated so that assignments are completed on time.

Most large firms will utilize a computerized system for its tickler files. Smaller firms may also use a computerized system. Depending on the size of the firm, others may use a simple desk calendar, a card box with cards by month and date, or a file with folders by date. The most important part of any tickler file is that it is checked each day for the following day to determine what is due that day.

DOCKET CONTROL SYSTEMS

The docket control system contains all due dates, including deadlines for filing documents, appointments, court dates, dates for meetings and depositions, and dates for following up and for reminders. If a comprehensive docket control system is utilized by the firm, deadlines will be met and malpractice cases will be reduced.

The size of the law firm usually dictates the sophistication of the docket control system. A small firm may use a desk calendar to note all due dates. As the firm gets larger, the system may be transferred to the computer.

In a large law firm, all deadlines may be entered on a centralized calendar that is controlled by a docket control clerk. This is often a first job for the aspiring legal assistant. The centralized calendar contains all due dates for all attorneys in the law firm, including deadlines for documents, court dates, meeting dates, and dates for depositions or other more informal hearings. Usually a computerized system accessible to all members of the law firm is used. Each member of the law office is responsible for updating her own calendar information on the system, which will then be accessible to other members of the firm. Generally, the attorney's name, date, time, case name, client name, subject (such as "trial" or "deposition"), and location are included. A typical entry may be written as follows:

> Wed. 8/5
> 9:00 a.m.   JAD—Hearing, ICC;
>   Washington, DC;
>   SantaFe v. NYC RR.

This entry may be interpreted as follows:

> An attorney with the firm with the initials JAD has a hearing with the Interstate Commerce Commission at 9:00 a.m. on August 5, in the case of *Santa Fe v. Central Railroad*.

If more information is needed about this particular hearing, the reader would contact JAD's legal assistant to receive additional material. For instance, if there is an urgent matter that requires JAD's attention immediately, the legal assistant would know how to reach the attorney.

Each individual member of the law firm must also have the pertinent information that is included on the centralized calendar on her own calendar, and this information should also appear on the calendar of the legal assistant involved. However, only the information pertaining to that particular attorney would be entered on the individual "tickler file." Included therein would be that particular attorney's deadlines, including trial dates, court dates, meeting dates, and due dates. The legal professional would also note additional dates in her tickler file with lead time for the completion of items that have deadlines. For instance, if the attorney is deposing the adverse party in a lawsuit, the legal professional should note not only the date of the deposition but an additional date approximately one week ahead of time to remind the attorney that she should begin preparing questions for the deposition. Every item noted in the individual tickler file should contain a notation three times:

1. on the due date or date of trial or meeting
2. three days before the due date as a last-minute reminder
3. one or two weeks before the due date depending on the complexity of the matter.

With a computerized docket control system, all items that require action on the part of the attorney keep appearing on the calendar until they are completed. Once local court holidays are inputted, the system will automatically adjust court deadlines for holidays and weekends. The master calendar may be printed after inputting the information one time for each item, as well as individual calendars, group calendars, and client and court calendars The master calendar may be checked for conflicts and appointments may be rescheduled in a few seconds.

Court deadlines may be automatically scheduled for different cases, different practice areas, or multiple locations. When an event is rescheduled, all related events will be automatically rescheduled at the same time.

Samples of a court docket and a printout of a weekly calendar appear as Exhibits 10–2 and 10–3.

DESK CALENDAR

Each individual in the law office will have a personal desk calendar on her desk, which may be in the form of a small desk calendar, with a space on each day for noting items under the time of day with a separate page for notes. Some attorneys prefer a binder that is covered and has spaces on each date for notations. Each office will have its own calendars in place and the legal professional should adapt to whatever type is being utilized. With a computerized system, each individual calendar will be automatically updated whenever the notation is placed on the master calendar if it involves that particular individual.

EXHIBIT 10–2   A Sample Court Docket

Source: From Judy Long, *Office Procedures for the Legal Professional*, 1st ed. (Clifton Park, NY: Thomson/Delmar, 2005). Reprinted with permission of Delmar Learning, a division of Thomson Learning: http://www.thomsonrights.com. Fax 800-730-2215.

SUPERIOR COURT DOCKET SLIP

Weiss & Richardson

June 23, 200x

Time	Case	Courtroom	Attorney
9:00 a.m.	Wilson v. Beck	B22, North Superior Court	Evans
9:00 a.m.	Sanchez v. Johns	D44, Hadley Municipal Court	Richardson
2:00 p.m.	Alter v. Rio	B25, North Superior Court	Michaels
3:00 p.m.	Stand v. Ross	C44, North Superior Court	Richardson

COMPUTERIZED SYSTEMS

One particularly comprehensive computerized docket control system is offered by AbacusLaw, whose Web site may be found at

http://www.abacuslaw.com

This company builds its systems so that the least computer-literate person in the law firm will be able to use the system effectively with a very short introduction. Their systems include computer systems for calendars, case files, conflicts of interest, contacts, communications, court rules, documents, e-mails, time and billing, and accounting functions. Exhibit 10–4 shows an example of their computerized calendar system for the law office.

These computerized calendars eliminate duplicate work on several calendars. All changes to the calendar are made at one time, on the master calendar, and individual calendars are always correct. When a docket date is entered using court rules, the legal professional will enter just the major events, such as the trial date, and all dependent deadlines will be accurately calendared based on local court rules or the individual practice requirements. If an event is rescheduled, the dependent deadlines will be automatically rescheduled.

For those offices requiring a conflict of interest system, a system is available that will check all potential opposing party names and/or social security numbers instantly against every former contact, calendar event, case file, and note in the law office. This avoids a situation where a client is retained by the firm but must be "conflicted out" at a later date because it is learned that she has a relationship to a former client.

EXHIBIT 10–3   A Sample Printout of a Weekly Calendar

COMPULAW, LTD.
WEEK AT A GLANCE

Page 1

Report for Courtney C. Richards
For the week beginning March 18, 2007

Monday 18	Tuesday 19	Wednesday 20	Thursday 21	Friday 22
9:00 a.m. Case Tools Corporation CTC v. Bren Industries, Inc. 10056.003 Hearing Los Angeles Superior Court Defendant's motions to dismiss.	9:30 a.m. to 12:00 p.m. Apex Construction Company v. Jones APEX-001 Deposition Office Depo of Lawrence G. Smith at the offices of West & Rains, 1400 West North Street, 21st floor.	No Time Precision Parts, Inc. v. United Systems, Inc. PREC-001 Discovery Office LAST COURT DAY FOR RESPONSE TO INTERROGATORIES TO BE SERVED. See Document #11.	No Time Apex Construction Company v. Jones APEX-001 Discovery Office LAST COURT DAY FOR RESPONSE TO INTERROGATORIES TO BE SERVED.	8:30 a.m. to 10:00 a.m. Office Administration Meetings 0000-001 Meeting: Office Related Office Meeting to discuss the great new features of our calendar program. The new WEEK AT A GLANCE report can be printed in land-scape format. We have the option to print the TRI-CAL on top or bottom. Quick review should make it very easy for attorneys to look at their schedules.
1:00 p.m. to 4:00 p.m. Apex Construction Company v. Jones APEX-001 Meeting: Client Office Discuss settlement offer.	*Due on 05/28/2005 No Time Acme Refrigeration Acme vs. The March Group ACME-001 Trial and Pretrial Dates Santa Monica Superior Court THE DATE THAT THIS CASE IS SET FOR JURY OR NONJURY TRIAL.	10:00 a.m. Precision Parts, Inc. v. United Systems, Inc. PREC-001 Deposition Opposing counsel's office Depo. of Lois West at the offices of Smith, Jones, Adams & Johnson, 21st floor.	12:00 p.m. Case Tools Corporation CTC v. Bren Industries, Inc. 10056.003 Meeting: Client Restaurant: Business Lunch with Howard Jones of CTC. Wong Chu Chinese Restaurant, 444 East April Lane.	5:00 p.m. Acme Refrigeration Acme v. The March Group ACME-001 Trial and Pretrial Dates Santa Monica Superior Court LAST COURT DAY TO FILE AND SERVE (BY HAND) NOTICE OF MOTION FOR SUM-MARY JUDGMENT. *** CHECK CURRENT LAW AND MOTION CALENDAR TO ASSURE AVAILABILITY OF HEARING DATE.
		5:00 p.m. Acme Refrigeration Acme v. The March Groupl ACME-001 Discovery Santa Monica Superior Court LAST COURT DAY TO SERVE (BY MAIL) REQUESTS FOR THE PRODUCTION OF DOCUMENTS. *** BE SURE TO ALLOW ENOUGH TIME TO MAKE A MOTION TO COMPEL.	5:00 p.m. Bell Computer Products Bell v. Delta Chips of GA 100092.001 Last day to file this action Los Angeles Superior Court Last court day to apply for correction of award. CCP 1284.	

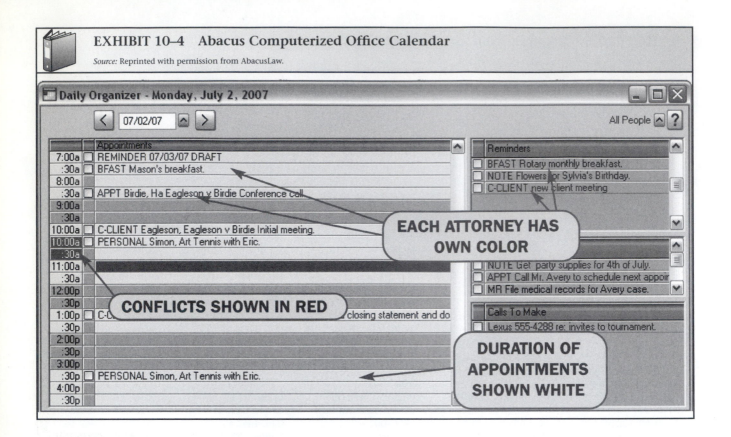

EXHIBIT 10–4 Abacus Computerized Office Calendar

Source: Reprinted with permission from AbacusLaw.

COMPUTERIZED DOCUMENT ASSEMBLY SYSTEMS

Abacus also offers a **computerized document assembly system** that integrates information into many different documents. When the document is scheduled to be completed, the system will automatically complete the document within a specified timeline. If an event with a timeline is calendared, all related events and documents will also be calendared. The legal professional would then click on "today's documents" to create the documents scheduled for each case. Any document may be linked to the documents database regardless of where it was created.

computerized document assembly system a system that integrates information into many different documents. When the document is scheduled to be completed, the system will automatically complete the document within the specified timeline

COMPUTERIZED TIMEKEEPING SYSTEMS

Abacus has also developed a unique timekeeping and accounting system whereby client data is input into the computer one time. The time spent working on the client's case is easily recorded and the fee calculated. The value of the service provided is added to the client's bill. A billing invoice is printed out for submittal to the client with the click of a mouse. All of these functions are completed upon the entry of one set of data. An example of this system is shown in Exhibit 10–5.

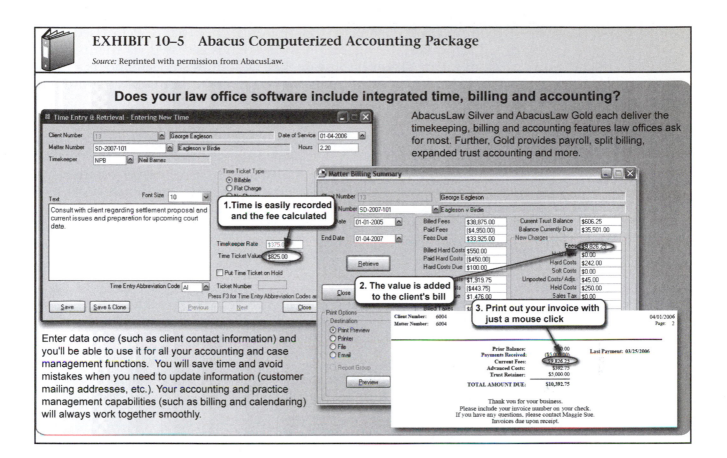

EXHIBIT 10–5   Abacus Computerized Accounting Package

Source: Reprinted with permission from AbacusLaw.

ONLINE CALENDARING AND DOCKET CONTROL PROGRAMS

A user-friendly calendaring program has been created by Deadlines On Demand™, LLC, a subsidiary of CompuLaw, LLC, and is available at

http://www.deadlines.com

The system is designed primarily for smaller law firms but is often used by larger firms as well. Forms are provided online for the user to enter the jurisdiction location, area of law, court location and date of the event (such as the trial date). The system then provides a complete and accurate list of all court deadlines in a matter of seconds. The list is displayed, e-mailed to the user, printed (if required) and can also be sent to the user's Microsoft Outlook® desktop calendar. Deadlines On Demand covers all 50 states, as well as federal jurisdictions.

A Unique Deadlines On Demand feature is the Change Notification System (CNS), provided to alert attorneys of recent court rules updates. E-mails are automatically sent to users when new court rule changes impact one or more of their recent searches, and Deadlines On Demand provides a convenient link to rerun each search that was affected. Since courts may issue changes in calendaring rules at any time, the change may be overlooked in a manual system. However, with the Deadlines On Demand system, the user is notified immediately and deadlines can be recalculated to reflect the new changes.

Deadlines On Demand is a subscription service that is Web-based. That is, all information available on the system is accessed via the Internet.

CompuLaw Vision™ software, like Deadlines On Demand, is a rules-based calendaring program. However, several other useful features are available with the CompuLaw Vision system, including:

1. **Matter Database Management**
   Records of key case information, event details, and other data may be stored and linked to documents, case notes, and other matter information. The Matter Information screen enables you to reach events, case notes, and documents with a single mouse click.

2. **Documents Database**
   All documents and information related to cases may be tracked and viewed. Documents stored in a central file location may be accessed.

3. **Report Writer**
   This function enables the user to design, filter, and print reports in several different formats, including options to send reports to other members of the law firm via e-mail.

4. **Case Notes**
   Unlimited case notes may be kept on the system and exported into other litigation management applications for case preparation or other functions.

5. **Related Parties Database**
   All parties related to every case may be tracked, including opposing counsel, judges, witnesses, experts, parties, and others. This item enables the user to find history on contacts and the parties they represented.

6. **Audit Trail System**
   Each time a change is made to the calendar, the system keeps track of the individual who made the change, the reasons for it, and the date the change was made.

The CompuLaw Vision system may be used with both centralized and decentralized data input methods. The system may send information to a centralized system, to individual calendars (Microsoft Outlook®, Novell GroupWise® and Lotus Notes™), or one may view events through the CompuLaw Vision Web Portal™, which gives browser-based access to data using Microsoft Internet Information Services.

Exhibit 10–6 shows a sample of the Vision system for a daily calendar for a week's time.

E-MAIL

E-mail should be treated in the same manner as incoming correspondence. The attorney may require you to obtain her e-mail for purposes of logging and calendaring. In other cases, the attorney may receive her own e-mail and dispose of it. However, be sure that you are aware of each business-related piece of e-mail that is received by the attorney so that you may follow up on any pending items.

EXHIBIT 10–6   Vision Weekly Calendar

Source: From Deadlines On Demand and Compulaw Vision legal calendaring products. Reprinted with permission.

Report Preview

April, 2006	May, 2006	June, 2006	For the week beginning Monday, April 03, 2006

Master Calendar

Monday 4/3	Tuesday 4/4	Wednesday 4/5	Thursday 4/6	Friday 4/7
DEADLINES	**DEADLINES**	**DEADLINES**	**DEADLINES**	**DEADLINES**
ABC Corp. v. Howard Inc., Sample Rule 84(a), DATE OF SERVICE (BY MAIL) OF NOTICE OF RELATED CASE.	ABC Corp. v. Howard Inc., Sample Rule 4586, LCD TO COMPLETE DISCOVERY PRIOR TO ARBITRATION HEARING.	Ruby Blue v. 23 Loft Corp., Sample Rule 491(c), 50(d), LCD TO SERVE (BY FAX) INTERROGATORIES AND REQUESTS FOR ADMISSION. *** SERVICE BY FAX PERMITTED ONLY BY WRITTEN AGREEMENT.	ABC Corp. v. Howard Inc., Sample Rule 203(f), 56(a)(1), LCD TO SERVE (BY ELECTRONIC MEANS) NOTICES OF DEPOSITIONS.	ABC Corp. v. Howard Inc., Sample Rule 203(f), LCD TO SERVE (BY HAND) NOTICES OF DEPOSITIONS.
ABC Corp. v. Howard Inc., Sample Rule 203(f), 67(r), LCD TO SERVE (BY MAIL) NOTICES OF DEPOSITIONS.	Reginald v. Smithson St. Assoc., Sample Rule 613(c), LCD TO SERVE (BY HAND) WITNESS STATEMENTS TO BE OFFERED AS EVIDENCE AT ARBITRATION HEARING.	Jones v. Skyline Sewers, Sample Rule 203(f), 56(a)(1), LCD TO SERVE (BY ELECTRONIC MEANS) NOTICES OF DEPOSITIONS.	Ruby Blue v. 23 Loft Corp., Sample Rule 78.43, LCD TO ISSUE SUBPOENA DUCES TECUM REGARDING THE PRODUCTION OF BUSINESS RECORDS INCLUDING PERSONAL RECORDS PERTAINING TO A CONSUMER. *** NOTE: THE DATE OF PRODUCTION SHALL BE NO EARLIER THAN 20 DAYS AFTER ISSUANCE, OR 10 DAYS AFTER THE SERVICE OF THE SUBPOENA, WHICHEVER DATE IS LATER.	Nielson v. Chiman, Sample Rule 16(a), LCD TO FILE STIPULATION TO ARBITRATE.
Ruby Blue v. 23 Loft Corp., Sample Rule 592(a), 27(c), LCD BEFORE TRIAL TO SERVE (BY ELECTRONIC MEANS) NOTICE OF MSJ AND SUPPORTING PAPERS.		Jones v. Skyline Sewers, Sample Rule 4986(f), 13(g), LCD TO SERVE (BY FAX) TO PROPONENT OF ANY WITNESS STATEMENTS A WRITTEN DEMAND THAT THE WITNESS BE PRODUCED IN PERSON TO TESTIFY AT THE ARBITRATION HEARING. *** SERVICE BY FAX PERMITTED ONLY BY WRITTEN AGREEMENT.		Collins Termination, Sample Rule 234, DATE OF CASE MANAGEMENT CONFERENCE.
Sancom Investments v. Rzinhad Capital, Sample Rule 529(c), 36(a), (e), LCD FOR PARTY OPPOSING MOTION FOR NEW TRIAL TO FILE AND SERVE OPPOSING AFFIDAVITS.			Collins Termination, Sample Rule 8(d), LCD TO WITHDRAW REQUEST TO APPEAR BY TELEPHONE AT CASE MANAGEMENT CONFERENCE.	Titan 16th Holdings v. Mountain Air, Sample Rule 4597, 4598, LCD FOR ANY PARTY TO MAKE APPLICATION FOR CORRECTION OF ARBITRATION AWARD.
			D.T.V. v. Solano, Sample Rule 369, DATE OF SETTLEMENT CONFERENCE.	

Close   Page # 1   Print Range

In some cases, the prompt answering of e-mail may be more critical than answering correspondence. Individuals who write e-mails to you or the attorney usually will expect an answer within a day. It is important to read the e-mail promptly after receipt to determine whether it should be answered immediately.

E-mail should be read at least twice a day, and more often when expecting an item of significance. In an office where many e-mails are received each day, plan to read e-mail every few hours.

Some people use e-mail as a substitute for returning telephone calls when the purpose of the call is to disseminate information. It is often faster to compose an e-mail at the computer, letting the client know the required information, instead of playing telephone tag.

One of the questions to ask at the initial client interview is the client's e-mail address. E-mail is becoming so popular that many businesses and law firms list their e-mail address on their business cards. It is a considerably more efficient method of communication.

The legal professional must be careful regarding confidential communications sent in e-mails. Many firms have programs on their computers to protect the release of confidential information via e-mail. Encoding programs are also available to protect against e-mail "theft." Investigate to determine whether your firm has any protections for confidential e-mail communications. If none is in place, consider examining what programs are available for this purpose.

PERIODIC FILE EXAMINATION ■

If the law office and/or attorney has many different files and cases, it will be easy to forget to take some action on one of the less active ones. For instance, suppose that you are working for a divorce attorney in a state that requires the attorney to file a formal document with the court to finalize the divorce a year after filing the first papers. Unless a regular file examination system is in place, it would be difficult to remember to file these final papers. However, in some states the client's divorce is not final until the paperwork is filed with the court and, should the client remarry thinking the previous divorce is final, she could be considered a bigamist.

A special docket control system for examining files should be in place on the computer. You may obtain one of these systems along with the computerized docket control system from one of the companies listed in Exhibit 10–4.

Generally, each file should be assessed on a monthly basis. All files should be listed on the computer and by date on the date they are due to be reviewed. Once the file is reviewed, the date should be moved up to the same date the following month. The file folder should also contain a check-off sheet with a space for the date the file was evaluated and the person who performed the review.

Most attorneys prefer to have an experienced paralegal or legal assistant review the file rather than doing it themselves. The examination date should be docketed on the tickler file of the individual who will be performing the review. If the firm uses a sophisticated computer system, the file name and review requirements will appear on the appropriate individual's tickler file on the appropriate date. A typical entry follows:

October 2   Review file for *James v. James* #D-8624

A system should also be in place for those files that sit dormant for a long period of time but require that action be taken after a certain number of months elapse. For instance, if the state requires that final divorce papers be filed six months after the initial complaint or petition is filed, the docket control system should show the following information a week before the papers are due, three days before the papers are due, and again on the due date. However, the client should be contacted before the final papers are prepared in the event that the couple has reconciled. A typical entry appears below:

October 20   Contact Mrs. James about final papers in *James v. James,* #D-8624

If Mrs. James would like the final papers to be filed, then the following entries would be appropriate if the paperwork must be filed by November 1:

October 22   Reminder: Mrs. James's final divorce papers due November 1 in *James v. James,* #D-8624

October 28   Have the final papers for Mrs. James's divorce been prepared in *James v. James,* #D-8624? (due November 1)

October 31   Mrs. James's final divorce papers due tomorrow—#D-8624.

November 1   Due date for filing Mrs. James' final divorce papers in #D-8624

Each month when the file is reviewed, a short letter should be sent to the client informing her of the status of her case. Many clients complain that attorneys do not contact them often enough about the status of their cases. This short informative letter will establish better client relations and enable the client to know what action has been taken on her case. The legal professional should prepare a template on her computer for these short informational letters. A sample letter is shown in Exhibit 10–7. Exhibit 10–8 shows a sample letter for a client whose final divorce papers are due.

These letters may be adapted to a number of situations where your review of the file shows that a due date will occur in the near future. In some cases, you may wish to either telephone or send an e-mail to the client when due dates will occur in the near future. Be particularly sensitive about sending an e-mail to the client if you think that another person may be reading the client's e-mail. Sometimes family members have access to each other's e-mail addresses and know their passwords.

ROUTINE CORRESPONDENCE   ■

Whenever you find that you are sending out the same or a similar letter a number of times, it may be appropriate to prepare a template in your word-processing program for the letter. In this way, you may send the same type letter out quickly to a number of individuals by making a few changes. Some of the letters might include:

1. letter informing client of a court date or meeting date
2. letter requesting an extension of time
3. letter informing client of the status of the file
4. letter requesting information from the court, another attorney, or others

These letters are usually quite short and use the same or similar wording. For instance, a typical letter for informing the client of a meeting date might state "We are scheduled to meet with Mr. Jones, our medical expert witness, on June 17 in my office at 2:00 p.m."

In most cases, the client will have been to your office for the initial interview. Otherwise, you might include directions with the letter. If the client must take something with her to the interview, you would need another sentence indicating the item required.

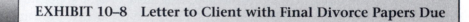

EXHIBIT 10–7   Informational Status Letter to Client

<Law Firm Letterhead>

<Today's Date>

<Client's Name and Address>

RE: <Case Name> Status

Dear <Client>:

Following our monthly review of your file, we find that <status>. We will follow up with the adverse party on <date> to determine whether this matter may be expedited.

Very truly yours,
NAME OF LAW FIRM
<Attorney Name>

EXHIBIT 10–8   Letter to Client with Final Divorce Papers Due

<Law Firm Letterhead>

<Today's Date>

<Client's Name and Address>

RE: <Case Name> Status

Dear <Client>:

Following our review of your file, we find that the final papers are due in your divorce. Please contact this office by October 22 if you would like us to file these final papers.

We will not file the papers unless we hear from you in the event that you have reconciled with your former spouse.

Very truly yours,
LAW FIRM
<Attorney Name>

■ KEY TERMS

Computerized document assembly system   Incoming mail log

■ SELF TEST

1. Prepare a one-page incoming mail log with the following entries:

   a. Letter dated two days ago, received today, from Client Perkins, asking for status of her case.

   b. Notice from local court dated three days ago with trial date 30 days from today in *Jones v. Roberts*, PI-22255. Our client is Mrs. Linda Jones.

2. Prepare a letter to Mrs. Jones informing her of the trial date. Her address is: 1699 Thimble Lane, Your town, Your state.

■ NOTEBOOK PROJECTS

1. Obtain sales literature for a computerized docket control system.

2. Prepare a memorandum to your instructor with an analysis of the advantages and disadvantages of the system in #1.

For additional resources, visit our Web site at **www.westlegalstudies.com**

NALS MODEL CODE OF ETHICS*

Members of NALS are bound by the objectives of this association and the standards of conduct required of the legal profession.

Every member shall

- Encourage respect for the law and the administration of justice;
- Observe rules governing privileged communications and confidential information;
- Promote and exemplify high standards of loyalty, cooperation, and courtesy;
- Perform all duties of the profession with integrity and competence; and
- Pursue a high order of professional attainment.

Integrity and high standards of conduct are fundamental to the success of our professional association. This Code is promulgated by the NALS and accepted by its members to accomplish these ends.

Canon 1. Members of this association shall maintain a high degree of competency and integrity through continuing education to better assist the legal profession in fulfilling its duty to provide quality legal services to the public.

Canon 2. Members of this association shall maintain a high standard of ethical conduct and shall contribute to the integrity of the association and the legal profession.

Canon 3. Members of this association shall avoid a conflict of interest pertaining to a client matter.

Canon 4. Members of this association shall preserve and protect the confidences and privileged communications of a client.

Canon 5. Members of this association shall exercise care in using independent professional judgment and in determining the extent to which a client may be assisted without the presence of a lawyer and shall not act in matters involving professional legal judgment.

*Reprinted with permission from NALS.

Canon 6.   Members of this association shall not solicit legal business on behalf of a lawyer.

Canon 7.   Members of this association, unless permitted by law, shall not perform paralegal functions except under the direct supervision of a lawyer and shall not advertise or contract with members of the general public for the performance of paralegal functions.

Canon 8.   Members of this association, unless permitted by law, shall not perform any of the duties restricted to lawyers or do things which lawyers themselves may not do and shall assist in preventing the unauthorized practice of law.

Canon 9.   Members of this association not licensed to practice law shall not engage in the practice of law as defined by statutes or court decisions.

Canon 10.   Members of this association shall do all other things incidental, necessary, or expedient to enhance professional responsibility and participation in the administration of justice and public service in cooperation with the legal profession.

NALA Model Standards and Guidelines for Utilization of Legal Assistants/Paralegals*

INTRODUCTION

The purpose of this annotated version of the National Association of Legal Assistants, Inc. Model Standards and Guidelines for the Utilization of Legal Assistants (the "Model," "Standards" and/or the "Guidelines") is to provide references to the existing case law and other authorities where the underlying issues have been considered. The authorities cited will serve as a basis upon which conduct of a legal assistant may be analyzed as proper or improper.

The Guidelines represent a statement of how the legal assistant may function. The Guidelines are not intended to be a comprehensive or exhaustive list of the proper duties of a legal assistant. Rather, they are designed as guides to what may or may not be proper conduct for the legal assistant. In formulating the Guidelines, the reasoning and rules of law in many reported decisions of disciplinary cases and unauthorized practice of law cases have been analyzed and considered. In addition, the provisions of the American Bar Association's Model Rules of Professional Conduct, as well as the ethical promulgations of various state courts and bar associations have been considered in the development of the Guidelines.

These Guidelines form a sound basis for the legal assistant and the supervising attorney to follow. This Model will serve as a comprehensive resource document and as a definitive, well-reasoned guide to those considering voluntary standards and guidelines for legal assistants.

I
PREAMBLE

Proper utilization of the services of legal assistants contributes to the delivery of cost-effective, high-quality legal services. Legal assistants and the legal profession should be assured that measures exist for identifying legal assistants and their role in assisting attorneys in the delivery of legal services. Therefore, the National Association of Legal Assistants, Inc., hereby adopts these Standards and Guidelines as an educational document for the benefit of legal assistants and the legal profession.

*Reprinted with permission from NALA.

Comment

The three most frequently raised questions concerning legal assistants are (1) How do you define a legal assistant; (2) Who is qualified to be identified as a legal assistant; and (3) What duties may a legal assistant perform? The definition adopted in 1984 by the National Association of Legal Assistants answers the first question. The Model sets forth minimum education, training and experience through standards which will assure that an individual utilizing the title "legal assistant" or "paralegal" has the qualifications to be held out to the legal community and the public in that capacity. The Guidelines identify those acts which the reported cases hold to be proscribed and give examples of services which the legal assistant may perform under the supervision of a licensed attorney.

These Guidelines constitute a statement relating to services performed by legal assistants, as defined herein, as approved by court decisions and other sources of authority. The purpose of the Guidelines is not to place limitations or restrictions on the legal assistant profession. Rather, the Guidelines are intended to outline for the legal profession an acceptable course of conduct. Voluntary recognition and utilization of the Standards and Guidelines will benefit the entire legal profession and the public it serves.

II
DEFINITION

The National Association of Legal Assistants adopted the following definition in 1984:

> Legal assistants, also known as paralegals, are a distinguishable group of persons who assist attorneys in the delivery of legal services. Through formal education, training, and experience, legal assistants have knowledge and expertise regarding the legal system and substantive and procedural law which qualify them to do work of a legal nature under the supervision of an attorney.

In recognition of the similarity of the definitions and the need for one clear definition, in July 2001, the NALA membership approved a resolution to adopt the definition of the American Bar Association as well. The ABA definition reads as follows:

> A legal assistant or paralegal is a person qualified by education, training or work experience who is employed or retained by a lawyer, law office, corporation, governmental agency or other entity who performs specifically delegated substantive legal work for which a lawyer is responsible. (Adopted by the ABA in 1997)

Comment

These definitions emphasize the knowledge and expertise of legal assistants in substantive and procedural law obtained through education and work experience. They further define the legal assistant or paralegal as a professional working under the supervision of an attorney as distinguished from a non-lawyer who delivers services directly to the public without any intervention or review of work product by an attorney. Such unsupervised services, unless authorized by court or agency rules, constitute the unauthorized practice of law.

Statutes, court rules, case law and bar association documents are additional sources for legal assistant or paralegal definitions. In applying the Standards and Guidelines, it is important to remember that they were developed to apply to the legal assistant as defined herein. Lawyers should refrain from labeling those as paralegals or legal assistants who do not meet the criteria set forth in these definitions and/or the definitions set forth by state rules, guidelines or bar associations. Labeling secretaries and other administrative staff as legal assistants/paralegals is inaccurate.

For billing purposes, the services of a legal secretary are considered part of overhead costs and are not recoverable in fee awards. However, the courts have held that fees for paralegal services are recoverable as long as they are not clerical functions, such as organizing files, copying documents, checking docket, updating files, checking court dates and delivering papers. As established in *Missouri v. Jenkins,* 491 U.S.274, 109 S.Ct. 2463, 2471, n.10 (1989) tasks performed by legal assistants must be substantive in nature which, absent the legal assistant, the attorney would perform.

There are also case law and Supreme Court Rules addressing the issue of a disbarred attorney serving in the capacity of a legal assistant.

III
STANDARDS

A legal assistant should meet certain minimum qualifications. The following standards may be used to determine an individual's qualifications as a legal assistant:

1. Successful completion of the Certified Legal Assistant (CLA)/ Certified Paralegal (CP) certifying examination of the National Association of Legal Assistants, Inc.;

2. Graduation from an ABA approved program of study for legal assistants;

3. Graduation from a course of study for legal assistants which is institutionally accredited but not ABA approved, and which requires not less than the equivalent of 60 semester hours of classroom study;

4. Graduation from a course of study for legal assistants, other than those set forth in (2) and (3) above, plus not less than six months of in-house training as a legal assistant;

5. A baccalaureate degree in any field, plus not less than six months in-house training as a legal assistant;

6. A minimum of three years of law-related experience under the supervision of an attorney, including at least six months of in-house training as a legal assistant; or

7. Two years of in-house training as a legal assistant.

For purposes of these Standards, "in-house training as a legal assistant" means attorney education of the employee concerning legal assistant duties and these Guidelines. In addition to review and analysis of assignments, the legal assistant should receive a reasonable amount of instruction directly related to the duties and obligations of the legal assistant.

Comment

The Standards set forth suggest minimum qualifications for a legal assistant. These minimum qualifications, as adopted, recognize legal related work backgrounds and formal education backgrounds, both of which provide the legal assistant with a broad base in exposure to and knowledge of the legal profession. This background is necessary to assure the public and the legal profession that the employee identified as a legal assistant is qualified.

The Certified Legal Assistant (CLA)/Certified Paralegal (CP) examination established by NALA in 1976 is a voluntary nationwide certification program for legal assistants. (*CLA and CP are federally registered certification marks owned by NALA.*) The CLA/CP designation is a statement to the legal profession and the public that the legal assistant has met the high levels of knowledge and professionalism required by NALA's certification program. Continuing education requirements, which all certified legal assistants must meet, assure that high standards are maintained. The CLA/CP designation has been recognized as a means of establishing the qualifications of a legal assistant in supreme court rules, state court and bar association standards and utilization guidelines.

Certification through NALA is available to all legal assistants meeting the educational and experience requirements. Certified Legal Assistants may also pursue advanced certification in specialty practice areas through the APC, Advanced Paralegal Certification, credentialing program. Legal assistants/paralegals may also pursue certification based on state laws and procedures in California, Florida, Louisiana and Texas.

IV
GUIDELINES

These Guidelines relating to standards of performance and professional responsibility are intended to aid legal assistants and attorneys. The ultimate responsibility rests with an attorney who employs legal assistants to educate them with respect to the duties they are assigned and to supervise the manner in which such duties are accomplished.

Comment

In general, a legal assistant is allowed to perform any task which is properly delegated and supervised by an attorney, as long as the attorney is ultimately responsible to the client and assumes complete professional responsibility for the work product.

ABA Model Rules of Professional Conduct, Rule 5.3 provides:

With respect to a non-lawyer employed or retained by or associated with a lawyer:

(a) a partner in a law firm shall make reasonable efforts to ensure that the firm has in effect measures giving reasonable assurance that the person's conduct is compatible with the professional obligations of the lawyer;

(b) a lawyer having direct supervisory authority over the non-lawyer shall make reasonable efforts to ensure that the person's conduct is compatible with the professional obligations of the lawyer; and

(c) a lawyer shall be responsible for conduct of such a person that would be a violation of the rules of professional conduct if engaged in by a lawyer if:

    (1) the lawyer orders or, with the knowledge of the specific conduct ratifies the conduct involved; or

    (2) the lawyer is a partner in the law firm in which the person is employed, or has direct supervisory authority over the person, and knows of the conduct at a time when its consequences can be avoided or mitigated but fails to take remedial action.

There are many interesting and complex issues involving the use of legal assistants. In any discussion of the proper role of a legal assistant, attention must be directed to what constitutes the practice of law. Proper delegation to legal assistants is further complicated and confused by the lack of an adequate definition of the practice of law.

Kentucky became the first state to adopt a Paralegal Code by Supreme Court Rule. This Code sets forth certain exclusions to the unauthorized practice of law:

For purposes of this rule, the unauthorized practice of law shall not include any service rendered involving legal knowledge or advice, whether representation, counsel or advocacy, in or out of court, rendered in respect to the acts, duties, obligations, liabilities or business relations of the one requiring services where:

    A. The client understands that the paralegal is not a lawyer;

    B. The lawyer supervises the paralegal in the performance of his or her duties; and

    C. The lawyer remains fully responsible for such representation including all actions taken or not taken in connection therewith by the paralegal to the same extent as if such representation had been furnished entirely by the lawyer and all such actions had been taken or not taken directly by the attorney. Paralegal Code, Ky.S.Ct.R3.700, Sub-Rule 2.

South Dakota Supreme Court Rule 97-25 Utilization Rule a(4) states:

The attorney remains responsible for the services performed by the legal assistant to the same extent as though such services had been furnished entirely by the attorney and such actions were those of the attorney.

Guideline 1

Legal assistants should:

1. Disclose their status as legal assistants at the outset of any professional relationship with a client, other attorneys, a court or

administrative agency or personnel thereof, or members of the general public;

2. Preserve the confidences and secrets of all clients; and

3. Understand the attorney's Rules of Professional Responsibility and these Guidelines in order to avoid any action which would involve the attorney in a violation of the Rules, or give the appearance of professional impropriety.

Comment

Routine early disclosure of the paralegal's status when dealing with persons outside the attorney's office is necessary to assure that there will be no misunderstanding as to the responsibilities and role of the legal assistant. Disclosure may be made in any way that avoids confusion. If the person dealing with the legal assistant already knows of his/her status, further disclosure is unnecessary. If at any time in written or oral communication the legal assistant becomes aware that the other person may believe the legal assistant is an attorney, immediate disclosure should be made as to the legal assistant's status.

The attorney should exercise care that the legal assistant preserves and refrains from using any confidence or secrets of a client, and should instruct the legal assistant not to disclose or use any such confidences or secrets.

The legal assistant must take any and all steps necessary to prevent conflicts of interest and fully disclose such conflicts to the supervising attorney. Failure to do so may jeopardize both the attorney's representation of the client and the case itself.

Guidelines for the Utilization of Legal Assistant Services adopted December 3, 1994 by the Washington State Bar Association Board of Governors states:

> "Guideline 7: A lawyer shall take reasonable measures to prevent conflicts of interest resulting from a legal assistant's other employment or interest insofar as such other employment or interests would present a conflict of interest if it were that of the lawyer."

In Re Complex Asbestos Litigation, 232 Cal. App. 3d 572 (Cal. 1991), addresses the issue wherein a law firm was disqualified due to possession of attorney-client confidences by a legal assistant employee resulting from previous employment by opposing counsel.

In Oklahoma, in an order issued July 12, 2001, in the matter of *Mark A. Hayes, M.D. v. Central States Orthopedic Specialists, Inc.,* a Tulsa County District Court Judge disqualified a law firm from representation of a client on the basis that an ethical screen was an impermissible device to protect from disclosure confidences gained by a non-lawyer employee while employed by another law firm. In applying the same rules that govern attorneys, the court found that the Rules of Professional Conduct pertaining to confidentiality apply to non-lawyers who leave firms with actual knowledge of material, confidential information and a screening device is not an appropriate alternative to the imputed disqualification of an incoming legal assistant who has moved from one firm to another during ongoing litigation and has actual knowledge of material, confidential information. The decision was appealed and the Oklahoma Supreme Court determined that, under certain circumstances, screening is an appropriate management tool for non-lawyer staff.

In 2004 the Nevada Supreme Court also addressed this issue at the urging of the state's paralegals. The Nevada Supreme Court granted a petition to rescind the Court's 1997 ruling in *Ciaffone v. District Court.* In this case, the court clarified the original ruling, stating "mere opportunity to access confidential information does not merit disqualification." The opinion stated instances in which screening may be appropriate, and listed minimum screening requirements. The opinion also set forth guidelines that a district court may use to determine if screening has been or may be effective. These considerations are:

1. substantiality of the relationship between the former and current matters
2. the time elapsed between the matters
3. size of the firm
4. number of individuals presumed to have confidential information
5. nature of their involvement in the former matter
6. timing and features of any measures taken to reduce the danger of disclosure
7. whether the old firm and the new firm represent adverse parties in the same proceeding rather than in different proceedings.

The ultimate responsibility for compliance with approved standards of professional conduct rests with the supervising attorney. The burden rests upon the attorney who employs a legal assistant to educate the latter with respect to the duties which may be assigned and then to supervise the manner in which the legal assistant carries out such duties. However, this does not relieve the legal assistant from an independent obligation to refrain from illegal conduct. Additionally, and notwithstanding that the Rules are not binding upon non-lawyers, the very nature of a legal assistant's employment imposes an obligation not to engage in conduct which would involve the supervising attorney in a violation of the Rules.

The attorney must make sufficient background investigation of the prior activities and character and integrity of his or her legal assistants.

Further, the attorney must take all measures necessary to avoid and fully disclose conflicts of interest due to other employment or interests. Failure to do so may jeopardize both the attorney's representation of the client and the case itself.

Legal assistant associations strive to maintain the high level of integrity and competence expected of the legal profession and, further, strive to uphold the high standards of ethics.

NALA's Code of Ethics and Professional Responsibility states "A legal assistant's conduct is guided by bar associations' codes of professional responsibility and rules of professional conduct."

Guideline 2

Legal assistants should not:

1. Establish attorney-client relationships; set legal fees; give legal opinions or advice; or represent a client before a court, unless authorized to do so by said court; nor

2. Engage in, encourage, or contribute to any act which could constitute the unauthorized practice law.

Comment:

Case law, court rules, codes of ethics and professional responsibilities, as well as bar ethics opinions now hold which acts can and cannot be performed by a legal assistant. Generally, the determination of what acts constitute the unauthorized practice of law is made by state supreme courts.

Numerous cases exist relating to the unauthorized practice of law. Courts have gone so far as to prohibit the legal assistant from preparation of divorce kits and assisting in preparation of bankruptcy forms and, more specifically, from providing basic information about procedures and requirements, deciding where information should be placed on forms, and responding to questions from debtors regarding the interpretation or definition of terms.

Cases have identified certain areas in which an attorney has a duty to act, but it is interesting to note that none of these cases state that it is improper for an attorney to have the initial work performed by the legal assistant. This again points out the importance of adequate supervision by the employing attorney.

An attorney can be found to have aided in the unauthorized practice of law when delegating acts which cannot be performed by a legal assistant.

Guideline 3

Legal assistants may perform services for an attorney in the representation of a client, provided:

1. The services performed by the legal assistant do not require the exercise of independent professional legal judgment;

2. The attorney maintains a direct relationship with the client and maintains control of all client matters;

3. The attorney supervises the legal assistant;

4. The attorney remains professionally responsible for all work on behalf of the client, including any actions taken or not taken by the legal assistant in connection therewith; and

5. The services performed supplement, merge with and become the attorney's work product.

Comment:

Paralegals, whether employees or independent contractors, perform services for the attorney in the representation of a client. Attorneys should delegate work to legal assistants commensurate with their knowledge and experience and provide appropriate instruction and supervision concerning the delegated work, as well as ethical acts of their employment. Ultimate responsibility for the work product of a legal assistant rests with the attorney. However, a legal assistant must use discretion and professional judgment and must not render independent legal judgment in place of an attorney.

The work product of a legal assistant is subject to civil rules governing discovery of materials prepared in anticipation of litigation, whether the legal assistant is viewed as an extension of the attorney or as another representative of the party itself. Fed.R.Civ.P. 26 (b) (3) and (5).

Guideline 4

In the supervision of a legal assistant, consideration should be given to

1. Designating work assignments that correspond to the legal assistant's abilities, knowledge, training and experience;
2. Educating and training the legal assistant with respect to professional responsibility, local rules and practices, and firm policies;
3. Monitoring the work and professional conduct of the legal assistant to ensure that the work is substantively correct and timely performed;
4. Providing continuing education for the legal assistant in substantive matters through courses, institutes, workshops, seminars and in-house training; and
5. Encouraging and supporting membership and active participation in professional organizations.

Comment:

Attorneys are responsible for the actions of their employees in both malpractice and disciplinary proceedings. In the vast majority of cases, the courts have not censured attorneys for a particular act delegated to the legal assistant, but rather, have been critical of and imposed sanctions against attorneys for failure to adequately supervise the legal assistant. The attorney's responsibility for supervision of his or her legal assistant must be more than a willingness to accept responsibility and liability for the legal assistant's work. Supervision of a legal assistant must be offered in both the procedural and substantive legal areas. The attorney must delegate work based upon the education, knowledge and abilities of the legal assistant and must monitor the work product and conduct of the legal assistant to insure that the work performed is substantively correct and competently performed in a professional manner.

Michigan State Board of Commissioners has adopted Guidelines for the Utilization of Legal Assistants (April 23, 1993). These guidelines, in part, encourage employers to support legal assistant participation in continuing education programs to ensure that the legal assistant remains competent in the fields of practice in which the legal assistant is assigned.

The working relationship between the lawyer and the legal assistant should extend to cooperative efforts on public service activities wherever possible. Participation in pro bono activities is encouraged in ABA Guideline 10.

Guideline 5

Except as otherwise provided by statute, court rule or decision, administrative rule or regulation, or the attorney's rules of professional responsibility, and within the preceding parameters and proscriptions, a legal assistant may perform any function delegated by an attorney, including, but not limited to the following:

1. Conduct client interviews and maintain general contact with the client after the establishment of the attorney-client relationship, so long as the client is aware of the status and function of the legal assistant, and the client contact is under the supervision of the attorney.

2. Locate and interview witnesses, so long as the witnesses are aware of the status and function of the legal assistant.

3. Conduct investigations and statistical and documentary research for review by the attorney.

4. Conduct legal research for review by the attorney.

5. Draft legal documents for review by the attorney.

6. Draft correspondence and pleadings for review by and signature of the attorney.

7. Summarize depositions, interrogatories and testimony for review by the attorney.

8. Attend executions of wills, real estate closings, depositions, court or administrative hearings and trials with the attorney.

9. Author and sign letters providing the legal assistant's status is clearly indicated and the correspondence does not contain independent legal opinions or legal advice.

Comment:

The United States Supreme Court has recognized the variety of tasks being performed by legal assistants and has noted that use of legal assistants encourages cost-effective delivery of legal services, *Missouri v. Jenkins,* 491 U.S.274, 109 S.Ct. 2463, 2471, n.10 (1989). In *Jenkins,* the court further held that legal assistant time should be included in compensation for attorney fee awards at the market rate of the relevant community to bill legal assistant time.

Courts have held that legal assistant fees are not a part of the overall overhead of a law firm. Legal assistant services are billed separately by attorneys, and decrease litigation expenses. Tasks performed by legal assistants must contain substantive legal work under the direction or supervision of an attorney, such that if the legal assistant were not present, the work would be performed by the attorney.

In *Taylor v. Chubb,* 874 P.2d 806 (Okla. 1994), the Court ruled that attorney fees awarded should include fees for services performed by legal assistants and, further, defined tasks which may be performed by the legal assistant under the supervision of an attorney including, among others: interview clients; draft pleadings and other documents; carry on legal research, both conventional and computer aided; research public records; prepare discovery requests and responses; schedule depositions and prepare notices and subpoenas; summarize depositions and other discovery responses; coordinate and manage document production; locate and interview witnesses; organize pleadings, trial exhibits and other documents; prepare witness and exhibit lists; prepare trial notebooks; prepare for the attendance of witnesses at trial; and assist lawyers at trials.

Except for the specific proscription contained in Guideline 1, the reported cases do not limit the duties which may be performed by a legal assistant under the supervision of the attorney.

An attorney may not split legal fees with a legal assistant, nor pay a legal assistant for the referral of legal business. An attorney may compensate a legal assistant based on the quantity and quality of the legal assistant's work and value of that work to a law practice.

CONCLUSION

These Standards and Guidelines were developed from generally accepted practices. Each supervising attorney must be aware of the specific rules, decisions and statutes applicable to legal assistants within his/her jurisdiction.

NFPA MODEL CODE OF ETHICS AND PROFESSIONAL RESPONSIBILITY AND GUIDELINES FOR ENFORCEMENT*

PREAMBLE

The National Federation of Paralegal Associations, Inc. ("NFPA") is a professional organization comprised of paralegal associations and individual paralegals throughout the United States and Canada. Members of NFPA have varying backgrounds, experiences, education and job responsibilities that reflect the diversity of the paralegal profession. NFPA promotes the growth, development and recognition of the paralegal profession as an integral partner in the delivery of legal services.

In May 1993 NFPA adopted its Model Code of Ethics and Professional Responsibility ("Model Code") to delineate the principles for ethics and conduct to which every paralegal should aspire.

Many paralegal associations throughout the United States have endorsed the concept and content of NFPA's Model Code through the adoption of their own ethical codes. In doing so, paralegals have confirmed the profession's commitment to increase the quality and efficiency of legal services, as well as recognized its responsibilities to the public, the legal community, and colleagues.

Paralegals have recognized, and will continue to recognize, that the profession must continue to evolve to enhance their roles in the delivery of legal services. With increased levels of responsibility comes the need to define and enforce mandatory rules of professional conduct. Enforcement of codes of paralegal conduct is a logical and necessary step to enhance and ensure the confidence of the legal community and the public in the integrity and professional responsibility of paralegals.

In April 1997 NFPA adopted the Model Disciplinary Rules ("Model Rules") to make possible the enforcement of the Canons and Ethical Considerations contained in the NFPA Model Code. A concurrent determination was made that the Model Code of Ethics and Professional Responsibility, formerly aspirational in nature, should be recognized as setting forth the enforceable obligations of all paralegals.

The Model Code and Model Rules offer a framework for professional discipline, either voluntarily or through formal regulatory programs.

*Reprinted with permission from NFPA.

§1. NFPA Model Disciplinary Rules and Ethical Considerations

1.1 A Paralegal shall Achieve and Maintain a High Level of Competence.

Ethical Considerations

EC-1.1(a) A paralegal shall achieve competency through education, training, and work experience.

EC-1.1(b) A paralegal shall aspire to participate in a minimum of twelve (12) hours of continuing legal education, to include at least one (1) hour of ethics education, every two (2) years in order to remain current on developments in the law.

EC-1.1(c) A paralegal shall perform all assignments promptly and efficiently.

1.2 A Paralegal shall Maintain a High Level of Personal and Professional Integrity.

Ethical Considerations

EC-1.2(a) A paralegal shall not engage in any ex parte communications involving the courts or any other adjudicatory body in an attempt to exert undue influence or to obtain advantage or the benefit of only one party.

EC-1.2(b) A paralegal shall not communicate, or cause another to communicate, with a party the paralegal knows to be represented by a lawyer in a pending matter without the prior consent of the lawyer representing such other party.

EC-1.2(c) A paralegal shall ensure that all timekeeping and billing records prepared by the paralegal are thorough, accurate, honest, and complete.

EC-1.2(d) A paralegal shall not knowingly engage in fraudulent billing practices. Such practices may include, but are not limited to: inflation of hours billed to a client or employer; misrepresentation of the nature of tasks performed; and/or submission of fraudulent expense and disbursement documentation.

EC-1.2(e) A paralegal shall be scrupulous, thorough and honest in the identification and maintenance of all funds, securities, and other assets of a client and shall provide accurate accounting as appropriate.

EC-1.2(f) A paralegal shall advise the proper authority of non-confidential knowledge of any dishonest or fraudulent acts by any person pertaining to the handling of the funds, securities or other assets of a client. The authority to whom the report is made shall depend on the nature and circumstances of the possible misconduct, (e.g., ethics committees of law firms, corporations and/or paralegal associations, local or state bar associations, local prosecutors, administrative agencies, etc.). Failure to report such knowledge is in itself misconduct and shall be treated as such under these rules.

1.3   A Paralegal shall Maintain a High Standard of Professional Conduct.

Ethical Considerations

EC-1.3(a)   A paralegal shall refrain from engaging in any conduct that offends the dignity and decorum of proceedings before a court or other adjudicatory body and shall be respectful of all rules and procedures.

EC-1.3(b)   A paralegal shall avoid impropriety and the appearance of impropriety and shall not engage in any conduct that would adversely affect his/her fitness to practice. Such conduct may include, but is not limited to: violence, dishonesty, interference with the administration of justice, and/or abuse of a professional position or public office.

EC-1.3(c)   Should a paralegal's fitness to practice be compromised by physical or mental illness, causing that paralegal to commit an act that is in direct violation of the Model Code/Model Rules and/or the rules and/or laws governing the jurisdiction in which the paralegal practices, that paralegal may be protected from sanction upon review of the nature and circumstances of that illness.

EC-1.3(d)   A paralegal shall advise the proper authority of non-confidential knowledge of any action of another legal professional that clearly demonstrates fraud, deceit, dishonesty, or misrepresentation. The authority to whom the report is made shall depend on the nature and circumstances of the possible misconduct, (e.g., ethics committees of law firms, corporations and/or paralegal associations, local or state bar associations, local prosecutors, administrative agencies, etc.). Failure to report such knowledge is in itself misconduct and shall be treated as such under these rules.

EC-1.3(e)   A paralegal shall not knowingly assist any individual with the commission of an act that is in direct violation of the Model Code/Model Rules and/or the rules and/or laws governing the jurisdiction in which the paralegal practices.

EC-1.3(f)   If a paralegal possesses knowledge of future criminal activity, that knowledge must be reported to the appropriate authority immediately.

1.4   A Paralegal shall Serve the Public Interest by Contributing to the Improvement of the Legal System and Delivery of Quality Legal Services, Including Pro Bono Publico Services.

Ethical Considerations

EC-1.4(a)   A paralegal shall be sensitive to the legal needs of the public and shall promote the development and implementation of programs that address those needs.

EC-1.4(b)   A paralegal shall support efforts to improve the legal system and access thereto and shall assist in making changes.

Continued

EC-1.4(c) A paralegal shall support and participate in the delivery of Pro Bono Publico services directed toward implementing and improving access to justice, the law, the legal system or the paralegal and legal professions.

EC-1.4(d) A paralegal should aspire annually to contribute twenty-four (24) hours of Pro Bono Publico services under the supervision of an attorney or as authorized by administrative, statutory or court authority to:

1. persons of limited means; or

2. charitable, religious, civic, community, governmental and educational organizations in matters that are designed primarily to address the legal needs of persons with limited means; or

3. individuals, groups or organizations seeking to secure or protect civil rights, civil liberties or public rights.

The twenty-four (24) hours of Pro Bono Publico services contributed annually by a paralegal may consist of such services as detailed in this EC-1.4(d), and/or administrative matters designed to develop and implement the attainment of this aspiration as detailed above in EC-1.4(a) B (c), or any combination of the two.

1.5 A Paralegal shall Preserve all Confidential Information Provided by the Client or Acquired from Other Sources Before, During, and After the Course of the Professional Relationship.

Ethical Considerations

EC-1.5(a) A paralegal shall be aware of and abide by all legal authority governing confidential information in the jurisdiction in which the paralegal practices.

EC-1.5(b) A paralegal shall not use confidential information to the disadvantage of the client.

EC-1.5(c) A paralegal shall not use confidential information to the advantage of the paralegal or of a third person.

EC-1.5(d) A paralegal may reveal confidential information only after full disclosure and with the client's written consent; or, when required by law or court order; or, when necessary to prevent the client from committing an act that could result in death or serious bodily harm.

EC-1.5(e) A paralegal shall keep those individuals responsible for the legal representation of a client fully informed of any confidential information the paralegal may have pertaining to that client.

EC-1.5(f) A paralegal shall not engage in any indiscreet communications concerning clients.

1.6   A Paralegal shall Avoid Conflicts of Interest and shall Disclose any Possible Conflict to the Employer or Client, as well as to the Prospective Employers or Clients.

Ethical Considerations

EC-1.6(a)   A paralegal shall act within the bounds of the law, solely for the benefit of the client, and shall be free of compromising influences and loyalties. Neither the paralegal's personal or business interest, nor those of other clients or third persons, should compromise the paralegal's professional judgment and loyalty to the client.

EC-1.6(b)   A paralegal shall avoid conflicts of interest that may arise from previous assignments, whether for a present or past employer or client.

EC-1.6(c)   A paralegal shall avoid conflicts of interest that may arise from family relationships and from personal and business interests.

EC-1.6(d)   In order to be able to determine whether an actual or potential conflict of interest exists a paralegal shall create and maintain an effective recordkeeping system that identifies clients, matters, and parties with which the paralegal has worked.

EC-1.6(e)   A paralegal shall reveal sufficient non-confidential information about a client or former client to reasonably ascertain if an actual or potential conflict of interest exists.

EC-1.6(f)   A paralegal shall not participate in or conduct work on any matter where a conflict of interest has been identified.

EC-1.6(g)   In matters where a conflict of interest has been identified and the client consents to continued representation, a paralegal shall comply fully with the implementation and maintenance of an Ethical Wall.

1.7   A Paralegal's Title shall be Fully Disclosed.

Ethical Considerations

EC-1.7(a)   A paralegal's title shall clearly indicate the individual's status and shall be disclosed in all business and professional communications to avoid misunderstandings and misconceptions about the paralegal's role and responsibilities.

EC-1.7(b)   A paralegal's title shall be included if the paralegal's name appears on business cards, letterhead, brochures, directories, and advertisements.

EC-1.7(c)   A paralegal shall not use letterhead, business cards or other promotional materials to create a fraudulent impression of

Continued

his/her status or ability to practice in the jurisdiction in which the paralegal practices.

EC-1.7(d)   A paralegal shall not practice under color of any record, diploma, or certificate that has been illegally or fraudulently obtained or issued or which is misrepresentative in any way.

EC-1.7(e)   A paralegal shall not participate in the creation, issuance, or dissemination of fraudulent records, diplomas, or certificates.

1.8   A Paralegal shall not Engage in the Unauthorized Practice of Law.

Ethical Considerations

EC-1.8(a)   A paralegal shall comply with the applicable legal authority governing the unauthorized practice of law in the jurisdiction in which the paralegal practices.

§2.   NFPA Guidelines for the Enforcement of the Model Code of Ethics and Professional Responsibility

2.1   Basis for Discipline

2.1(a)   Disciplinary investigations and proceedings brought under authority of the Rules shall be conducted in accord with obligations imposed on the paralegal professional by the Model Code of Ethics and Professional Responsibility.

2.2   Structure of Disciplinary Committee

2.2(a)   The Disciplinary Committee ("Committee") shall be made up of nine (9) members including the Chair.

2.2(b)   Each member of the Committee, including any temporary replacement members, shall have demonstrated working knowledge of ethics/professional responsibility-related issues and activities.

2.2(c)   The Committee shall represent a cross-section of practice areas and work experience. The following recommendations are made regarding the members of the Committee.

1) At least one paralegal with one to three years of law-related work experience.

2) At least one paralegal with five to seven years of law related work experience.

3) At least one paralegal with over ten years of law related work experience.

4) One paralegal educator with five to seven years of work experience; preferably in the area of ethics/professional responsibility.

5) One paralegal manager.

6) One lawyer with five to seven years of law-related work experience.

7) One lay member.

2.2(d) The Chair of the Committee shall be appointed within thirty (30) days of its members' induction. The Chair shall have no fewer than ten (10) years of law-related work experience.

2.2(e) The terms of all members of the Committee shall be staggered. Of those members initially appointed, a simple majority plus one shall be appointed to a term of one year, and the remaining members shall be appointed to a term of two years. Thereafter, all members of the Committee shall be appointed to terms of two years.

2.2(f) If for any reason the terms of a majority of the Committee will expire at the same time, members may be appointed to terms of one year to maintain continuity of the Committee.

2.2(g) The Committee shall organize from its members a three-tiered structure to investigate, prosecute and/or adjudicate charges of misconduct. The members shall be rotated among the tiers.

2.3 Operation of Committee

2.3(a) The Committee shall meet on an as-needed basis to discuss, investigate, and/or adjudicate alleged violations of the Model Code/Model Rules.

2.3(b) A majority of the members of the Committee present at a meeting shall constitute a quorum.

2.3(c) A Recording Secretary shall be designated to maintain complete and accurate minutes of all Committee meetings. All such minutes shall be kept confidential until a decision has been made that the matter will be set for hearing as set forth in Section 6.1 below.

2.3(d) If any member of the Committee has a conflict of interest with the Charging Party, the Responding Party, or the allegations of misconduct, that member shall not take part in any hearing or deliberations concerning those allegations. If the absence of that member creates a lack of a quorum for the Committee, then a temporary replacement for the member shall be appointed.

2.3(e) Either the Charging Party or the Responding Party may request that, for good cause shown, any member of the Committee not participate in a hearing or deliberation. All such requests shall be honored. If the absence of a Committee member under those circumstances creates a lack of a quorum for the Committee, then a temporary replacement for that member shall be appointed.

2.3(f) All discussions and correspondence of the Committee shall be kept confidential until a decision has been made that the matter will be set for hearing as set forth in Section 6.1 below.

2.3(g) All correspondence from the Committee to the Responding Party regarding any charge of misconduct and any decisions made regarding the charge shall be mailed certified mail, return receipt requested, to the Responding Party's last known address and shall be clearly marked with a "Confidential" designation.

Continued

2.4 Procedure for the Reporting of Alleged Violations of the Model Code/Disciplinary Rules

2.4(a) An individual or entity in possession of non-confidential knowledge or information concerning possible instances of misconduct shall make a confidential written report to the Committee within thirty (30) days of obtaining same. This report shall include all details of the alleged misconduct.

2.4(b) The Committee so notified shall inform the Responding Party of the allegation(s) of misconduct no later than ten (10) business days after receiving the confidential written report from the Charging Party.

2.4(c) Notification to the Responding Party shall include the identity of the Charging Party, unless, for good cause shown, the Charging Party requests anonymity.

2.4(d) The Responding Party shall reply to the allegations within ten (10) business days of notification.

2.5 Procedure for the Investigation of a Charge of Misconduct

2.5(a) Upon receipt of a Charge of Misconduct ("Charge"), or on its own initiative, the Committee shall initiate an investigation.

2.5(b) If, upon initial or preliminary review, the Committee makes a determination that the charges are either without basis in fact or, if proven, would not constitute professional misconduct, the Committee shall dismiss the allegations of misconduct. If such determination of dismissal cannot be made, a formal investigation shall be initiated.

2.5(c) Upon the decision to conduct a formal investigation, the Committee shall:

1) mail to the Charging and Responding Parties within three (3) business days of that decision notice of the commencement of a formal investigation. That notification shall be in writing and shall contain a complete explanation of all Charge(s), as well as the reasons for a formal investigation and shall cite the applicable codes and rules;

2) allow the Responding Party thirty (30) days to prepare and submit a confidential response to the Committee, which response shall address each charge specifically and shall be in writing; and

3) upon receipt of the response to the notification, have thirty (30) days to investigate the Charge(s). If an extension of time is deemed necessary, that extension shall not exceed ninety (90) days.

2.5(d) Upon conclusion of the investigation, the Committee may:

1) dismiss the Charge upon the finding that it has no basis in fact;

2) dismiss the Charge upon the finding that, if proven, the Charge would not constitute Misconduct;

3) refer the matter for hearing by the Tribunal; or

4) in the case of criminal activity, refer the Charge(s) and all investigation results to the appropriate authority.

2.6   Procedure for a Misconduct Hearing Before a Tribunal

2.6(a)   Upon the decision by the Committee that a matter should be heard, all parties shall be notified and a hearing date shall be set. The hearing shall take place no more than thirty (30) days from the conclusion of the formal investigation.

2.6(b)   The Responding Party shall have the right to counsel. The parties and the Tribunal shall have the right to call any witnesses and introduce any documentation that they believe will lead to the fair and reasonable resolution of the matter.

2.6(c)   Upon completion of the hearing, the Tribunal shall deliberate and present a written decision to the parties in accordance with procedures as set forth by the Tribunal.

2.6(d)   Notice of the decision of the Tribunal shall be appropriately published.

2.7   Sanctions

2.7(a)   Upon a finding of the Tribunal that misconduct has occurred, any of the following sanctions, or others as may be deemed appropriate, may be imposed upon the Responding Party, either singularly or in combination:

1) letter of reprimand to the Responding Party; counseling;

2) attendance at an ethics course approved by the Tribunal; probation;

3) suspension of license/authority to practice; revocation of license/authority to practice;

4) imposition of a fine; assessment of costs; or

5) in the instance of criminal activity, referral to the appropriate authority.

2.7(b)   Upon the expiration of any period of probation, suspension, or revocation, the Responding Party may make application for reinstatement. With the application for reinstatement, the Responding Party must show proof of having complied with all aspects of the sanctions imposed by the Tribunal.

2.8   Appellate Procedures

2.8(a)   The parties shall have the right to appeal the decision of the Tribunal in accordance with the procedure as set forth by the Tribunal.

DEFINITIONS

"**Appellate Body**" means a body established to adjudicate an appeal to any decision made by a Tribunal or other decision-making body with respect to formally-heard Charges of Misconduct.

"**Charge of Misconduct**" means a written submission by any individual or entity to an ethics committee, paralegal association, bar association, law enforcement agency, judicial body, government agency, or other appropriate body or entity, that sets forth non-confidential information regarding any instance of alleged misconduct by an individual paralegal or paralegal entity.

"Charging Party" means any individual or entity who submits a Charge of Misconduct against an individual paralegal or paralegal entity.

"Competency" means the demonstration of: diligence, education, skill, and mental, emotional, and physical fitness reasonably necessary for the performance of paralegal services.

"Confidential Information" means information relating to a client, whatever its source, that is not public knowledge nor available to the public. ("Non-Confidential Information" would generally include the name of the client and the identity of the matter for which the paralegal provided services.)

"Disciplinary Hearing" means the confidential proceeding conducted by a committee or other designated body or entity concerning any instance of alleged misconduct by an individual paralegal or paralegal entity.

"Disciplinary Committee" means any committee that has been established by an entity such as a paralegal association, bar association, judicial body, or government agency to: (a) identify, define and investigate general ethical considerations and concerns with respect to paralegal practice; (b) administer and enforce the Model Code and Model Rules and; (c) discipline any individual paralegal or paralegal entity found to be in violation of same.

"Disclose" means communication of information reasonably sufficient to permit identification of the significance of the matter in question.

"Ethical Wall" means the screening method implemented in order to protect a client from a conflict of interest. An Ethical Wall generally includes, but is not limited to, the following elements: (1) prohibit the paralegal from having any connection with the matter; (2) ban discussions with or the transfer of documents to or from the paralegal; (3) restrict access to files; and (4) educate all members of the firm, corporation, or entity as to the separation of the paralegal (both organizationally and physically) from the pending matter. For more information regarding the Ethical Wall, see the NFPA publication entitled "The Ethical Wall—Its Application to Paralegals."

"Ex parte" means actions or communications conducted at the instance and for the benefit of one party only, and without notice to, or contestation by, any person adversely interested.

"Investigation" means the investigation of any charge(s) of misconduct filed against an individual paralegal or paralegal entity by a Committee.

"Letter of Reprimand" means a written notice of formal censure or severe reproof administered to an individual paralegal or paralegal entity for unethical or improper conduct.

"Misconduct" means the knowing or unknowing commission of an act that is in direct violation of those Canons and Ethical Considerations of any and all applicable codes and/or rules of conduct.

"Paralegal" is synonymous with "Legal Assistant" and is defined as a person qualified through education, training, or work experience to perform substantive legal work that requires knowledge of legal concepts and is customarily, but not exclusively performed by a lawyer. This person may be retained or employed by a lawyer, law office, governmental agency, or other entity or may be authorized by administrative, statutory, or court authority to perform this work.

"Pro Bono Publico" means providing or assisting to provide quality legal services in order to enhance access to justice for persons of limited means; charitable, religious, civic, community, governmental and educational organizations in matters that are designed primarily to address the legal needs of persons with limited means; or individuals, groups or organizations seeking to secure or protect civil rights, civil liberties or public rights.

"Proper Authority" means the local paralegal association, the local or state bar association, Committee(s) of the local paralegal or bar association(s), local prosecutor, administrative agency, or other tribunal empowered to investigate or act upon an instance of alleged misconduct.

"Responding Party" means an individual paralegal or paralegal entity against whom a Charge of Misconduct has been submitted.

"Revocation" means the recision of the license, certificate or other authority to practice of an individual paralegal or paralegal entity found in violation of those Canons and Ethical Considerations of any and all applicable codes and/or rules of conduct.

"Suspension" means the suspension of the license, certificate or other authority to practice of an individual paralegal or paralegal entity found in violation of those Canons and Ethical Considerations of any and all applicable codes and/or rules of conduct.

"Tribunal" means the body designated to adjudicate allegations of misconduct.

STATE FORMS

This appendix includes the following state forms:

Arizona Order Changing Name for an Adult

California Petition for Dissolution of Marriage

Florida Profit Articles of Incorporation

Illinois Certificate of Limited Partnership

Massachusetts UCC Financing Statement

Nevada Application for Amendment of Notary Public Appointment/Information

New Jersey Registration of Alternate Name

New York Notice of Client's Right to Arbitrate a Dispute over Attorneys Fees

Oregon Assumed Business Name—New Registration

Texas Abstract of Judgment

Washington Indigent Defense Form

Additional state forms may be found on the following web pages:

Illinois—Limited Partnership Forms	http://www.cyberdriveillinois.com/departments/business_services/publications_and_forms/lp.html
Massachusetts UCC Forms	http://www.sec.state.ma.us/cor/corpweb/corucc/uccfrm.htm
Nevada Notary Forms	http://sos.state.nv.us/notary/notforms/index.htm
New Jersey Corporate Formation Forms	http://www.state.nj.us/njbgs/bgsclientreg.htm
New York Attorney Client Fee Dispute Resolution Forms	http://www.nycourts.gov/admin/feedispute/model_forms.shtml
New York Name Change Forms	http://www.nycourts.gov/forms/namechange.shtml
Oregon Business Registry Forms	http://www.filinginoregon.com/forms/index.htm#Business_Registry
Texas Civil Forms—US District Court—Northern District of Texas	http://www.txnd.uscourts.gov/forms/civil.html
Washington State Criminal Law Forms	http://www.courts.wa.gov/forms/index.cfm
Washington Courts Forms	Criminal Law:
	• http://www.courts.wa.gov/forms/?fa=forms.contribute&formID=22
	• http://www.courts.wa.gov/forms/?fa=forms.contribute&formID=18
	• http://www.courts.wa.gov/forms/?fa=forms.contribute&formID=21
	• http://www.courts.wa.gov/forms/?fa=forms.contribute&formID=27
	• http://www.courts.wa.gov/forms/?fa=forms.contribute&formID=11
	• http://www.courts.wa.gov/forms/?fa=forms.contribute&formID=43
	• http://www.courts.wa.gov/forms/?fa=forms.contribute&formID=38

Other state forms may be found at http://www.westlegalstudies.com on the Professional page.

For Clerk's Use Only

SUPERIOR COURT OF ARIZONA
IN MARICOPA COUNTY

In the Matter of:

_____
Name of Applicant

Case Number: _____

ORDER CHANGING NAME OF AN ADULT

THE COURT FINDS:

1.   This case has come before this Court to change the legal name of the Applicant.
2.   This Court has jurisdiction to change the legal name of the Applicant.
3.   Good cause exists to grant the application for change of name.

THE COURT ORDERS:

1.   **The name on the Birth Certificate OR** ☐ **the Current Legal Name:**

First	Middle	Last

Date of Birth:_____
              Month   Day   Year

Place of Birth:_____
              City   State   Nation

IS CHANGED TO:

First	Middle	Last

2.   ☐ For a person born in the State of Arizona, the Office of Vital Records is ordered to amend the birth record to reflect the new name as ordered above.

☐ For a person born in a state other than Arizona, to the extent that the agency that maintains birth records in that state is authorized to honor an order of this Court, that agency is requested or ordered to amend its birth records to reflect the new name as ordered above.

3.   This Order does not release the Applicant from any obligations incurred or harm any rights of property or action in any original name.

4.   Other orders: _____

DONE IN OPEN COURT: _____.   _____
                           Date   Judicial Officer

CVNC81f
Use only most current version

FL-100

ATTORNEY OR PARTY WITHOUT ATTORNEY *(Name, State Bar number, and address):*	FOR COURT USE ONLY

TELEPHONE NO.:   FAX NO. *(Optional):*

E-MAIL ADDRESS *(Optional):*

ATTORNEY FOR *(Name):*

SUPERIOR COURT OF CALIFORNIA, COUNTY OF

STREET ADDRESS:

MAILING ADDRESS:

CITY AND ZIP CODE:

BRANCH NAME:

MARRIAGE OF

PETITIONER:

RESPONDENT:

PETITION FOR	CASE NUMBER:

☐ **Dissolution of Marriage**
☐ **Legal Separation**
☐ **Nullity of Marriage**   ☐ **AMENDED**

1. RESIDENCE (Dissolution only) ☐ Petitioner ☐ Respondent   has been a resident of this state for at least six months and of this county for at least three months immediately preceding the filing of this *Petition for Dissolution of Marriage.*

2. STATISTICAL FACTS
   a. Date of marriage:
   b. Date of separation:
   c. Time from date of marriage to date of separation *(specify):*
      Years: Months:

3. DECLARATION REGARDING MINOR CHILDREN *(include children of this relationship born prior to or during the marriage or adopted during the marriage):*
   a. ☐   There are no minor children.
   b. ☐   The minor children are:

Child's name	Birthdate	Age	Sex

   ☐ Continued on Attachment 3b.
   c. If there are minor children of the Petitioner and Respondent, a completed *Declaration Under Uniform Child Custody Jurisdiction and Enforcement Act (UCCJEA)* (form FL-105) must be attached.
   d. ☐   A completed voluntary declaration of paternity regarding minor children born to the Petitioner and Respondent prior to the marriage is attached.

4. SEPARATE PROPERTY
   Petitioner requests that the assets and debts listed ☐ in *Property Declaration* (form FL-160) ☐ in Attachment 4
   ☐ below   be confirmed as separate property.

Item	Confirm to

NOTICE: You may redact (black out) social security numbers from any written material filed with the court in this case other than a form used to collect child or spousal support.

Page 1 of 2

Form Adopted for Mandatory Use
Judicial Council of California
FL-100 [Rev. January 1, 2005]

PETITION—MARRIAGE
(Family Law)

Family Code, §§ 2330, 3409;
www.courtinfo.ca.gov

American LegalNet, Inc.
www.USCourtForms.com

continued

Exhibit D–2 *continued*

MARRIAGE OF (last name, first name of parties):	CASE NUMBER:

5. DECLARATION REGARDING COMMUNITY AND QUASI-COMMUNITY ASSETS AND DEBTS AS CURRENTLY KNOWN
   a. ☐ There are no such assets or debts subject to disposition by the court in this proceeding.
   b. ☐ All such assets and debts are listed ☐ in *Property Declaration* (form FL-160) ☐ in Attachment 5b.
      ☐ below (specify):

6. **Petitioner requests**
   a. ☐ dissolution of the marriage based on
      (1) ☐ irreconcilable differences. (Fam. Code, § 2310(a).)
      (2) ☐ incurable insanity. (Fam. Code, § 2310(b).)
   b. ☐ legal separation of the parties based on
      (1) ☐ irreconcilable differences. (Fam. Code, § 2310(a).)
      (2) ☐ incurable insanity. (Fam. Code, § 2310(b).)
   c. ☐ nullity of void marriage based on
      (1) ☐ incestuous marriage. (Fam. Code, § 2200.)
      (2) ☐ bigamous marriage. (Fam. Code, § 2201.)

   d. ☐ nullity of voidable marriage based on
      (1) ☐ petitioner's age at time of marriage. (Fam. Code, § 2210(a).)
      (2) ☐ prior existing marriage. (Fam. Code, § 2210(b).)
      (3) ☐ unsound mind. (Fam. Code, § 2210(c).)
      (4) ☐ fraud. (Fam. Code, § 2210(d).)
      (5) ☐ force. (Fam. Code, § 2210(e).)
      (6) ☐ physical incapacity. (Fam. Code, § 2210(f).)

7. **Petitioner requests** that the court grant the above relief and make injunctive (including restraining) and other orders as follows:

	Petitioner	Respondent	Joint	Other
a. Legal custody of children to	☐	☐	☐	☐
b. Physical custody of children to	☐	☐	☐	☐
c. Child visitation be granted to	☐	☐		☐

      As requested in form: ☐ FL-311 ☐ FL-312 ☐ FL-341(C) ☐ FL-341(D) ☐ FL-341(E) ☐ Attachment 7c.
   d. ☐ Determination of parentage of any children born to the Petitioner and Respondent prior to the marriage.
   e. Attorney fees and costs payable by ☐ ☐
   f. Spousal support payable to (earnings assignment will be issued) ☐ ☐
   g. ☐ Terminate the court's jurisdiction (ability) to award spousal support to Respondent.
   h. ☐ Property rights be determined.
   i. ☐ Petitioner's former name be restored to (specify):
   j. ☐ Other (specify):

      ☐ Continued on Attachment 7j.

8. **Child support**—If there are minor children born to or adopted by the Petitioner and Respondent before or during this marriage, the court will make orders for the support of the children upon request and submission of financial forms by the requesting party. An earnings assignment may be issued without further notice. Any party required to pay support must pay interest on overdue amounts at the "legal" rate, which is currently 10 percent.

9. **I HAVE READ THE RESTRAINING ORDERS ON THE BACK OF THE SUMMONS, AND I UNDERSTAND THAT THEY APPLY TO ME WHEN THIS PETITION IS FILED.**

I declare under penalty of perjury under the laws of the State of California that the foregoing is true and correct.

Date:

_____ ▶ _____
(TYPE OR PRINT NAME) (SIGNATURE OF PETITIONER)

Date:

_____ ▶ _____
(TYPE OR PRINT NAME) (SIGNATURE OF ATTORNEY FOR PETITIONER)

NOTICE: Dissolution or legal separation may automatically cancel the rights of a spouse under the other spouse's will, trust, retirement plan, power of attorney, pay on death bank account, survivorship rights to any property owned in joint tenancy, and any other similar thing. It does not automatically cancel the right of a spouse as beneficiary of the other spouse's life insurance policy. You should review these matters, as well as any credit cards, other credit accounts, insurance polices, retirement plans, and credit reports to determine whether they should be changed or whether you should take any other actions. However, some changes may require the agreement of your spouse or a court order (see Family Code sections 231–235).

FL-100 [Rev. January 1, 2005]
PETITION—MARRIAGE
(Family Law)
Page 2 of 2

EXHIBIT D–3   Florida Profit Articles of Incorporation

Source: http://www.dos.state.fl.us/doc/pdf/cr2e010.pdf

FLORIDA DEPARTMENT OF STATE
DIVISION OF CORPORATIONS

INSTRUCTIONS FOR A PROFIT CORPORATION

The following are instructions, a cover letter and sample articles of incorporation pursuant to Chapter 607 and 621 Florida Statutes (F.S.).

NOTE: THIS IS A BASIC FORM MEETING MINIMAL REQUIREMENTS FOR FILING ARTICLES OF INCORPORATION.

The Division of Corporations strongly recommends that corporate documents be reviewed by your legal counsel. The Division is a filing agency and as such does not render any legal, accounting, or tax advice.

This office does not provide you with corporate seals, minute books, or stock certificates. It is the responsibility of the corporation to secure these items once the corporation has been filed with this office.

Questions concerning S Corporations should be directed to the Internal Revenue Service by telephoning 1-800-829-1040. This is an IRS designation, which is not determined by this office.

A preliminary search for name availability can be made on the Internet through the Division's records at www.sunbiz.org. Preliminary name searches and name reservations are no longer available from the Division of Corporations. You are responsible for any name infringement that may result from your corporate name selection.

Pursuant to Chapter 607 or 621 F.S., the articles of incorporation **must** set forth the following:

Article I: The name of the corporation **must** include a corporate suffix such as Corporation, Corp., Incorporated, Inc., Company, or Co.

A Professional Association **must** contain the word "chartered" or "professional association" or "P.A.".

Article II: The principal place of business and mailing address of the corporation.

Article III: **Specific Purpose for a "Professional Corporation"**

Article IV: The number of shares of stock that this corporation is authorized to have **must** be stated.

CR2E010 (8/05)

continued

Exhibit D–3 *continued*

Article V: The names, address and titles of the Directors/Officers **(optional).** The names of officers/directors may be required to apply for a license, open a bank account, etc.

Article VI: The name and **Florida Street address** (P.O. Box **NOT** acceptable) of the initial
Registered   Agent. The Registered Agent **must** sign in the space provided and type or
print his/her   name accepting the designation as registered agent.

Article VII: The name and address of the Incorporator. The Incorporator **must** sign in the space provided and type or print his/her name below signature.

An Effective Date: **Add a <u>separate</u> article if applicable or necessary**: An effective date **may** be added to the Articles of Incorporation, otherwise the date of receipt will be the file date. (An effective date can not be more than five (5) business days prior to the date of receipt or ninety (90) days after the date of filing).
****

The fee for filing a profit corporation is:
Filing Fee $35.00
Designation of Registered Agent $35.00
Certified Copy (optional) $ 8.75 (plus $1 per page for each page over 8, not to exceed a maximum of $52.50).

Certificate of Status (optional) $ 8.75
(Make checks payable to Florida Department of State)

Mailing Address:	Street Address:
Department of State	Department of State
Division of Corporations	Division of Corporations
P.O. Box 6327	Clifton Building
Tallahassee, FL 32314	2661 Executive Center Circle
(850) 245-6052	Tallahassee, FL 32301
	(850) 245-6052

continued

Exhibit D–3   *continued*

COVER LETTER

Department of State
Division of Corporations
P. O. Box 6327
Tallahassee, FL 32314

SUBJECT: _____

(PROPOSED CORPORATE NAME – <u>MUST INCLUDE SUFFIX</u>)

Enclosed are an original and one (1) copy of the articles of incorporation and a check for:

☐ $70.00
Filing Fee

☐ $78.75
Filing Fee
& Certificate of Status

☐ $78.75
Filing Fee
& Certified Copy

☐ $87.50
Filing Fee,
Certified Copy
& Certificate of
Status

ADDITIONAL COPY REQUIRED

FROM: _____

Name (Printed or typed)

_____

Address

_____

City, State & Zip

_____

Daytime Telephone number

NOTE: Please provide the original and one copy of the articles.

continued

Exhibit D–3   *continued*

ARTICLES OF INCORPORATION
In compliance with Chapter 607 and/or Chapter 621, F.S. (Profit)

ARTICLE I   NAME
The name of the corporation shall be:

ARTICLE II   PRINCIPAL OFFICE
The principal place of business/mailing address is:

ARTICLE III   PURPOSE
The purpose for which the corporation is organized is:

ARTICLE IV   SHARES
The number of shares of stock is:

ARTICLE V   INITIAL OFFICERS AND/OR DIRECTORS
List name(s), address(es) and specific title(s):

ARTICLE VI   REGISTERED AGENT
The **name and Florida street address** (P.O. Box **NOT** acceptable) of the registered agent is:

ARTICLE VII   INCORPORATOR
The **name and address** of the Incorporator is:

****

Having been named as registered agent to accept service of process for the above stated corporation at the place designated in this certificate, I am familiar with and accept the appointment as registered agent and agree to act in this capacity

_____   _____

Signature/Registered Agent   Date

_____   _____

Signature/Incorporator   Date

DO NOT STAPLE

Print   Reset

**Form LP 201
January 2005**

Filing Fee: $150
Submit in duplicate. Payment must be
made by certified check, cashier's check,
Illinois attorney's check, Illinois C.P.A.'s
check or money order, payable to
Secretary of State.
Please do not send cash.

Department of Business Services
Limited Partnership Division
357 Howlett Building
Springfield, IL 62756
217-785-8960
www.cyberdriveillinois.com

Correspondence regarding this filing will
be sent to the registered agent of the
Limited Partnership unless a self-
addressed, stamped envelope is
included.

**Illinois Secretary of State
Department of Business Services**
**Certificate of Limited Partnership
(Illinois Limited Partnership or LLLP)**

Please type or print clearly.

1. Limited Partnership Name:_____
    (must contain "Limited Partnership," "L.P." or "LP")

2. Address of office at which records required by Section 111 will be kept:

    _____
    Street Address (P.O. Box alone is unacceptable.)

    _____
    City, State, ZIP, County

3. Federal Employer Identification Number (F.E.I.N.): _____

4. Certificate of Limited Partnership is effective on (check one):
    ❑ filing date
    ❑ a later date, but not more than 60 days subsequent to filing date _____
                                                                            Date (month, day, year)

5. Registered Agent: _____
                                              Name

    Registered Office: _____
                                    Street Address (P.O. Box alone is unacceptable.)

    _____
    City (must be in Illinois), ZIP, County

6. Limited Partnership's Purpose(s): _____

    _____

7. IRS Business Code Number: _____

8. This entity is a Limited Liability Limited Partnership:
    ❑ Yes
    ❑ No

Printed by authority of the State of Illinois. June 2005 — 1 — CLP 3.14

continued

Exhibit D–4 *continued*

Form LP 201

9. **Total** aggregate **dollar amount** of cash, property and services contributed by all partners (optional):

$ _____

10. If agreed upon, brief statement of partners' membership termination and distribution rights (optional):

_____

_____

_____

_____

_____

Names and Business Addresses of all General Partners

The undersigned affirms, under penalties of perjury, that the facts stated herein are true. All general partners are required to sign the Certificate of Limited Partnership.

1. _____
   Signature

   _____
   Name and Title (type or print)

   _____
   General Partner Name if corporation or other entity

   _____
   Street Address

   _____
   City, State, ZIP, County

2. _____
   Signature

   _____
   Name and Title (type or print)

   _____
   General Partner Name if corporation or other entity

   _____
   Street Address

   _____
   City, State, ZIP, County

3. _____
   Signature

   _____
   Name and Title (type or print)

   _____
   General Partner Name if corporation or other entity

   _____
   Street Address

   _____
   City, State, ZIP, County

4. _____
   Signature

   _____
   Name and Title (type or print)

   _____
   General Partner Name if corporation or other entity

   _____
   Street Address

   _____
   City, State, ZIP, County

Signatures must be in black ink on an original document.
Carbon copy, photocopy or rubber stamp signatures
may only be used on conformed copies.

UCC FINANCING STATEMENT

FOLLOW INSTRUCTIONS (front and back) CAREFULLY

A. NAME & PHONE OF CONTACT AT FILER [optional]

B. SEND ACKNOWLEDGMENT TO: (Name and Address)

[Print]   [Reset]

THE ABOVE SPACE IS FOR FILING OFFICE USE ONLY

1. DEBTOR'S EXACT FULL LEGAL NAME - insert only one debtor name (1a or 1b) - do not abbreviate or combine names

1a. ORGANIZATION'S NAME			

OR

1b. INDIVIDUAL'S LAST NAME	FIRST NAME	MIDDLE NAME	SUFFIX

1c. MAILING ADDRESS	CITY	STATE	POSTAL CODE	COUNTRY

1d. SEE INSTRUCTIONS	ADD'L INFO RE ORGANIZATION DEBTOR	1e. TYPE OF ORGANIZATION	1f. JURISDICTION OF ORGANIZATION	1g. ORGANIZATIONAL ID #, if any ☐ NONE

2. ADDITIONAL DEBTOR'S EXACT FULL LEGAL NAME - insert only one debtor name (2a or 2b) - do not abbreviate or combine names

2a. ORGANIZATION'S NAME			

OR

2b. INDIVIDUAL'S LAST NAME	FIRST NAME	MIDDLE NAME	SUFFIX

2c. MAILING ADDRESS	CITY	STATE	POSTAL CODE	COUNTRY

2d. SEE INSTRUCTIONS	ADD'L INFO RE ORGANIZATION DEBTOR	2e. TYPE OF ORGANIZATION	2f. JURISDICTION OF ORGANIZATION	2g. ORGANIZATIONAL ID #, if any ☐ NONE

3. SECURED PARTY'S NAME (or NAME of TOTAL ASSIGNEE of ASSIGNOR S/P) - insert only one secured party name (3a or 3b)

3a. ORGANIZATION'S NAME			

OR

3b. INDIVIDUAL'S LAST NAME	FIRST NAME	MIDDLE NAME	SUFFIX

3c. MAILING ADDRESS	CITY	STATE	POSTAL CODE	COUNTRY

4. This FINANCING STATEMENT covers the following collateral:

5. ALTERNATIVE DESIGNATION [if applicable]: ☐ LESSEE/LESSOR ☐ CONSIGNEE/CONSIGNOR ☐ BAILEE/BAILOR ☐ SELLER/BUYER ☐ AG. LIEN ☐ NON-UCC FILING

6. ☐ This FINANCING STATEMENT is to be filed [for record] (or recorded) in the REAL ESTATE RECORDS.   Attach Addendum   [if applicable]   **7.** Check to REQUEST SEARCH REPORT(S) on Debtor(s) [ADDITIONAL FEE]   [optional] ☐ All Debtors ☐ Debtor 1 ☐ Debtor 2

8. OPTIONAL FILER REFERENCE DATA

FILING OFFICE COPY — UCC FINANCING STATEMENT (FORM UCC1) (REV. 05/22/02)

International Association of Commercial Administrators (IACA)

continued

Exhibit D–5 *continued*

Instructions for UCC Financing Statement (Form UCC1)

Please type or laser-print this form. Be sure it is completely legible. Read all Instructions, especially Instruction 1; correct Debtor name is crucial. Follow Instructions completely.

Fill in form very carefully; mistakes may have important legal consequences. If you have questions, consult your attorney. Filing office cannot give legal advice.

Do not insert anything in the open space in the upper portion of this form; it is reserved for filing office use.

When properly completed, send Filing Office Copy, with required fee, to filing office. If you want an acknowledgment, complete item B and, if filing in a filing office that returns an acknowledgment copy furnished by filer, you may also send Acknowledgment Copy; otherwise detach. If you want to make a search request, complete item 7 (after reading Instruction 7 below) and send Search Report Copy, otherwise detach. Always detach Debtor and Secured Party Copies.

If you need to use attachments, you are encouraged to use either Addendum (Form UCC1Ad) or Additional Party (Form UCC1AP).

A. To assist filing offices that might wish to communicate with filer, filer may provide information in item A. This item is optional.

B. Complete item B if you want an acknowledgment sent to you. If filing in a filing office that returns an acknowledgment copy furnished by filer, present simultaneously with this form a carbon or other copy of this form for use as an acknowledgment copy.

1. **Debtor name**: Enter only one Debtor name in item 1, an organization's name (1a) or an individual's name (1b). Enter Debtor's exact full legal name. Don't abbreviate.

1a. Organization Debtor. "Organization" means an entity having a legal identity separate from its owner. A partnership is an organization; a sole proprietorship is not an organization, even if it does business under a trade name. If Debtor is a partnership, enter exact full legal name of partnership; you need not enter names of partners as additional Debtors. If Debtor is a registered organization (e.g., corporation, limited partnership, limited liability company), it is advisable to examine Debtor's current filed charter documents to determine Debtor's correct name, organization type, and jurisdiction of organization.

1b. Individual Debtor. "Individual" means a natural person; this includes a sole proprietorship, whether or not operating under a trade name. Don't use prefixes (Mr., Mrs., Ms.). Use suffix box only for titles of lineage (Jr., Sr., III) and not for other suffixes or titles (e.g., M.D.). Use married woman's personal name (Mary Smith, not Mrs. John Smith). Enter individual Debtor's family name (surname) in Last Name box, first given name in First Name box, and all additional given names in Middle Name box.

For both organization and individual Debtors: Don't use Debtor's trade name, DBA, AKA, FKA, Division name, etc. in place of or combined with Debtor's legal name; you may add such other names as additional Debtors if you wish (but this is neither required nor recommended).

1c. An address is always required for the Debtor named in 1a or 1b.

1d. Reserved for Financing Statements to be filed in North Dakota or South Dakota only. If this Financing Statement is to be filed in North Dakota or South Dakota, the Debtor's taxpayer identification number (tax ID#) — social security number or employer identification number must be placed in this box.

1e,f,g. "Additional information re organization Debtor" is always required. Type of organization and jurisdiction of organization as well as Debtor's exact legal name can be determined from Debtor's current filed charter document. Organizational ID #, if any, is assigned by the agency where the charter document was filed; this is different from tax ID #; this should be entered preceded by the 2-character U.S. Postal identification of state of organization if one of the United States (e.g., CA12345, for a California corporation whose organizational ID # is 12345); if agency does not assign organizational ID #, check box in item 1g indicating "none."

Note: If Debtor is a trust or a trustee acting with respect to property held in trust, enter Debtor's name in item 1 and attach Addendum (Form UCC1Ad) and check appropriate box in item 17. If Debtor is a decedent's estate, enter name of deceased individual in item 1b and attach Addendum (Form UCC1Ad) and check appropriate box in item 17. If Debtor is a transmitting utility or this Financing Statement is filed in connection with a Manufactured-Home Transaction or a Public-Finance Transaction as defined in applicable Commercial Code, attach Addendum (Form UCC1Ad) and check appropriate box in item 18.

2. If an additional Debtor is included, complete item 2, determined and formatted per Instruction 1. To include further additional Debtors, attach either Addendum (Form UCC1Ad) or Additional Party (Form UCC1AP) and follow Instruction 1 for determining and formatting additional names.

3. Enter information for Secured Party or Total Assignee, determined and formatted per Instruction 1. To include further additional Secured Parties, attach either Addendum (Form UCC1Ad) or Additional Party (Form UCC1AP) and follow Instruction 1 for determining and formatting additional names. If there has been a total assignment of the Secured Party's interest prior to filing this form, you may either (1) enter Assignor S/P's name and address in item 3 and file an Amendment (Form UCC3) [see item 5 of that form]; or (2) enter Total Assignee's name and address in item 3 and, if you wish, also attaching Addendum (Form UCC1Ad) giving Assignor S/P's name and address in item 12.

4. Use item 4 to indicate the collateral covered by this Financing Statement. If space in item 4 is insufficient, put the entire collateral description or continuation of the collateral description on either Addendum (Form UCC1Ad) or other attached additional page(s).

5. If filer desires (at filer's option) to use titles of lessee and lessor, or consignee and consignor, or seller and buyer (in the case of accounts or chattel paper), or bailee and bailor instead of Debtor and Secured Party, check the appropriate box in item 5. If this is an agricultural lien (as defined in applicable Commercial Code) filing or is otherwise not a UCC security interest filing (e.g., a tax lien, judgment lien, etc.), check the appropriate box in item 5, complete items 1-7 as applicable and attach any other items required under other law.

6. If this Financing Statement is filed as a fixture filing or if the collateral consists of timber to be cut or as-extracted collateral, complete items 1-5, check the box in item 6, and complete the required information (items 13, 14 and/or 15) on Addendum (Form UCC1Ad).

7. This item is optional. Check appropriate box in item 7 to request Search Report(s) on all or some of the Debtors named in this Financing Statement. The Report will list all Financing Statements on file against the designated Debtor on the date of the Report, including this Financing Statement. There is an additional fee for each Report. If you have checked a box in item 7, file Search Report Copy together with Filing Officer Copy (and Acknowledgment Copy). Note: Not all states do searches and not all states will honor a search request made via this form; some states require a separate request form.

8. This item is optional and is for filer's use only. For filer's convenience of reference, filer may enter in item 8 any identifying information (e.g., Secured Party's loan number, law firm file number, Debtor's name or other identification, state in which form is being filed, etc.) that filer may find useful.

EXHIBIT D–6   Nevada Application for Amendment of Notary Public Appointment/Information

Source: http://sos.state.nv.us/notary/notforms/amend_omfm.pdf

Application for Amendment of
Notary Public Appointment/Information   *State of Nevada*

AMEND THE FOLLOWING: (please mark one)

Mailing Address ☐   Name ☐   County ☐ $ 10.00

Duplicate Certificate ☐ $ 10.00

Amount Attached $ _____

Name of Applicant: _____

Mailing Address: _____

Phone Number: _____

Length of Residence in County: _____

Date of Expiration of Present Appointment: _____

Notary Number: _____

Applicant's Signature: (Please sign this application exactly as you wish it to read on your appointment.)

Signature _____

Please print your name exactly as you wish it to read on your appointment.

_____

Prior Name: _____

Prior County: _____

SUBMIT A COPY OF YOUR CURRENT NOTARY
CERTIFICATE WITH THE FEE OF $10.00 TO:

Secretary of State
101 North Carson Street - Suite 3
Carson City, Nevada 89701-3714
Phone (775) 684-5708

Reset

EXHIBIT D–7   New Jersey Registration of Alternate Name

Source: http://www.state.nj.us/treasury/revenue/pdforms/c150.pdf

Mail to:	PO Box 308 Trenton, NJ 08646	**STATE OF NEW JERSEY** **DIVISION OF REVENUE**	Overnight to:	225 West State St. 3rd Floor Trenton, NJ 08608-1001

FEE REQUIRED

REGISTRATION OF ALTERNATE NAME

C-150G

Complete the following applicable information, and sign in the space provided. Please note that once filed, the information contained in the filed form is considered <u>public</u>. **Refer to the instructions on page 26 for filing fees and field-by-field requirements.** Remember to remit the appropriate fee amount. Use attachments if more space is required for any field.

Check Appropriate Statute:

[ ] Title 14A:2-2.1 (2) New Jersey Business Corporation Act   [ ] Title 42:2B-4 Limited Liability Company

[ ] Title 15A:2-2-3 (b) New Jersey Nonprofit Corporation Act   [ ] Title 42:2A-6 Limited Partnership

Pursuant to the provisions of the appropriate statute, checked above, of the New Jersey Statutes, the undersigned corporation/business entity hereby applies for the registration of an Alternate Name in New Jersey for a period of five (5) years, and for that purpose submits the following application:

1.   Name of Corporation/Business: _____

2.   NJ 10-digit ID number: _____

3.   Set forth state of Original Incorporation/Formation: _____

4.   Date of Incorporation/Formation: _____

     Date of Authorization (Foreign): _____

5.   Alternate Name to be used: _____

6.   State the purpose or activity to be conducted using the Alternate Name: _____

7.   The Business intends to use the Alternate Name in this State.

8.   The Business has not previously used the Alternate Name in this State in violation of this Statute, or; if it has, the month and year in which it commenced such use is: _____

Signature requirements:

For Corporations   Chairman of the Board., President, Vice-President
For Limited Partnerships   General Partner
For all Other Business Types   Authorized Representative

SIGNATURE: _____   TITLE: _____

NAME (please type): _____   DATE: _____

THE PURPOSE OF THIS FORM IS TO SIMPLIFY THE FILING REQUIREMENTS. IT DOES NOT REPLACE THE NEED FOR COMPETENT LEGAL ADVICE.

- 25 -

continued

Exhibit D–7   *continued*

- Instructions -
Registration of Alternate Name (Form C-150G)

Page 25 Instructions -

<u>Important</u>: The completion of all items is mandatory in order to process your application.

First, check off the Statutory Authority that applies to your business.

Item 1 - Enter the name of the corporation/business exactly as it appears on the records of the Treasurer of the State New Jersey.

Item 2 - Enter the 10-digit Corporation/Business ID number as issued by the State of New Jersey.

Item 3 - Enter the name of the State in which the corporation was incorporated.

Item 4 - Enter the date of incorporation (domestic corporations) or the date of authorization (foreign corporations).

Item 5 - Enter the alternate name that you wish to have registered.

<u>Warning</u>: Do Not Use a name that is prohibited by other New Jersey State Laws - for example, those governing banking, insurance, and real estate, or involving the Professional Services Act in Title 14A. While checking on usage limitations is not a mandatory review element for the Corporate Filing Section, the Section will reject or void filings upon advice and guidance of regulatory and licensing authorities. The filer is responsible for researching regulatory and licensing issues.

Item 6 - State the purpose of the business or the primary type of activity performed by the business, using the alternate name given above.

Item 7 - No entry is required.

Item 8 - If the alternate name was previously used, enter the month and year such use commenced.

<u>ATTESTATIONS</u>:

Form C-150G provides the following statements: 1) the corporation intends to use the alternate name in New Jersey and 2) that the corporation has not used the name in violation of the law, or if it has, the month/year in which it commenced such use.

<u>EXECUTION</u>:

You must have the correct business representative sign and date form C-150G before submitting. Refer to the specific requirements for each type of business.

<u>FEE</u>:

You must attach the mandatory fee of $50.00 to the completed C-150G application.

These documents should be filed in duplicate. Non-profits should file in triplicate.
Make checks payable to: **Treasurer, State of New Jersey**. (No cash, please)
Mail to: **NJ Division of Revenue, PO Box 308, Trenton, NJ 08646**

EXHIBIT D–8   New York Notice of Client's Right to Arbitrate a Dispute over Attorneys Fees

Source: http://www.nycourts.gov/admin/feedispute/Forms/137_1.pdf

UCS 137-1 (11/01)

NOTICE OF CLIENT'S RIGHT TO ARBITRATE

A DISPUTE OVER ATTORNEYS FEES

The amount of $_____ is due and owing for the provision of legal services with respect to _____. If you dispute that you owe this amount, you have the right to elect to resolve this dispute by arbitration under Part 137 of the Rules of the Chief Administrator of the Courts. To do so, you must file the attached Request for Fee Arbitration within 30 days from the receipt of this Notice, as set forth in the attached instructions.   If you do not file a Request for Fee Arbitration within 30 days from the receipt of this Notice, you waive the right to resolve this dispute by arbitration under Part 137, and your attorney will be free to bring a lawsuit in court to seek payment of the fee.

Dated:_____   _____

                                   _____

                                   _____

                                   [Attorney's name and address]

EXHIBIT D–9   Oregon Assumed Business Name—New Registration

Source: http://www.fillinginoregon.com/forms/pdf/business/101.pdf

Phone: (503) 986-2200
Fax: (503) 378-4381

Assumed Business Name—New Registration

Secretary of State
Corporation Division
255 Capitol St. NE, Suite 151
Salem, OR 97310-1327
FilingInOregon.com

Print
Reset
Save As

REGISTRY NUMBER: _____

For office use only

In accordance with Oregon Revised Statute 192.410-192.490, the information on this application is public record.
We must release this information to all parties upon request and it will be posted on our website.

For office use only

Please Type or Print Legibly in **Black** Ink. Attach Additional Sheet if Necessary.

1) **ASSUMED BUSINESS NAME** (To be registered)

_____

Registration or filing of a name does not grant exclusive rights or interests in that name. A name may be available for registration; however, someone else may hold a prior right to that name, or the name may be too similar to another, and may result in a case of legal action brought against the registrant for dilution or unfair competition of someone else's business.

2) **DESCRIPTION OF BUSINESS** (Primary business activity)

4) **NAME OF AUTHORIZED REPRESENTATIVE** (One name only)

3) **PRINCIPAL PLACE OF BUSINESS** (Address, city, state, zip)

5) **MAILING ADDRESS OF AUTHORIZED REPRESENTATIVE**

6) **REGISTRANT'S/OWNER PUBLICLY AVAILABLE ADDRESS** (List name and street address of each person or entity who will conduct or transact business under the assumed business name.) (Attach a separate sheet if necessary.)

NAME	STREET ADDRESS	CITY/STATE/ZIP

7) **COUNTIES**

☐ ALL COUNTIES (Statewide)

☐ Baker	☐ Crook	☐ Harney	☐ Lake	☐ Morrow	☐ Union
☐ Benton	☐ Curry	☐ Hood River	☐ Lane	☐ Multnomah	☐ Wallowa
☐ Clackamas	☐ Deschutes	☐ Jackson	☐ Lincoln	☐ Polk	☐ Wasco
☐ Clatsop	☐ Douglas	☐ Jefferson	☐ Linn	☐ Sherman	☐ Washington
☐ Columbia	☐ Gilliam	☐ Josephine	☐ Malheur	☐ Tillamook	☐ Wheeler
☐ Coos	☐ Grant	☐ Klamath	☐ Marion	☐ Umatilla	☐ Yamhill

8) **SIGNATURES** (All registrants/owners must sign.)

FEES

Required Processing Fee $50
Confirmation Copy (Optional) $5

Processing Fees are nonrefundable.

Please make check payable to "Corporation Division."

NOTE:
Fees may be paid with VISA or MasterCard. The card number and expiration date should be submitted on a separate sheet for your protection.

9) **CONTACT NAME** (To resolve questions with this filing.)   **DAYTIME PHONE NUMBER** (Include area code.)

101 (Rev. 08/06)

EXHIBIT D–10   Texas Abstract of Judgment

Source: http://www.txnd.uscourts.gov/pdf/forms/Abstract.pdf

IN THE UNITED STATES DISTRICT COURT
FOR THE NORTHERN DISTRICT OF TEXAS

<u>Abilene</u> DIVISION

(Name All Plaintiffs and Defendants)

CIVIL NUMBER _____

Complete the following if judgment
was rendered in another District:

vs.

District: _____
Docket Number: _____
Date Entered: _____

ABSTRACT OF JUDGMENT

In the above entitled and numbered cause a judgment was rendered in this Court, or other United States

District Court as indicated above and registered herein, on the _____ day of _____,_____, in

favor of _____

against _____

_____

in the sum of $ _____ with interest at the rate of

_____ per cent per annum from the _____ day of _____, _____.

Costs have been taxed by the Clerk of Court in the sum of $ _____.

Credits reflected by returns on execution in the sum of $_____.

The address of the defendant shown in this suit in which said judgment was rendered:_____

_____or nature of

citation and date and place citation served:

_____.

I certify that the above and foregoing is a true and correct abstract of judgment rendered or registered in this
Court.

Witness my hand and seal of the Court this _____ day of _____, 20____.

KAREN MITCHELL, CLERK

By _____
Deputy Clerk

EXHIBIT D–11   Washington Indigent Defense Form

Source: http://www.courts.wa.gov/forms/documents/indigent_E.doc

STATE OF WASHINGTON
Determination Of Indigency Report

I. Identification

County_____ Court_____

Jurisdiction (check one) (   ) Superior (   ) District   (   ) Municipal   Name of City_____

Applicant's Name _____ Case Number: _____

Case Type
(check the category corresponding to the most serious charge)

_____(1) Felony - Class A+   _____(5) Juvenile Felony - Class A+   _____(9) Dependency

_____(2) Felony - Class A   _____(6) Juvenile Felony - Class A   _____(10) Civil Commitment

_____(3) Felony - Class B or C   _____(7) Juvenile Felony - Class B or C   _____(11) Civil Contempt

_____(4) Misdemeanor   _____(8) Juvenile - Misdemeanor   _____(12) Other (specify)_____

Charges_____

Applicant's Address_____

            (Street)   (City)   (State)   (Zip Code)

Applicant's Telephone (____) ____ - _____ Date of Birth ____ /____ /____ Social Security # (optional) ____ /____ /____

Occupation_____ Employer_____

                              (Name)   (Address)   (Telephone)

II. Support Obligations

Total Number Dependents (include applicant in count) _____ If juvenile defendant, does he/she live with parents? (circle) Y   N

If yes: Father's name _____ Mother's name (include maiden) _____

III. Presumptive Eligibility (check all that apply)

a. __ Party is indigent because receives public assistance in form of: ( ) AFDC[1] ( ) General Assistance ( ) Food Stamps
( ) Medicaid ( ) Poverty-Related V.A.[2] Benefits ( ) SSI[3] ( ) Refugee Resettlement Benefits ( ) Other; specify_____

Case Number_____Verified? _____ Method_____

b. __ Party is indigent because committed to a public mental health facility.

Verified? _____ Method: _____

c. __ Party is indigent because annual income, after taxes, is 125% or less of current federally established poverty level.

$_____ Specify annual income after taxes

Verified? _____ Method: _____

If Section III, a, b, or c applies, complete only Sections VIII, X and XI. Submit report to Court. If Section III is not applicable, complete all remaining sections.

IV. Monthly Income   Verified?

a. Monthly take-home pay (after deductions) $_____   Y   N

b. Spouse's take-home pay (enter N/A if conflict) $_____   Y   N

c. Contribution from any person domiciled with applicant and helping defray his/her basic living costs $_____   Y   N

d. Interest, dividends, or other earnings $_____   Y   N

e. Non-poverty based assistance (Unemployment, Social Security, Workers Compensation, pension,
annuities) **(DON'T include poverty-based assistance. See IV. a)** $_____   Y   N

f. Other income (specify) _____ $_____   Y   N

                                                          Total Income $_____

V. Monthly Expenses (for applicant and dependents; average where applicable)

a. Basic Living Costs - Shelter (rent, mortgage, board) $_____   Y   N

   Utilities (heat, electricity, water); enter 0 if included in cost of shelter $_____   Y   N

   Food $_____   Y   N

   Clothing $_____   Y   N

   Health Care $_____   Y   N

   Transportation $_____   Y   N

   Loan Payments (specify)_____ $_____   Y   N

b. Court imposed obligations (check) ___fines ___court costs ___restitution ___support ___other $_____   Y   N

c. Bail/bond paid or anticipated (this offense) $_____   Y   N

d. Other expenses (specify) _____ $_____   Y   N

                                                          Total Expenses $_____

[1] Aid to Families with Dependent Children
[2] Veterans' Administration
[3] Supplemental Security Income

continued

Exhibit D–11 *continued*

VI. Total Income Part IV, minus Total Expenses Part V   Disposable Net Monthly Income $_____

VII. Liquid Assets   **Verified?**

a. Cash, savings, bank accounts (include joint accounts) $_____   Y   N

b. Stocks, bonds, certificates of deposit $_____   Y   N

c. Equity in real estate $_____   Y   N

d. Equity in motor vehicle required for employment, IF over $3,000 (list overage: value minus $3,000) $_____   Y   N

    Make of car_____ Year_____

e. Equity in additional vehicles (list total value) $_____   Y   N

f. Personal property (jewelry, boat, stereo, etc.) $_____   Y   N

                                           Total Liquid Assets $_____

VIII. Affidavit and Notification

I, _____(print name) do hereby certify (or declare) under penalty of perjury under the Laws of the State of Washington that the foregoing is true and correct (RCW 9A.72.085). By my signature below, I authorize the court to verify all information provided here. I further swear to immediately report any change in financial status to the court. I understand that if bail is imposed in this matter or if my financial condition changes I may request a redetermination.

Signed_____ Date_____

Place_____

IX. Determination of Indigency

a. Disposable Net Monthly Income (from Section VI) $_____

b. Total Liquid Assets (from Section VII)   + $_____

c. **Total Available Funds** (a plus b)   = $_____

d. Anticipated Cost of Counsel for Offense Type(s) $_____

_____If (c) is zero (0) or less, party is **INDIGENT**.   _____If (c) is greater than (d), party is **NOT INDIGENT**.

_____If (c) is more than zero (0) but less than (d), party is **INDIGENT AND ABLE TO CONTRIBUTE**.

                                           Assessment Amount $_____

X. Recommendation

Should this recommendation be modified due to anticipated length or complexity of case? (circle one)   Yes   No

If yes, explain _____

_____

_____

_____

Other considerations or comments _____

_____

_____

_____

The above constitutes my recommendation to the court. I have explained my recommendation to the party.

Screening Agent/Witness (please print)_____ Date_____

Signature_____ Agency/Organization_____

XI. Finding

_____Indigent   _____Not Indigent   _____Indigent and Able to Contribute   Assessment $_____

Judge or Judge's Designee_____ Title_____

OAC INDIG 1A691

GLOSSARY

A

administrative manager individual responsible for managing all administrative functions of the office

alphabetical filing system client files arranged alphabetically with last name (surname) first; generally used by smaller law firms

annotation a note or commentary explaining the meaning of a passage in a book or document

associates lawyers who are employed by the firm; they receive a salary and not a percentage of the profits

B

billable hours the hours that are spent working on a client's case that may be billed to the client

C

caption the heading of the document or pleading that identifies it

centralized files central filing system where all files are located in a central file room

chronological file file of outgoing correspondence kept by date with most recent date on top

Circuit Courts of Appeal intermediate courts that hear appeals from the federal district court

citation a reference for a particular legal authority and where it is found, such as a case citation

client trust account a separate bank account for client funds that must be kept separate from the funds of the firm

closing line before the signature line used in formal communications

codes compilations of statutes by subject

common law case law that creates a precedent for future cases

computer filing systems software programs used for automating the filing system; categorize files and assign numbers if utilizing a numerical system

computerized document assembly system a system that integrates information into many different documents. When the document is scheduled to be completed, the system will automatically complete the document within the specified timeline

computerized filing systems software programs used for automating the filing system

contempt an act that obstructs a court's work or lessens the dignity of the court; court sanction for inappropriate behavior in court

contingency fees attorney's fees set as a percentage of the award that the client receives from the defendant.

court forms forms developed by the courts that are used instead of office-typed pleadings

D

decentralized or local filing system a local filing system located in the legal professional's office and generally used in small law offices

disbar take away a lawyer's right to practice law

E

e-mail electronic mail sent on the computer via the Internet

H

hourly fee the fee the attorney bills the client for each hour spent working on her case

I

incoming mail log a notebook or other type of log that will indicate the date of the incoming mail, the date received, the sender, the recipient, the subject, and the disposition

L

law office manager individual with the responsibilities of not only the administrative manager but the managing attorney as well

law reviews published by law schools; compilations of articles on current legal issues

lawyer/attorney individual who has graduated from law school and passed his state's bar examination

legal cap lined and numbered paper used for preparing pleadings and legal documents in most states

limited liability corporations corporations managed by the individual members, or their management may be delegated to officers or managers who are similar to corporate directors

M

malpractice professional misconduct or unreasonable lack of skill

managing attorney manages the law firm on a day-to-day basis

N

nonbillable hours the hours spent working in the law office that cannot be billed directly to a client

numerical filing systems files are numbered sequentially with cross-reference lists kept separately from the name of the client

O

oral communications communicating via your voice by telephone or in person

P

Pacer system that provides court opinions of the federal courts

partner attorney owner of the law firm; receives a percentage of the profits of the firm

partnership a law firm that is composed of two or more attorneys who share the expenses and profits of the partnership

pleading formal legal document of allegations by the parties in a lawsuit where they state their claims and defenses and documents

pocket parts updates to volumes of the annotated codes that are filed in a pocket at the back of each book

primary authority binding authority that includes statutes, court decisions, administrative regulations, and other similar sources of law rather than interpretive or indirect information from secondary sources

probate account a separate bank account for the funds of an estate; used by the law office when the attorney is representing the personal representative of the decedent

professional corporation corporation governed by state law that may be made up of attorneys, doctors, architects, accountants, or other professionals to form a special type of corporation to manage their business

project fees flat fees charged to the client based on the project to be completed

public reproval notice to the attorney's clients that the attorney has committed a violation of the ethical codes, admonishment is also considered a punishment in some states

R

research memorandum informal memorandum sent to a member of the law firm answering a legal question

restatements comprehensive explanations of the law authored by judges, law school professors, and attorneys; restatements are available for contracts and tort law

retainer fees special fees charged by some attorneys that are payable at the outset of the case or at the time the client retains the attorney to work on her case

S

salutation greeting at the beginning of correspondence

secondary authority persuasive authority that is not actual law; includes various writings about law such as legal encyclopedias and law review articles

senior partners lawyers who are the founders of the law firm and have an ownership interest therein

Shepardize updating a case by finding the citation in Shepard's volumes

sole proprietorship a law office operated by a single attorney who owns the practice

solicitation directly seeking business from prospective clients for the attorney and being paid a fee for this service; this practice is not allowed by state law

stare decisis earlier case decisions that set precedents for later cases that the court decides

statutes laws established by the state and federal legislatures

statutory fees attorney fees set by state statute, such as those used in probate and workers' compensation cases

T

time sheet used by each employee of the firm to keep track of the billable hours; may be computerized or done by hand

U

U.S. District Court trial court on the federal level

United States Supreme Court highest court in the United States

f indicates a reference to a figure and not the text